Discourses on violence

Discourses on violence

Conflict analysis reconsidered

Vivienne Jabri

Manchester University Press

Manchester and New York

distributed exclusively in the USA and Canada by St. Martin's Press

Copyright © Vivienne Jabri 1996
Published by Manchester University Press
Oxford Road, Manchester M13 9NR, UK
and Room 400, 175 Fifth Avenue, New York, NY 10010, USA

Distributed exclusively in the USA and Canada
by St. Martin's Press, Inc., 175 Fifth Avenue, New York,
NY 10010, USA

British Library Cataloguing-in-Publication Data
A catalogue record for this book is available from the British Library

Library of Congress Cataloging-in-Publication Data
Jabri, Vivienne, 1958–
Discourses on violence: conflict analysis reconsidered / Vivienne Jabri
    p.   cm.
  ISBN 1–7190–3958–4 (hard : alk. paper).
  ISBN 00–7190–3959–2 (pbk. : alk. paper)
  1. Violence. 2. War. 3. Conflict management.
  4. Mediation, International I. Title.
hm281.j32 1996
303.6—dc20   95–30847
                                                                  cip
ISBN   0 7190 3958 4   hardback
          0 7290 3959 2   paperback

First published in 1996
00 99 98 97 96   10 9 8 7 6 5 4 3 2 1

Typeset by Carnegie Publishing, Preston
Printed in Great Britain
by Bell & Bain Ltd, Glasgow

Contents

Preface and acknowledgements

The objective of this book is to uncover the discursive and institutional processes which reproduce war and violent conflict as aspects of the human condition. My work on conflict resolution has led to a recognition that developing technical expertise in modes of resolution must remain inadequate in the absence of an understanding of the social processes which generate war and support for violent human interaction.

The book specifically utilises a structurationist analysis, inspired by the writings of Anthony Giddens, to develop a critical analysis of war. More specifically, this approach allows an ontological discourse on the place of war in the constitutive relationship between self and society, the construction of identity, and the institutional and normative orders which are implicated in the reproduction of violent conflict as a social continuity.

In arguing that war as a social phenomenon can only be understood within a wider understanding of human action and social reproduction, the structurationist theory of war provided in these pages takes human conduct and discursive and institutional continuities within social systems as mutually constitutive processes implicated in the reproduction of violence as an aspect of social and political life. Of central importance in this critical perspective are the roles played by social discourse and institutional formations in the generation of exclusionist identities which reproduce the legitimating orders underpinning violent human interaction.

This study is normative in orientation in that it seeks both understanding and emancipation. It calls for a transformation of the human condition, its exclusionist discourses and institutions, and suggests that such transformation must be situated in altered interactions which incorporate difference and celebrate such agency.

I owe a special debt to Dr Stephen Chan for his thorough reading of this text and for his continuing encouragement and generosity of spirit. I am deeply grateful to Richard Purslow of Manchester

University Press for his patience and faith in my work. Our telephone conversations were a vital reminder of fast approaching deadlines and the practicalities involved in the production of this work. I also thank other members of the team at MUP, including Vivienne Robertson, for their invaluable contributions. I am grateful to Mark Hoffman, Eleanor O'Gorman, Michael Banks, Professor Chris Mitchell, Professor John Groom and Professor Trevor Salmon for their intellectual and professional support.

I am dependent on my friends and family for the unconditional love which provides the lifeline for my work. My special gratitude goes to Mary Nankivell for her support and endurance of my eccentricities. I also owe a debt to Dorian Jabri and Chris Smith for being a source of encouragement, good food and good talk.

Chapter one

Introduction:
conflict analysis reconsidered

*War is not only a state of affairs, but a process of gradual
realisation. First, one has to get used to the idea of it. The idea then
has to become part of everyday life. Then rules can change, rules of
behaviour, of language, of expectations.*

Slavenca Draculic, *Balkan Express* (1993)

War is a widespread human phenomenon. It is an option that
is available to states and communities as conflicts emerge
and relations break down. With the exception of pacifism, the belief
that war is unacceptable under any circumstances, the predominant view is that violence may be resorted to in conditions of high
salience, for causes that are deemed worthy of the human and
material destruction which is war. The constitutive element of war
as violent conflict is that it is aimed at social/political objectives
requiring human sacrifice in an environment of threat. As a form
of behaviour, violent conflict is not confined to inter-state relations,
but involves communities within and across state boundaries involved either directly in combat or indirectly through economic
and symbolic support. Our understanding of war cannot, therefore,
be limited to inter-state conduct or to the definition of world politics
as the external relations of states as behavioural entities. War as
a social phenomenon involves individuals, communities and states
and any attempt to uncover its genesis must incorporate the discursive and institutional continuities which render violent conflict
a legitimate and widely accepted mode of human conduct.

The advent of nuclear weapons and the Cold War stand-off in the
European arena invited suggestions that war had come to be an ob-
solete phenomenon, its ramifications too costly for its continuance

as a technique of statecraft. Increasing economic interdependence and the spread of international organisations instituted linkages which enabled the resolution of conflicts and competition over resources within cooperative interactions. The "war generation" was a label applied to those who had directly experienced the First and Second World Wars. Future generations would not again be allowed to experience such devastation. Nuclear weaponry and a policy of deterrence would be their insurance policy against the onset of further wars. Any conflicts and competitions for global influence would be fought out by proxy, in arenas outside the European "theatre", involving combatants from elsewhere, "clients" engaged in "hot" wars to sustain the North's "cold" conflict.

The end of the Cold War was deemed to have brought forth a "new world order", free of threat, concerned with progress, international trade, and individual material contentment. Protracted conflicts such as the Arab-Israeli conflict and conflict in southern Africa witnessed transformations towards resolution, possibilities unforeseen and unpredicted in the previous era. The breakdown of the Soviet Union, the democratisation of formerly authoritarian states, and increasing calls for popular democracy elsewhere focused attention on a world politics based on representation and human rights. Security could no longer be defined in military terms but in terms of shared threats and concerns the resolution of which demanded cooperation rather than confrontation.

However, just as the Cold War era was based on violence and high military expenditure, so too the post-Cold War situation has produced new uncertainties, new demands for sovereignty, intercommunal violence, and military intervention. The war in former Yugoslavia and the 1991 conflict in the Gulf brought into sharp focus the readiness with which leaders and their populations resort to violence as a form of behaviour in emergent conflicts. These and other conflicts throughout Europe, Africa, the Middle East, Asia, and the American continent show that violence for political ends continues to constitute an aspect of the human condition. The inter-state conflict in the Gulf and inter-communal conflicts in Rwanda, Yugoslavia, Algeria and elsewhere illustrate with vivid clarity the ability of leaderships to mobilise support for violence and, in certain civil wars, the involvement of mass populations in direct combat against former neighbours and fellow citizens. The phenomenon of violent conflict cannot, therefore, be understood simply through analyses of leadership decision-making, but calls for uncovering the continuities in social life which enable war and give it legitimacy, backed by discursive and institutional structures.

The study of war has produced a number of often conflicting answers to Quincy Wright's question, "Why is war thought? Why is war fought?"[1] The history of human political violence has shown that we cannot produce monocausal explanations of war. Studies which concentrate on assumed innate human characteristics fail to account for the societal factors which are implicated in what is essentially an interactive and dynamic process. Similarly, investigations which link attributes of the international system, such as balances of power, not only produce contradictory findings, but seem to negate human decision-making and psychological processes in the onset of war in specific conditions. Studies of violent conflict aspire to uncover, through empirical investigation, patterns of behaviour which lead to war. As indicated by Holsti, studies of war may be divided into those which emphasise structural or "ecological" variables, such as the distribution of power capabilities within the system, and those which emphasise "decision-making, values, and perceptions of policy-makers" in attempts to isolate common features leading up to the decision for war.[2]

This book does not aim to review the empirical findings of the above investigations. Rather, it seeks to use social and political theory in an attempt to locate violence in the relationship between self and society. It is primarily an ontological investigation of the constitution of self and society, or action and social structure, and the place of war therein. The primary assumption made in the study is that war or violent conflict are social phenomena emerging through, and constitutive of, social practices which have, through time and across space, rendered war an institutional form that is largely seen as an inevitable and at times acceptable form of human conduct. The study specifically utilises Giddens's structuration theory,[3] a statement on the ontological relationship between action and structure, in seeking to understand the institutionalisation of war as human practice. The assumption is that our understanding of violent human conflict cannot simply be based on instrumental rationality but must situate the agent, or acting subject, in relation to the structural properties which render war a continuity in social systems. The relationship between human action and social structure is at the heart of social theory and is central to developing an understanding of violent conflict if we assume that this mode of conduct is a continuity in patterned social systems. As stated by Giddens, structuration theory is concerned with the "conditions governing the continuity or transformation of structures, and therefore the reproduction of systems", which in turn are "reproduced relations between actors or collectivities, organised as regular social practices".[4] The relevance of structuration theory for developing an understanding of war is located in this theory's concern with the reproduction of social systems, or aspects of social life, through the activities of situated actors drawing upon and reproducing the structural features of social systems. The starting assumption is that violent conflict is not a product of characteristics innate within the "make-up" of human beings or of instrumental reason, nor is it a product of the structure of the international system, but derives from the ontological relationship between agency and structure, where war as human action is a product of human decisions made within the context of structured social relations. The argument is that violent conflict is itself structurated through the actions of agents situated in relation to discursive and institutional continuities which both enable war's occurrence and legitimate it as a form of human behaviour.

Structuration theory and its relevance to the understanding of violent conflict will be returned to in chapter three. The remaining sections of this chapter begin with a discussion of the implication of violent conflict as a human condition. The second section locates the parameters of conflict analysis as currently defined by the field of conflict studies. The third and final section of the chapter identifies the premises made in a specifically critical approach to the study of conflict.

The social meaning of war

Slavenca Draculic's description quoted at the outset of this chapter is based on her experience of the ethnic nationalist wars which led to the breakdown of Yugoslavia. It illustrates with vivid clarity the two prominent aspects of that peculiarly human condition which is war, namely its cruel reality and its immediate impact on the everyday and the mundane. Its physical manifestation has an equivalent impact upon discourse which, in a self-fulfilling prophecy, renders the destructive element of human violence acceptable or legitimate to those who perceive war in strategic terms.

War has no exclusionary clauses. As shown by the civil wars in the former Yugoslavia, Somalia, Angola, Rwanda, and the 1991 war in the Gulf, while the decision to go to war is confined to the few making up the "war cabinet", its consequences go far beyond and affect the armed as well as the unarmed. Telecommunications advances also render proximate events which could, in the past, be perceived as sufficiently distant to warrant inaction or indifference. Combatants vie for the onlookers' support and their actions, even in combat, may be directed more at these external others than at the enemy. Official and non-official responses to a conflict are greatly influenced by the proximity of the media to a particular conflict. Protracted and ongoing conflicts perceived as unnewsworthy in the editorial rooms remain hidden from view and therefore beyond any ethical or moral consideration by policy-makers and/or audiences.

War brings with it other socially constitutive manifestations. Affiliation and identity come to be defined in terms of exclusionist social boundaries. To be a dissenting voice is to be an outsider, who is often branded as traitor to the cause and, therefore, deserving of sacrifice at the mythical altar of solidarity. What would previously have been blurred social boundaries become sharpened primarily through a discursive focus upon features, both symbolic and material, which divide communities to the extent that the desire for destruction of the enemy is perceived to be the only legitimate or honourable course to follow. Again, Slavenca Draculic expresses this experience of war:

> After a year of violence, with the dead numbering approximately 200,000, with many more wounded and over two million refugees flooding Europe, there came the story of concentration camps. And all of a sudden in a thin desperate man behind barbed wire the world recognized not a Moslem, but a human being. That picture, the words "concentration camp" and "holocaust" finally translated the true meaning of "ethnic cleansing". At last people in the West began to grasp what was going on. It was suddenly clear that Europe had not learned its lesson, that history always repeats itself and that someone is always a Jew. Once the concept of "otherness"

takes root, the unimaginable becomes possible. Not in some mythological country but to ordinary urban citizens, as I discovered all too painfully.[5]

As a conflict escalates towards violence and as the "war mood"[6] takes hold of entire populations, the dissident from either camp or the peacemaker from the onlooking external world can become subject to social contempt and censure rather than admiration.

Once violent destruction of the enemy and its valued resources comes to define a relationship, the rules of the game or the rules of "everyday life" change. Behaviour that is unacceptable in peacetime becomes legitimate in time of war. Specifically killing, torture, rape, mass expulsions, ethnic cleansing and the creation of concentration camps are explained by such terms which essentially state that while war goes on we must expect such occurrences, or simply not be surprised by them. They form part of the strategic calculations perceived as necessary when the prime motivation is winning in war.[7] The existence of conventions on the conduct of war, on such matters as the treatment of prisoners of war, or of populations under occupation, may suggest a basis of ethical norms which interconnect international society. The very existence of these laws may, on the other hand, be interpreted as humanity's acknowledgement of war as an unavoidable aspect of social interaction.

War has a certain dialectic which incorporates both normality and abnormality. Its normality derives from the assumption, held predominantly by the "realist" school of thought in international relations,[8] that war has always been a tool, or a mode of behaviour, to which individuals and groups may have recourse in times of conflict with other individuals and groups. The Hobbesian emphasis on the state of nature as being inherently conflictual and violent suggests that non-violent interaction is an artificial condition achieved only through an imposed contractual order. The breakdown of social order, according to Hobbes, is a mere reversion back to what is naturally human: "Hereby it is manifest, that during the time men live without a common Power to keep them all in awe, they are in that condition which is called Warre; and such a warre, as is of every man, against every man."[9] As pointed out by Chanteur, the Hobbesian analysis is based on an ahistorical and apolitical state of nature where the universal driving forces are centred at one and the same time around fear and desire.

Human beings fear not so much the natural world around them but other human beings where the desire to dominate is the basic need defining what it is to be human.[10]

War is also an abnormal condition. War implies the breakdown of an existing order defining either domestic or international situations. War constitutes behaviour which is unacceptable in times of peace, or non-war. War breaks down taboos against killing and the deliberate and direct infliction of suffering against fellow human beings. The mechanism by which war specifically breaks down taboos is distinguished by the relatively short timespan between the existence of a taboo, its breakdown and its re-establishment. The moral boundary between war and non-war is defined by the acceptance or legitimacy conferred on violence as a form of human behaviour.

The discourse of war aims at the construction of a mythology based on inclusion and exclusion. This categorisation sharply contrasts the insiders from the outsiders who are the "others", or the deserving enemy. This process cannot be confined to the definition of the enemy but incorporates the inclusion of texts which valorise the history and cause of one party to a conflict while depicting the claims of the enemy as unfounded, unjust or even diabolical. The discourse of inclusion and exclusion cannot allow uncertainty or doubt, so if such are expressed, they must be represented as irrational or even treacherous. Any representation which blurs the inclusion/exclusion boundary breaks down certainties constructed in the name of war and forms a counter-discourse which deconstructs and delegitimates war and thereby fragments myths of unity, duty and conformity.

Conflict, and specifically violent conflict, is constitutively defined in terms of inclusion and exclusion and any understanding of war must incorporate the means through which such systems are perpetuated and implicated in violent action. Linklater rightly points out that "questions of inclusion and exclusion are central to international relations, since states and the state system are, in themselves, systems of inclusion and exclusion".[11] Systems of inclusion and exclusion generate a "normative" discourse concerned with the justifications of such formations, a "sociological" discourse centred around the workings and maintenance of systems of inclusion and exclusion, and "praxeological" questions related to the practical implications of such systems.[12] While the normative implications of such systems defined in the cosmopolitan/communitarian debate will not be dealt with,[13] the sociological and praxeological components form a central focus for the framework of understanding developed in this study. As will be argued later, systems of inclusion and exclusion are structurated through identiational discursive and institutional practices implicated in the legitimation of and support for violent conflict.

War is a social condition and takes place within the realm of society. Analyses of war based on notions of innate drives or basic needs fail to recognise the social and political origins of what Diderot referred to as "the convulsive and violent disease of the body politic".[14] To conceive of the individual as somehow separate from society is to negate the constitutive implications of normative and discursive processes which define the institutional continuities of social life. War is a product of social interaction. It emerges or is made possible through processes of group formation; for example, the institutionalisation of difference as reflected in the division of humanity into a world of separate states, and the establishment of machineries aimed specifically at the war-making process. The interplay between self and society comes into sharp focus especially in time of war when identity, affiliation and the will to sacrifice are tested against criteria defining loyal citizenship.

Although war is a product of social life, it reflects a drastic change in the rules of conduct where actions take forms which are qualitatively different from interaction in times of non-war. Quincy Wright's seminal work on the study of war concentrates on inter-state war in pointing to the "legal condition which equally permits two or more hostile groups to carry on a conflict by armed force". The term conflict, according to Wright, suggests that "war is a definite and mutually understood pattern of behaviour, distinguishable not only from other patterns of behaviour in general but from other forms of conflict".[15] War reflects a breakdown in the rules of everyday life, possesses its own socialised customs, but is, even so, a product of social and inter-social formations.

In answer to the question "where are the major causes of war to be found?", Kenneth Waltz suggests three "images" encompassing individual traits, internal structures of states, and the inter-state system as having prevalence in Western political thought.[16] He provides a devastating critique of the first two and concludes that any explanation of war must recognise that it is a product of social formations and more specifically the anarchical inter-state system. In relation to perspectives which assume innate human characteristics, his conclusion is that "To attempt to explain social forms on the basis of psychological data is to commit the error of psychologism: the analysis of individual behaviour used uncritically to explain group phenomena."[17] This view has its supporters in the field of social anthropology where researchers argue both against essentialism and in support of the view that war is a distinctly social phenomenon.[18] In rejecting universalist premises on human characteristics, Howell and Willis point to the implications of essentialist criteria for social research:

> An accepted notion that aggression is a given characteristic in humans everywhere leads to a search for it in various social settings. This, however, begs the question and determines the formulation of research, phrasing the questions in terms of how aggressive drives are handled. The vocabulary of the debates reflects this, for the contrast is drawn between aggression and non-aggression, violence and non-violence; it is the absence of conflict not the presence of something else that is noted.[19]

Just as inter-personal and inter-societal behaviour must be located within the ideological and cultural settings of societies, so too the linguistic constructs within research derive from and construct the settings which they seek to understand.

Waltz argues that explanations of war based on the internal structures of states are similarly reductionist in orientation and remain inadequate as bases for explaining inter-state violent conflict. He specifically directs his attack against the liberal assumption that "democracy is preeminently the peaceful form of the state" arguing that "faith in public opinion or, more generally, faith in the uniformly peaceful proclivities of democracies has proved utopian".[20] Instead of providing an alternative theory of the state, Waltz suggests that inter-state war must be situated in the anarchical structure of the inter-state system which contains specific characteristics peculiar to the game of international politics where "(1) . . . the stakes of the game are considered to be of unusual importance and (2) . . . in international politics the use of force is not excluded as a means of influencing the outcome".[21] This forms the basis of Kenneth Waltz's neo-realist perspective on international relations generally and on war in particular. It is a perspective which Waltz later develops as a specifically structural approach to the study of international relations and which Gilpin adopts in his analysis of the impact of war on change in world politics.[22] Structure is here recognised as both determining and constraining the behaviour of states within the anarchic condition of the inter-state system, and the distribution of capabilities is a central feature in the analysis of state behaviour.

Does this structuralist orientation to the explanation of violent human conflict provide an improvement on explanations based on individual traits or instrumental reason? The first argument against the approach is that it suffers from the same linguistic determinism as that which Howell and Willis direct against the essentialist premises which underpin explanations based on individual innate characteristics.[23] The second argument is that, as Wendt has pointed out, Waltz's understanding of system structure is "ontologically reductionist"[24] in that it conceives structure as constraining the agency of pre-existing states rather than as "generating" state agents themselves. Given this, the theory fails to provide a social conception of the state or of agency. The third argument against the approach that is relevant to our present objectives is that it fails to provide an adequate framework for understanding the social formations which generate violent human conflict across the boundaries of the state. Conflict is not confined to inter-state relations but, as argued above, involves both state and non-state actors. The state itself is a container of individuals and communities existing within shared worlds of meaning, symbolic orders, and institutional frameworks which are, as will be argued in this study, implicated in the generation of violent human conflict. The agent-structure problem will be returned to in an elaboration of structuration theory later in this study. The following section provides a brief overview of the field which is specifically devoted to developing explanations of conflict and conflict resolution.

Conflict analysis and the understanding of war

The study of conflict seeks to broaden the analysis of political violence beyond the inter-state level of analysis and adopts a more specifically decision-making framework. The boundaries of conflict and peace studies relate to two fundamental assumptions: firstly, conflict is a generic phenomenon, and as such requires a multi-disciplinary approach; and secondly, the field has a normative orientation based on a concern to alleviate the dysfunctional aspects of violent conflict. These central assumptions, while providing a basis of identity for the conflict researcher, do not immediately suggest the existence of a hard core of theory around which what Lakatos terms a "scientific research programme" is conducted.[25] Groom suggests a division of the field between conflict research and peace research, where the former considers conflict as a subjective phenomenon resulting from individual and group decision-making, while the latter concerns structural inequalities and exploitation as bases of conflict.[26] Nicholson suggests that the former constitutes a "social science" as it concerns "a description of how social groups actually behave" while the latter constitutes "social engineering" as it is a "prescription for achieving specified goals in the light of the propositions discovered by the social scientists".[27] The two approaches have been presented as a dichotomy whereby the hard core of conflict research is rational actor decision-making while the hard core of peace research looks to structures which perpetuate domination and dependency, defined by Galtung as "structural violence".[28]

The debate has its origins in the 1960s when neo-Marxist West European peace researchers, such as Herman Schmid, criticised the empiricist and uncritical orientation of the field, calling for an explicit statement on the concept of peace as a clearly-defined value orientation.[29] The call was for a critical mode of inquiry that would transcend the behaviouralist consensus which became prevalent in the late 1960s and early 1970s, as evidenced by the nature of articles published in the United States-based *Journal of Conflict Resolution*. Krippendorff, for example, suggested that while this methodological consensus brought peace research a certain legitimacy, the cost was that it "lost its significance for a reorientation of the social sciences",[30] which could only be restored by a return to fundamental questions of ontology and epistemology. Despite such calls for reorientation and theoretical and methodological clarity, the conflict research/peace research dichotomy has largely remained static. The field has not experienced the level of theoretical debate prevalent in other social sciences, including international relations. As pointed out by Reid and Yanarella,

The controversy has simply run aground as the concern for communication and dialogue across schools of peace research has dwindled. Radical peace researchers have an important stake in renewing this controversy, going beyond the limits of the earlier phase of conflict.[31]

The field has been so dominated by a positivist orientation that questions of ontology and epistemology have been largely ignored, since the methods of the natural sciences have been assumed to be applicable to the study of social phenomena such as conflict.

As succinctly pointed out by Burton, conflict studies is "not merely concerned with conflict as a specific and overt happening, but with the underlying human and institutional problems that create it".[32] The primary aim of conflict research may be explanation, but the field also has a self-consciously practical aim. It is assumed that greater understanding of conflict processes leads to the amelioration of their most destructive implications. As pointed out by Nardin, "Conflict research reflects a commitment to what is regarded as theoretical illumination, but it is also practically motivated. Like many other branches of inquiry, it is the offspring of a wish to ameliorate the human condition."[33]

The parameters of conflict research start from explanations of the causes of conflict, and develop into analyses of its dynamics and development, namely escalation and de-escalation processes, to conflict resolution. Developments in the latter theme have focused on mediation and negotiation processes and, as a result of Burton's unparalled contributions to the field, on innovative modes of conflict resolution.[34]

Conflict research is based on the assumption that conflict is a generic phenomenon and that any separation of types of conflict based on levels of societal interaction is an artificial one built on the exigencies of the division of the social sciences into separate academic disciplines. Inter-personal conflict becomes as much a valid point of departure as conflict between states. The focus of investigation is, therefore, on what Kriesberg terms "social conflict", where it is assumed that theories on the origins, dynamics and termination of conflict have explanatory potential in investigations of such seemingly diverse conflicts as college-based disputes, gender-related, inter-racial and international conflicts.[35] The basic mode of inquiry is to isolate the conflict system, which becomes the unit of analysis. Propositions linking sets of variables are tested against empirical observations. Sets of interrelated hypotheses deemed successful after empirical testing are then formulated into an empirical theory.[36] The most important feature of this approach is that it is dependent on a *decision-making framework* which seeks to explain the interaction process between parties in conflict and the social environmental influences on this interaction.

One major focus of inquiry has been what Kriesberg terms "conflict mitigation" which suggests that "one seeks to control the adverse consequences of the way a conflict is waged".[37] This approach takes as its baseline the specific conflict under investigation and focuses on the modes by which it may be resolved, from negotiation, to mediation, to problem-solving.[38] This form of research has produced ideas on the suitability of different modes of peacemaking in international conflict and has been successful in highlighting the dynamics of the conflict resolution process. If empirical theory is the primary aim of this research, then the combined efforts of empirical researchers have pointed to the nature of the conflict resolution process; the spectrum of activity which defines it; and the suitability of different modes of peacemaking in different conflict situations.[39] The practical aim is to develop frameworks which may be applied in the international arena both through the incorporation of mediation within institutional settings,[40] and through the direct participation of conflict researchers as conflict resolvers.

The analysis of conflict, investigations of the dynamic processes involved in the generation and escalation of conflict, have the purpose of informing conflict mitigation. The question of "why war?" is approached by defining factors, or independent variables, which explain the escalation of conflict situations towards the use of violence. War is defined as a contest or conflict over valued resources and belief systems carried out through the use of violence by one group against another. The aim is to uncover a causal sequence specifying factors which may lead to war in a specific situation. As Vasquez points out, "war is fundamentally a political institution that serves crucial political functions".[41] This instrumentalist view sees war as a tool of policy that is available to the decision-maker where conflicts of interest escalate to such a degree of intensity that violence is deemed an appropriate method of achieving desired outcomes. Whether a contention over issues and desired outcomes is carried out violently or through non-violent modes of interaction is dependent on a number of factors related to the issues at stake, the relationship between the parties, resources available to the parties, the ideological disposition of the parties, and the impact of the social environment.[42] This last factor also incorporates the "institutional context" in which issues arise, agendas are formed and interaction between contending parties regulated.[43] Violence, whether used by state or non-state actors, is one form of conflict behaviour and a component part of the life cycle of a conflict. War is understood as part of a wider interaction process. The emergence of goal incompatibilities between contending parties leads to the adoption of behaviours aimed at achieving desired outcomes.

The framework of analysis which underpins empirical investigations in the study of conflict is one of *interactive decision-making* and the model is a "modified rational actor model".[44] It is "modified" since it incorporates subjective expected utilities, recognising the potential diversity of conflict goals which may range from the economic to the ideological, and of subjective probabilities influenced by misperceptions, informational distortion and ideological biases. The approach centres around conflict processes within the life cycle of a conflict which can be considered as having "causal importance"[45] in escalation to the use of force. Such factors as misunderstood signals, perceived changes in the balance of advantage between the protagonists, prior relationships, and the input of allies and interested others could, either singly or in combination, influence the course of a conflict and behaviours therein.

The notion of "intent" or purposeful behaviour is central to the perspective outlined above. Mitchell defines conflict behaviour as aimed specifically at gaining desired outcomes by influencing the adversary's evaluations of the issues in conflict and altering their perceptions of the merits of their actions.[46] Himes defines social conflicts as "purposeful struggles between collective actors who use social power to defeat or remove opponents and to gain status, power, resources, and other scarce values".[47] The idea of purposeful behaviour suggests the existence of an element of choice between alternative courses of action. Kriesberg suggests that the "use of the word choice should not be interpreted to mean that all alternatives are consciously weighed by each party and that, after due calculation, a course of action is selected". Interest is, rather, focused on the "factors that influence and constrain the course followed".[48] Such influences and constraints derive from the dynamics of the conflict and its social environment. The purposefulness of conflict behaviour is stressed by Kriesberg when he states that "there must be an intention to induce the other side to yield what the coercer wishes to obtain".[49]

Two questions emerge from the above. The first relates to the influences and constraints which determine the course of action adopted. An instrumentalist perspective suggests that primary constraining or enabling factors would include the balance of advantage between the protagonists, prior relationships linking the parties, as well as constituency and third party input. Enabling and constraining factors could also be conceptualised in terms of structural continuities within which decision-making takes place. The constraining and enabling inputs which determine the mode of behaviour within situations of conflict cannot merely be analysed in terms of immediate cost/benefit evaluations, but must also incorporate the institutional and discursive continuities which form the backdrop to conflict behaviour. This second concern is central to a "critical" approach adopted in this study and will be returned to later.

The concern of the remainder of this chapter is to highlight the questions and the research problems which have emerged from the "modified rationality" model or the interactive decision-making approach. The focus of the review is drawn to two interrelated analytical problems, namely the parties to a conflict and the issues which lead to the emergence of violent conflict.

The first question relates to the "parties" in conflict and the ways in which these are defined in the conflict research literature. One method is to adopt Bueno de Mesquita's assumption that decisions about the onset of war are controlled by either a single leader or a centralised and well-defined leadership such as a "war cabinet", both of which are taken to act as "rational expected utility maximisers". According to Bueno de Mesquita, a necessary condition for a nation or a party to go to war is that its leader must calculate it to be in his or her interest which is itself equated with the "national" or group interest.[50] While Bueno de Mesquita "recognizes that decision making about the use of force is a process of social choice, he adopts a simplifying assumption that collapses the process into the hands of a single dominant leader".[51] As Haney *et al.* rightly point out, this is consistent with the assumptions of the realist approach in international relations which views states as single, unitary, rational actors.

The central problem with Bueno de Mesquita's treatment of the problem is that it precludes analysis of the involvement of non-leadership levels of society which are involved in the process of war. How do we, therefore, delimit the boundaries of the "parties" in conflict? The answer has a number of implications for both conflict analysis and practical concerns with conflict resolution. Leaderships may choose war, but it is the entire social framework which becomes involved in war, defining itself in terms of the con-tending sides to the conflict. How we define the parties to a conflict may also be a reflection of dominant discourses around a particular conflict situation which legitimise or render visible the claims of one while delegitimising those of the other. Scholarly analyses or journalistic accounts of particular conflicts may also directly or indirectly influence practical approaches adopted by potential mediators in the resolution of conflict such that mediation becomes a legitimating exercise for those chosen as "representatives" of the protagonists.

That party boundaries are, in some types of conflict, difficult to define is especially reflected in conflicts involving diffuse categories such as classes, genders or ethnic groups. As indicated by Blalock, "In such instances there may be highly active members of both parties but also many others whose behaviours and loyalties are difficult to classify as being clearly on the one side or the other."[52]

Difficulties in unambiguously classifying parties emerge espe-cially in inter-communal civil war where the boundaries between the armed and the "unarmed" become seriously blurred. The diffuse nature of the conflict in the former Yugoslavia and that in Rwanda demonstrates that in certain conflicts the combatant/ civilian divide is problematic. Within the former Yugoslavia, an already armed and militarised civilian population rapidly became involved in inter-communal hostilities involving households, neighbourhoods and ultimately entire regions. Inter-communal violence on a massive scale in Rwanda similarly shows the ease with which a civilian population is recruited directly into active combat. The dividing line between decision-makers and combat-ants on the one hand and the non-combatant population on the other in situations of inter-communal conflict is not as un-ambiguous as in inter-state conflict. Even in such seemingly

well-defined conflicts, however, it is important to analyse the relationship between the war-making machinery of the state (which
includes the war cabinet as well as the armed forces) and the
civilian population, whose support is mobilised towards the war
effort. The gathering of information and its dissemination may in
such instances be used to ensure popular support for a military
solution to an emergent dispute. Tilly's emphasis on "resource
mobilisation" as a central aspect of the escalation of conflict towards violence becomes highly relevant in investigations of the
legitimation of violence as a mode of conflict behaviour. It also
provides a behavioural link between decisions made by policy-
makers and the support conferred on these decisions by the wider
constituency.[53] To confine analysis to the role of leadership
decision-making and instrumentalist calculation is, therefore, to
negate the crucial role played through societal processes in the
legitimation of war.

Empirical investigations of conflict have also sought to analyse
the relationship between issue type and the emergence of violent
conflict. The consensus in the literature is that, rather than
developing typologies of issues around which conflicts evolve, it is
more fruitful to uncover processes through which some issues
become so salient as to enable leaders to mobilise support for a
course of war as opposed to peaceful resolutions of emerging disputes.

A number of typologies have been suggested as a means to understanding the role that issues play in the emergence of violent conflict. Aubert defines issues in terms of those which are "consensual"
as opposed to those which are "dissensual".[54] Consensual conflicts
are where parties agree about the value of what they seek, but a
conflict arises where one obtains more of what it wants and the
other achieves less. These are conflicts of interest where there is
agreement on the value of the resources sought and disagreement
over the distribution of scarce resources such as territory, leadership positions, access rights and competitions over markets. Dissensual conflicts, on the other hand, exist where parties differ in
belief systems and where one seeks the conversion, persecution, or
even the destruction of the other.

The sources of differences or incompatibilities between individuals, groups and states are variously labelled the "conflict situation", the "bases of conflict", or the "structure of conflict".[55]

Empirical observations suggest that contentions over territorial boundaries and ethnic separation seem to be the dominant sources of violent disputes in present-day world society. The rise of ethnic nationalism in the former territories of the Soviet Union, the breakdown of Yugoslavia, the Israeli-Palestinian conflict, and the Hutu-Tutsi warfare in Rwanda and Burundi seem to confirm the relationship between ethnic territoriality and the escalation of conflict towards violence. Conflicts of belief systems relating to the organisation and governance of society can also be a source of violent conflict and tend to be a more intractable form of conflict. Mere difference in belief is not in itself a basis for conflict but becomes so when one party seeks to convert, undermine, or, in extreme situations, eliminate members of groups holding differing belief systems. The rise of Islamist groups in certain Middle Eastern states has led to conflicts between these and adherents of secular modes of governance. Conflicts of interest over tangible resources are rendered graver in intensity where they overlap an ideological or religious conflict. As pointed out by Druckman, "conflicts of interest linked to differences in ideology are more difficult to resolve than conflicts that do not derive from contrasting ideological orientations and . . . the more polarized the parties in ideological orientation, the more difficult it is to resolve a related conflict of interest."[56]

One difficulty associated with the identification of issues as bases of conflict is that specific disputes could reflect both consensual and dissensual differences. As pointed out by Kriesberg, "The relative importance of each varies in different conflicts, it also varies among the different segments of each party and probably changes in the course of a struggle."[57] Thus, even in cases where there is a clear case of dissensual conflict, such as exists between those striving for theocratic governance as opposed to secularist leaders, both antagonists value the same leadership positions which are seen as the vehicles for social control. The dynamic nature of the conflict process also means that the issues which lead to the emergence of conflict are not necessarily those which cause its intractability or longevity.

Another difficulty in attempting to build an empirical relationship between issues and violence relates to the salience of grievances which underpin a conflict. As indicated by Paul Diehl,

It is even more problematic to develop an empirical measure

of the salience of those issues involved in the conflict. In some conflicts, the stakes in the conflict are not as tangible as might be the case with conflicts over territory or markets. Scholars also cannot easily point to characteristics of the issues to identify which, if any, are most salient. Furthermore, one runs into the problem of perception; it is difficult to determine if what appears objectively to be very salient is perceived as such by decision-makers (or vice versa).[58]

It would seem, therefore, that identification of the issues is not as clear-cut as would be suggested by Clausewitz when he suggests that "The political object – the original motive/issue for the war – will thus determine both the military objective to be reached and the amount of effort it requires."[59] A conflict is not merely constituted by a set of incompatibilities, but incorporates salience of desires and beliefs which could determine the choice of violence as a mode of conflict behaviour. Salience as identified by the investigator may not reflect the "operating frames of reference"[60] influencing policy-makers' choices of action.

Empirical investigations of the role of issues in the generation of violent conflict assume that policy-makers are purposive actors seeking particular ends through action deemed as the most effective in achieving desirable outcomes. One purpose which seems to have led overwhelmingly to the emergence of war is the creation of states. As indicated by Holsti:

> When we aggregate three issues – national liberation/state creation, national unification/consolidation, and secession – we deal with similar values and stakes if not behaviours. They all identify efforts to create states and symbolize that long historical process that began in Europe in the fifteenth and sixteenth centuries and that has extended into the non-European parts of the world in the twentieth century.[61]

In his inductive study of the role of issues in generating war, Holsti finds that state creation ranks highest as the cause of war, standing at 52 per cent of the wars of the post-1945 period. He also finds that ideological conflicts, those concerned with the political principles which underpin governance, have also been a frequent cause of international conflict, standing at 42 per cent of post-1945 conflicts, constituting "the second highest issue cluster after state creation".[62] Another major cause of war is found to be what Holsti refers to as "human sympathy" with those considered ethnic, religious or ideological kin, vindicating the importance or salience of identity as the basis of conflict while conflicts over tangible resources, such as territory and wealth have declined in relative importance. It also shows that while conflicts over tangible resources may be amenable to compromise or the creation of regimes aimed at the management of such disputes, conflicts centred around national self-determination and belief systems seem to be less amenable to compromise and accommodation.

The dichotomous distinction between conflicts over belief systems and those over tangible resources and the related assumption that the former are less amenable to resolution than the latter becomes questionable when we distinguish between *values* underlying a conflict, the specific *issues* which define a conflict situation, and the *stakes* involved (cf. Holsti, 1991). An example which could be used to illustrate this distinction may be drawn from the Israeli-Palestinian conflict. This particular conflict may be broken down into a number of issues which are salient to the parties involved and around which negotiation has taken place. These include territorial boundaries, the nature of Palestinian autonomy in the disputed territories, the numbers and location of Jewish settlements in these territories, economic rights, the future of diaspora Palestinians, the treatment of political prisoners, and the maintenance of law and order. The values which underlie these issues centre around national identity, political self-determination, and the right to security. The stakes for the leaderships of either side include the maintenance of unity, legitimacy and support from their respective constituencies and allies in the external world. The success or failure of a process of conflict resolution may be determined by whether it begins with addressing the underlying values, the specific issues or the stakes involved.

Apart from the practical conflict resolution implications of the distinction between values, issues and stakes, the theoretical concerns which emerge from this trilateral conception relate more immediately to the concerns of this study. One central question revolves around processes which constitute underlying values, including the construction of social identity, and how these come to dominate discourse around a particular conflict. A related concern is how one form of identity, namely national identity, acquires primacy over other formations which could identify cross-cutting interests across the conflict divide. Understanding social conflict must begin with these continuities of social life, namely the processes through which a value system or a mode of discourse come to define the relationship between the individual and society. It is only then that we may begin to analyse how dominant values and discourses translate into specific issues and stakes around which parties come to be willing participants in violent conflict.

Vasquez distinguishes between "underlying" and "proximate" causes of conflict where "Underlying causes are fundamental causes that set off a train of events (the proximate causes) that end in war."[63] War is the outcome of sequences of actions and decisions carried out by defined decision-makers: "Those who made war decisions implicitly or explicitly calculated that the potential costs of men, *matériel*, property, and the possibility of humiliating defeats and terms of surrender did not outweigh the values and purposes that they sought or that were being challenged or threatened by opponents."[64] This approach to the study of conflict assumes that the emergence of violent conflict is an extraordinary activity undertaken in response to extraordinary circumstances. In confining analysis to the decision-making process in specific conflicts, taken as discrete events, this form of investigation precludes an understanding of the relationship between everyday forms of interaction and the emergence of support for war as a form of conflict behaviour. Furthermore, it fails to develop an understanding of the relationship between the discursive and institutional continuities of social life and their role in the relationship between the individual and society and the place of war therein.

A critical investigation

The aim of conflict studies from its inception has been to explain war, or human violence in time of conflict, in terms of its origins, its dynamics in escalation and de-escalation, its consequences, and the means by which it comes to an end. While we may explain the peculiar and the specific, the central aim of the field must lie in explaining the basis of support for war and its legitimation through time and geographic space.

Historical accounts of major wars, inter-state or civil, concentrate on those who make decisions, the leaders as opposed to the led, ignoring thereby the internalisation of war which inevitably leads to its normalisation. Until an explanation is elaborated of the non-combatants' willingness to support war, violence as a mode of conflict behaviour will remain a central element of the human condition.

Any investigation of war as a form of human action must begin with a conceptualisation of action itself. War is a consequence of human actions and human decisions. The central focus of this study is violence used in time of social conflict. Such conflict may be at the inter-communal level within domestic society, as for example in times of civil war or civil insurrection, or it may be located at the transnational level, where both state and non-state actors are involved in conflict, or at the inter-state level, where two or more states become involved in conflict.

The methodology conventionally adopted in the field of conflict research is the search for explanation, defined in terms of scientific statements of the cause-effect variety. The object for explanation, or the dependent variable, requires the identification of independent variables which "explain" the phenomenon under observation. The methods of the natural sciences are assumed to apply to the social sciences in general and to the study of war in particular. The aim is to discover objective laws which would be devoid of normative considerations and as such would lend legitimacy to a field which could easily be accused of activist-led emotionalism. To discover a statement of the "if X then Y" variety would be to emulate the methods of the natural sciences, perceived as the harder, more legitimate sciences. Under the behaviouralist revolution, a correlation between events was seen as a means of discovering explanation. Under this epistemological framework, theories are based on regularities which, if they withstand empirical testing, stand as explanations. If anomalies arise, the theories are either modified or rejected altogether. This is essentially the positivist idea that hypotheses can be tested by comparing their implications with objective, neutral facts of experience.[65]

The objective of this book is to develop a critical understanding of war as a social continuity. While it appreciates the empirical studies of conflict reviewed above, it seeks a critical understanding by situating war and violent conflict in the constitution of the human self and human society. It assumes that specific instances of war are a manifestation of the longer-term processes which have established war as a form of institution linked to discursive and institutional practices which define societal continuities. Further-more, the study assumes that a critical interpretation must incor-porate both understanding and the practical intent of promoting emancipatory social transformation. It seeks to uncover the ideo-logical basis of discourses on any social phenomenon and their relations to the constitution of human practices. It assumes that knowledge of human phenomena such as war is, in itself, a con-stitutive part of the world of meaning and practice. Any critical interpretation situates knowledge within specific historical con-texts and in doing so sees knowledge and history as the products of the constituting labour of the human species. Knowledge as such is both historically bound and interest bound. As pointed out by Held, "The plausibility of critical social theory depends on an ac-ceptable explication of the relation between language, action and history."[66] Tradition, or the historical context, must be an integral part of understanding, and knowledge itself is generated and made possible within the framework of traditions. Chapter two, therefore, starts this project by locating understandings of war within political theory and moral philosophy as discourses which have influenced our assumptions about human political violence. While the sym-bolic mediation of social action is central to understanding action, the world of meaning is in itself part of a wider complex shaped by material conditions.[67] Such material conditions situate the worlds of meaning and practice within the wider institutional con-tinuities which define particular social formations. Chapter three provides an analysis of human action which takes human conduct and social discursive and institutional continuities as mutually constitutive processes and, for this purpose, makes use of the writ-ings of Anthony Giddens and his theory of structuration. The aim of this chapter is to argue that (i) war can only be understood within a wider understanding of human action, and (ii) war is both a product and a constitutive part of the relationship between the self (agency) and societal structures.

Any critical interpretation of a social phenomenon must incorporate within its conceptual scheme the two themes men-tioned above, namely the place of discursive practices as well as structural systems of domination which have homogenising and conforming tendencies. As pointed out by Best and Kellner, "Using the dialectical category of mediation, critical theory attempts to describe how concrete particulars are constituted by more general and abstract social forces, undertaking an analysis of particulars to illuminate these broader social forces."[68] A critical interpretation thus seeks to analyse the connection or mediation between particularities and totalities, parts and wholes, individual artifacts and events and social processes and structures. The central focus is therefore on the constitution of phenomena and the interconnections between them. Thought and knowledge are a product of discourses, social experiences, and institutions while society is a product of language, social determination and human practices. Chapter four seeks to analyse the discursive orders and ideological frameworks which have legitimated war across time and space. It specifically concentrates on a "language of war" based on militarism and notions of justice which have structurated war as a continuity in social systems. The relationship between specific decisions for war, support for war, and the institutional frameworks of society are located in the construction of identity which, it is argued in chapter five, must remain the central focus in our attempts at understanding war as a social continuity. Emancipatory knowledge incorporates the basis of social transformation and, with this in mind, chapter six seeks to define discourses on peace. This chapter argues that the condition of peace and the elimination of war must rest upon transformed discursive and institutional practices which have legitimated violence in human history. Language and forms of communication are seen as central to the development of new forms of social solidarity which reject discourses based on the dichotomy of inclusion and exclusion, self and other, and processes which legitimate violent fragmentation. The concluding chapter seven provides a critical reflection on the approach adopted in this study.

Notes

1. Q. Wright, *A Study of War* (University of Chicago Press, Chicago and London, 1966), p. 20.
2. K.J. Holsti, *Peace and War: Armed Conflicts and International Order 1648–1989* (Cambridge University Press, Cambridge, 1991), p. 5.
3. Anthony Giddens defines his theory of structuration in *Central Problems in Social Theory* (Macmillan, London, 1979) and *The Constitution of Society* (Polity Press, Cambridge, 1984).

4. A. Giddens, *op. cit.*, p. 66.
5. S. Draculic, *Balkan Express* (Hutchinson, London, 1993), p. 3.
6. L.F. Richardson, "War Moods", *Psychometrica*, Vol. 13, Part 1 (1948), pp. 147–174.
7. Vanessa Vasic Janekovic illustrates this point in relation to ethnic cleansing in the Bosnian conflict where, in geographic areas containing Muslim populations which complicated Serb aspirations of a Greater Serbia, "the Serbs came to a simple solution: displacement. The improvised mass murder that evolved was only a logical extension of the game." See Vanessa Vasic Janekovic, "Beyond the Detention Camps", War Report, *Bulletin of the Institute for War and Peace Reporting* (October 1992), p. 12, quoted in L. Freedman (ed.), *War* (Oxford University Press, Oxford, 1994), p. 63.
8. Representatives of this school include K. Waltz, *Man, the State and War* (Columbia University Press, New York, 1954) and H.J. Morgenthau, *Politics Among Nations* (Alfred Knopf, New York, 1985).
9. T. Hobbes, *Leviathan* (Penguin Classics, Harmondsworth, 1985), p. 185.
10. J. Chanteur, *From War to Peace* (Westview Press, Boulder, CO, 1992), pp. 42–50.
11. A. Linklater, "The Question of the Next Stage in International Relations Theory: A Critical-Theoretical Point of View", *Millennium*, Vol. 21, No. 1 (1992), p. 78.
12. *Ibid.*, p. 78.
13. For the normative divide between cosmopolitanism and communitarianism in international relations, see C. Brown, *International Relations Theory: New Normative Approaches* (Harvester Wheatsheaf, Hemel Hempstead, 1993); A. Linklater, *Men and Citizens in the Theory of International Relations* (Macmillan, London, 1990). For a philosophical discourse on the liberal/communitarian debate, see S. Mulhall and A. Swift, *Liberals and Communitarians* (Blackwell Publishers, Oxford, 1992).
14. Quoted in Wright, *op. cit.*, p. 10.
15. Wright, *op. cit.*, pp. 8–9.
16. Waltz, *op. cit.*, p. 12.
17. *Ibid.*, p. 28.
18. See R.B. Ferguson (ed.), *Warfare, Culture and Environment* (Academic Press, Orlando, FL, 1984); P. Marsh and A. Campbell (eds), *Aggression and Violence* (Blackwell, Oxford, 1982); D. Riches, *The Anthropology of Violence* (Blackwell, Oxford, 1986); and G. Siann, *Accounting for Aggression: Perspectives on Aggression and Violence* (Allen and Unwin, Boston, 1985).

19. S. Howell and R. Willis (eds), *Societies at Peace: Anthropological Perspectives* (Routledge, London and New York, 1989), p. 8.
20. Waltz, *op. cit.*, pp. 101–102.
21. *Ibid.*, p. 205.
22. K.N. Waltz, *Theory of International Politics* (Addison-Wesley, Reading, MA, and London, 1979); R. Gilpin, *War and Change in World Politics* (Cambridge University Press, Cambridge, 1981).
23. See note 19 above.
24. A.E. Wendt, "The Agent-Structure Problem in International Relations Theory", *International Organisation*, Vol. 41, No. 3 (1987), p. 342.
25. I. Lakatos, "Falsification and the Methodology of Scientific Research Programmes", in I. Lakatos and A. Musgrove (eds), *Criticism and the Growth of Knowledge* (Cambridge University Press, Cambridge, 1970).
26. A.J.R. Groom, "Paradigms in Conflict: The Strategist, the Conflict Researcher and the Peace Researcher", in J.W. Burton and F. Dukes (eds), *Conflict: Readings in Management and Resolution* (Macmillan, London, 1990).
27. M. Nicholson, *Rationality and the Analysis of International Conflict* (Cambridge University Press, Cambridge, 1992), p. 22.
28. J. Galtung, "Violence, Peace, and Peace Research", *Journal of Peace Research*, Vol. 6, No. 3 (1969), pp. 167–191.
29. H. Schmid, "Peace Research and Politics", *Journal of Peace Research*, 5 (1968), pp. 217–232. For a discussion of this early debate, see A. Eide, "Dialogue and Confrontation in Europe", *Journal of Conflict Resolution*, Vol. 16 (1972), pp. 511–522.
30. E. Krippendorff, "Peace Research and the Industrial Revolution", *Journal of Peace Research*, Vol. 10 (1973), p. 184.
31. H.G. Reid and E.J. Yanarella, "Toward a Critical Theory of Peace Research in the United States; The Search for an 'Intelligible Core'", *Journal of Peace Research*, Vol. 13 (1976), p. 318.
32. J.W. Burton, "Introduction", in J.W. Burton and F. Dukes (eds), *Conflict: Readings in Management and Resolution* (Macmillan, London, 1990), p. 2.
33. T. Nardin, "Theory and Practice in Conflict Research", in T.R. Gurr (ed.), *Handbook of Political Conflict* (Free Press, New York, 1980), p. 463.
34. For the major themes of inquiry in the field, see C.R. Mitchell, "Conflict Research", in M. Light, and A.J.R. Groom (eds), *Contemporary International Relations: A Guide to Theory* (Pinter, London, 1994). For Burton's work on conflict resolution, see his *Resolving Deep-Rooted Conflict* (University Press of America, Lanham, MD, 1987) and *Conflict Resolution and Provention* (Macmillan, London, 1990).

35. L. Kriesberg, *Social Conflicts* (Prentice Hall, Englewood Cliffs, NJ, 1982).
36. This is the approach adopted by H. Blalock in *Power and Conflict: Toward a General Theory* (Sage, London, 1989), and by M. Nicholson, *Rationality and the Analysis of International Conflict* (Cambridge University Press, Cambridge, 1992).
37. L. Kriesberg, "Conflict Resolution Applications to Peace Studies", *Peace and Change*, Vol. 16, No. 4 (1991), p. 404.
38. Conflict resolution is one of the fastest growing research areas in the field of conflict studies. See C.R. Mitchell and K. Webb (eds), *New Approaches to International Mediation* (Greenwood Press, Westport, CT, 1989).
39. V. Jabri, *Mediating Conflict* (Manchester University Press, Manchester, 1990); K. Kressel and D. Pruitt (eds), *Mediation Research* (Jossey-Bass, San Francisco, 1989); S. Touval and I.W. Zartman (eds), *International Mediation in Theory and Practice* (Westview Press, Boulder, CO, 1985).
40. The development of a mediation framework within the CSCE to prevent the escalation of ethnic conflict in Eastern Europe is an area which may potentially benefit from the conflict resolution literature.
41. J.A. Vasquez, *The War Puzzle* (Cambridge University Press, Cambridge, 1993), p. 44.
42. For general reviews of the relationship between these factors and the onset of violent conflict, see Kriesberg (1982), *op. cit.*, pp. 66–106; Vasquez, *op. cit.*, chapters 4 and 5; and Blalock, *op cit.*, chapters 2, 3 and 6.
43. Vasquez, *op. cit.*, p. 46.
44. Blalock, *op. cit.*, p. 5.
45. *Ibid.*, p. 6.
46. C.R. Mitchell, *Structure of International Conflict* (Macmillan, London, 1981), pp. 120–121.
47. J.S. Himes, *Conflict and Conflict Management* (Georgia University Press, Athens, GA, 1980), p. 14.
48. Kriesberg (1982), *op. cit.*, p. 114.
49. *Ibid.*, p. 115.
50. B. Bueno de Mesquita, *The War Trap* (Yale University Press, New Haven, CT, 1981), p. 20.
51. P.J. Haney *et al.*, "Unitary Actors, Advisory Models, and Experimental Tests", *Journal of Conflict Resolution*, Vol. 36, No. 4 (1992), p. 605.
52. Blalock, *op. cit.*, p. 11.
53. On the concept of resource mobilisation, see C. Tilly, "Do Communities Act?", *Sociological Inquiry*, Vol. 43 (1974), pp. 209–240, and C. Tilly, *From Mobilization to Revolution* (Addison-Wesley, Reading, MA, 1978).

54. V. Aubert, "Competition and Dissensus: Two Types of Conflict and Conflict Resolution", *Journal of Conflict Resolution*, Vol. 7 (1963), pp. 26–42.
55. See D. Druckman, "An Analytical Research Agenda for Conflict and Conflict Resolution", in D.J.D. Sandole and H. van der Merwe (eds), *Conflict Resolution Theory and Practice* (Manchester University Press, Manchester, 1993).
56. *Ibid.*, p. 28.
57. Kriesberg (1982), *op. cit.*, p. 42.
58. R.F. Diehl, "What Are They Fighting For? The Importance of Issues in International Conflict Research", *Journal of Peace Research*, Vol. 29, No. 3 (1992), p. 335.
59. C. von Clausewitz, *On War*, translated by J.J. Graham (Routledge and Kegan Paul, London, 1966), p. 81.
60. Holsti, *op. cit.*, p. 18.
61. *Ibid.*, p. 311.
62. *Ibid.*, p. 313.
63. Vasquez, *op. cit.*, p. 7.
64. Holsti, *op. cit.*, p. 306.
65. M. Hollis and S. Smith, *Explaining and Understanding International Relations* (Clarendon, Oxford, 1991), p. 54.
66. D. Held, *Introduction to Critical Theory* (Polity Press, Cambridge, 1980), p. 311.
67. See J. Habermas, "A Review of Gadamer's *Truth and Method*", in F. Dallmayr and T. McCarthy (eds), *Understanding Social Inquiry* (Notre Dame Press, Notre Dame, IN, 1977), quoted in Held, *op. cit.*, p. 316. Also see J. Habermas, *Knowledge and Human Interests*, trans. J.J. Shapiro (Heinemann, London, 1972). For an international relations perspective, see M. Hoffman, "Critical Theory and the Inter-Paradigm Debate", *Millennium*, Vol. 16, No. 2 (1987), pp. 231–250.
68. S. Best and D. Kellner, *Postmodern Theory: Critical Interrogations* (Macmillan, London, 1991), p. 223.

Chapter two

The political foundations of a theory of war

We have to admit that the greatest evils which oppress civilized nations are the result of war – not so much of actual wars in the past or present as of the unremitting, indeed ever-increasing preparation for war in the future.

Immanuel Kant, *Political Writings* (ed. Reiss, 1991)

Western political thought on war and the causes of political violence is constructed on two foundations. The first is based on the notion that violent conflict emerges from characteristics inherent to the essence of "man". These are transcendental features which define individuals irrespective of the temporal and spatial domains constituting their social environment. War, according to this conception, originates in biological drives and instinctual aggression. War is as much part of "nature" as are other physical processes which constitute the natural order.

The "naturalist" foundation must be juxtaposed against thought which places war and violent conflict firmly within the dynamics of social interaction and the individual's membership of a wider social and political community. The assumption here is that while there may exist universal needs and drives across the human species, what distinguishes humanity from the order of nature is the social and cultural domain which shapes individuals and their interactions across time and space. War is here seen as a phenomenon which is peculiar to the human species and as, therefore, emerging from that which is distinctively social.

The aim of this chapter is to evaluate these two positions from the standpoint of political theory and to argue, in anticipation of chapter three, that our understanding of war as a human phenomenon can only take form by situating the individual within the wider realm of society in a mutually constitutive relationship.

The war–society interface

War is a social phenomenon involving two or more entities of mobilised groups and individuals purely for the purpose of war fighting. The creation and conduct of conflict parties involved in violent behaviour aimed specifically at a target adversary cannot simply be analysed as instrumentalist strategic decision-making. Such a Clausewitzian approach would merely be stating that the objective of a discourse on war is to determine the relative efficiency of each party as killing machine. Moreover, the war process is not confined to that part of society which is professionally concerned with war, namely the military. War as stated earlier involves entire societies, from those directly involved in the decision-making process and combat to onlookers whose lives are affected by war.

To state that war is a social phenomenon is to place war firmly within the context of social change. It is to assert that war is not only generated by and through social interaction, but is itself generative or constitutive of society. As argued by Martin Shaw, "war must be seen as a social activity related to the whole complex of social life and organisation".[1] While violent conflict emerges as a sudden and catastrophic condition disruptive of the everyday life of those directly involved, its progenitor in war preparation is precisely located in "'ordinary' social activity, integrated institutionally in all the structures of society – economic, political, and cultural".[2] The idea of a war-society interface suggests that war and society are mutually constitutive where the institutional and discursive continuities which define society come to form a central aspect of our understanding of violent conflict. Where strategic analyses of war have concentrated attention on the place of war in inter-state relations, the notion of a war-society interface suggests that even where war seems to be an external activity of the state, such activity is related to the dynamics of society within the state. Furthermore, the boundaries of the state within present-day world society "no longer insulates the 'inside' of the 'civil' from the violent 'outside'".[3] War emerges from the institutional and discursive pillars of society and recursively feeds back to reformulate, reconstitute and reproduce its constitutive elements.

A second means by which war preparation and war-making are centrally located within society is more directly apparent in the condition of "civil war", where the state's monopoly of force and internal sovereignty is challenged by political factions and/or ethnic communities seeking either the take-over of state machinery or total secession aimed at the creation of separate statehood. As is observed in such conflicts as the wars in Angola, Rwanda, Northern Ireland, and the former Yugoslavia, here society is directly involved and the distinction between state and civil society seems no longer relevant.

The individual's involvement in the war-society interface has a number of locations based on social role and autonomous individuality. That the individual may be a member of a "war cabinet", a civil servant in a government bureaucracy, a combatant, a worker in a defence-related establishment, a tax-payer or writer is an aspect of the relationship between individuality and social membership. Whether an individual's role has consequences for that individual's perspective on war is of central importance to understanding war as a social phenomenon. The form of investigation we adopt is dependent on the options available. As pointed out in chapter one, we may pursue the positivist mode where we seek to establish empirical regularities between, for example, social role and attitudes towards political violence or internal instability and external adventurism. While such studies are of significant value, the position of this writer is that they are better left to those who have greater expertise and interest in quantitative analysis.

The form of investigation the present work adopts is ontological. It is founded on discourses whose concern is the nature of individuality and society and the link these discourses make between individuality, society and that peculiarly human condition which is war. The themes which emerge in this chapter and provide the basis of the intellectual framework outlined in the next include the following:

- the relationship between individuality and social membership;
- war as a recurrent theme in human life and its position in the definition of individuality and social membership;
- the institutional and discursive continuities generative of war itself as a social and political continuity.

The aim in this chapter is not so much to treat each of these themes as separate and distinct analytical questions, but rather to look to discourses in political theory which have considered these questions. Clearly, justice cannot be done to the full writings of each of the theorists considered here and this is not the aim of this chapter. It is rather to interpret their discourses and others' interpretations of these as they relate to the themes outlined above. This chapter is a dialogue between interpretations or readings of textual material pertaining to the aims of this book. It is, therefore, undeniably selective and admits of the intellectual and social environment of the present writer whose biases will evidently be apparent as the reader moves through the text.

War and the "natural" order

A dominant and recurring theme in Western discourses on violence is that it emerges from natural tendencies inherent in man. A Machiavellian analysis of war and violent conflict starts from the premise that to be human is to seek self-preservation and the fulfilment of a desire for political power. This ahistorical assertion of a will to survive and a will to power leads Machiavelli to consider the implications of these drives for society and the state. His insights on the nature of the state and his notion of the *raison d'état* derive directly from his conception of the individual as a rational and self-interested entity.

Machiavelli distinguishes two types of war, namely that arising from need or the basic instinct for self-preservation and war which fulfils "desire". The instinctual drive for survival in the individual human being is here directly linked to war between societies and is a notion that is repeated by contemporary scholars in conflict research.[4] Machiavelli's primary interest, however, is in war as a distinctly political process and as a phenomenon originating in the human desire for domination. While the first type of war, that based on the need for survival, fails to provide a distinction between humanity and the rest of nature, the second type, that motivated by the desire for domination, is what distinguishes war as a specifically human activity. It is this second form, according to Machiavelli, which renders war a "political" as opposed to a "natural" phenomenon.[5]

Machiavelli's is a universalist language which assumes a human essence based on the desire for domination. The outcome of conflict is based on the relative distribution of resources which ultimately distinguishes winner from loser, the dominant and the dominated. If, as Chanteur points out, desire is the central concept in Machiavelli's contribution to our understanding of war, it becomes apparent that the remits of desire are those elements of existence which are contingent within the temporal and social realm of the individual human agent. To desire is to go into the realms of a remembered past or an imagined future. It is actively to seek that which is known to the human agent. As will be seen later in the book, such is the basis of identity-based conflicts and more specifically those centred around the "nation" and the ideology of ethnic nationalism. According to Chanteur's reading of Machiavelli, "Reason only mediates desire, furnishing it the best means for its fulfilment."[6] That which we desire, however, is contingent and situated within the realms of our experience. For Machiavelli, victory in war establishes leaders, war defines the political autonomy of territorial political units or states, and war which defends these against external others:

> A prince, therefore, must have no other object or thought, nor acquire skill in anything, except war, its organization, and its discipline. The art of war is all that is expected of a ruler; and it is so useful that besides enabling hereditary princes to maintain their rule it frequently enables ordinary citizens to become rulers.[7]

Ultimately, however, in Machiavelli's ontological project, war emerges as a constitutive element of desire, and desire as that which is essentially human. That which makes the individual social is not an affinity with other human beings but the desire to dominate, such desire being fulfilled ultimately through war.

Discourses on war as originating in biological drives, the natural order, are also founded on a Hobbesian analysis of the state of nature. The project defined by Hobbes in *Leviathan* calls for a contractual order which would contain man's capacity for violence. The individual male in Hobbes's *Leviathan* is driven by the instinct for self-preservation. Violence is used by the rational individual to avoid death in a state of nature defined by fear. Reason, for Hobbes, is a basis for both peace and violence so that "it is a precept or general rule of Reason that every man, ought to endeavour Peace, as farre as he has hope of obtaining it; and when he cannot obtain it, that he may seek, and use, all helps, and advantages of Warre".[8]

A Hobbesian analysis sees conflict and war as originating in the individual who is not naturally inclined to associate with a collectivity. Continuing on a theme developed by Machiavelli, the individual is driven by the instinct for self-preservation because of the fear that dominates human interaction. The genesis of this fear is the universal "inclination of all mankind, a perpetuall and restlesse desire of Power after power, that ceaseth only in Death".[9] The central element of a Hobbesian analysis of violent conflict is the basic need for survival in a world where all seek to dominate. Since not all have such a capacity to dominate, conflicts arise whose outcome is determined by war. The need for a contractual order is, therefore, evident where the individuals place the right to violence in the hands of an authority (the state) whose function is protection of its members. Reason thus becomes a basis for the renunciation of violence of individual against individual and the legitimator of violence between states which come to exist within an anarchical state of nature. The only rule which exists in a state of nature defining relations between states is that of self-preservation where "during the time men live without a common Power to keep them all in awe, they are in that condition which is called Warre".[10] War is not merely defined as that instance of war-fighting but as a general condition which is resorted to where necessary:

> For Warre, consisteth not in Battell onely, or the act of fighting; but in a tract of time, wherein the Will to contend by Battell is sufficiently known: and therefore the notion of Time, is to be considered in the nature of Warre; as it is in the nature of Weather. For as the nature of Foule weather, lyeth not in a shower or two of rain; but in an inclination thereto of many dayes together: So the nature of War, consisteth not in actuall fighting; but in the known disposition thereto, during all the time there is no assurance to the contrary. All other time is Peace.[11]

Hobbes "enjoys a paradigmatic status in international relations".[12] His assumptions on the state of nature, the rigid border between civic peace and international anarchy, and his conception of security form the basis of the "onto-theological foundations of an epistemic realism".[13] Hobbes's assumptions hold paradigmatic status in the field of international relations in that they form the foundation upon which contemporary realism, as the dominant discourse in international relations, is built. Hobbes's assumptions on the state of nature, the civic contract and international anarchy are taken as given, as are the consequences of these assumptions in the form of territoriality and sovereign statehood. Rather than attempts being made to deconstruct the textual foundation as situated in time and place, it is adopted as the teleological premise of realism. As pointed out by Campbell and Dillon, "Epistemic realism must actually continuously reproduce that which it claims, realistically, to presuppose."[14]

The state of nature is not, however, always characterised by war and the constant struggle for survival against the actions of other human beings. The Hobbesian definition of the state of nature has dominated realist thought in international relations, where the external affairs of states are determined by the assumed anarchical nature of the international system. Other thinkers in the Western tradition distinguish between the state of nature conceived as inherently peaceful and the external relations of states which are perceived as conflictual.

As pointed out by Chanteur, "In one way or another, all the social contract philosophers have invoked a state of nature for humanity and have pointed out its features. Though it is Locke who describes it as the original life of the human race, the state of nature plays the identical role of benchmark for all, however different – even contradictory – the attributes assigned to it."[15] The state of nature, according to Hobbes, defines an essence which is prone to war. Rousseau's state of nature is one of peaceful coexistence. Both, however, share an interest in a rationalist explanation of the creation of societies and its consequences for inter-societal relations. Both also share the view that individuals in the state of nature are not communal entities. Rousseau's individual is born in solitude, and peace is assured though the dispersion of the human species. The solitary life and the fulfilment of basic needs such as food and shelter are the basis of the state of nature which must remain inherently peaceful as the individual has a "natural repugnance to seeing any sentient being, especially our fellow man, perish or suffer".[16] The state of nature is prior to reason and is characterised by solitude and empathy with other members of the species.

In *The State of War is Born from the Social State*, Rousseau defines the conditions which transformed the peaceable state of nature into the warring state of social interaction. Such conditions were external to the human essence and derived from natural disasters which rendered nature an inhospitable environment for man's continued asocial freedom. Man's perfectibility, his potential ability to reason, enabled him to adapt to an increasingly hostile natural environment. The development of reason enabled humanity to observe and compare, to imagine future states, and analyse historical pasts. Human contact results from the awakening of reason and produces in its wake such social manifestations as ownership, interdependence, inequality, and ultimately war.[17]

Self, society and war

Discourses on war as a "natural" phenomenon must be juxtaposed with those conceptualisations of war as a social or cultural phenomenon. To state that war emanates from "society" is to state firstly, that it derives from the collectivity constituting more than its individual members and secondly, that those elements which make a society, institutions, norms and values, are in some way implicated in the generation of violent conflict. The relationship between individuality and membership of society, therefore, becomes crucial for our understanding of war. Can we frame an ontological discussion to uncover the forces which relate the individual to the actions of the wider collectivity? Can individuals stand alone as rational, autonomous beings or are they constituted by the group or polity which surrounds them? Is there a case for stating that both individuality and society are mutually constitutive and, if so, what is the place of war in this mutually constitutive relationship?

As indicated above, Rousseau identifies war as a product of society. However, the social state, which emerges through necessity, must at the same time preserve the freedom, equality, and peace that characterised the state of nature. The "social contract", a product of reason, requires that each individual surrenders his possessions and his rights to the community which only then is transformed into a community of equal individuals where civic peace is assured. The body politic which emerges through the social contract is both a product and a manifestation of reason and freedom and as such constitutes a moral community, or the "general will".[18] The individual as moral entity can only be mediated through the individual's membership of society in that the "passage from the state of nature to the civil state produces a remarkable change in man, for it substitutes justice for instinct in his behaviour and gives his actions a moral quality they previously lacked".[19] The individual, as moral entity, is therefore constituted through his or her social membership.

However, where reason enables the creation of civic peace, it does not impact on the state of nature between states which, at this inter-societal level, is defined by Rousseau as being ridden with war and destruction. The state of nature between states is unlike the peaceable state of nature that existed between individuals prior to reason since it is not characterised by solitude and empathy but rather by competition and fear of domination. The individual citizen's responsibility in these conditions is to the state which, in turn, has conferred on the individual his or her freedom and safety. A citizen's loyalty must be to the state and the will to sacrifice in the name of the state is a moral commitment made in the social contract. However, it is states that engage in war, where "private individuals are enemies only incidentally: not as men or even as citizens, but as soldiers; not as members of the homeland but as its defenders".[20] Human reason creates the social contract and in so doing renders the individual a moral entity having his or her primary duty to the state. Where Hobbes envisages an absolute sovereign as the outcome of the social contract, Rousseau's conception of sovereignty is democratised in the form of the "general will". Both, however, reify the state and territoriality with the latter clearly articulating a celebration of patriotism and self-sacrifice in the name of the body politic.

The transformation from the state of nature to society creates the conditions for war since war is a peculiarly social phenomenon. However, whereas civil society could be regulated by law, the only "law" that existed at the international level was that of the strongest, where order, as opposed to peace, could only be possible through a self-equilibrating balance of power system. In his *Project Towards a Perpetual Peace*,[21] Rousseau agrees with the Abbé Saint-Pierre's assertion that a social contract among states would generate the conditions for peace. He disagrees, however, with the notion that the rulers of Europe would actually act according to reason.

Rationality is only a potential attribute whose actuality is often prevented by the corrupt society which the individual inhabits.

For Rousseau, therefore, human reason is shaped by the society within which an individual is born and it is society and the place of the individual therein which generates the conditions for war. Can individuality, defined as reason and the free will, be conceived in universal terms, and can human reason extend morality to the realm of the universal so that duty and obligation are not confined to the boundaries of the state but extend beyond, to the rest of humanity?

The Kantian individual is an autonomous, rational being whose actions are determined by a knowledge of the rationality of other individuals constituting humanity where "each person's freedom to promote his purposes was compatible with the equal freedom of all others".[22] What separates human beings from the rest of nature is their capacity to be moral agents and to be such they must recognise universal moral principles which derive, not from pre-scribed, bounded societies, but from the universality of reason.

Kant's ontological vision starts with his definition of individuality in terms of rationality or that which is separate from the order of nature or instinct. Kant's political thought sought an understanding of the relationship between the individual, the state and mankind as a universal moral community and his ideas on this relationship derive directly from his critical philosophy. Elaborated in the *Critique of Pure Reason*, his philosophy of science suggests that the laws of nature are not inherent in nature but are rather "constructions of the mind used for the purpose of understanding nature."[23] Understanding moral or political experience was also dependent on the construction of premises or rules about human life which are logically prior to experience. Understanding human experience is, therefore, dependent on the assumption of universal rationality and autonomous individuality. Kant's political vision was to derive ethical principles which all rational beings share. The order of reason was distinguishable from that of nature and contained within it the basis of moral conduct. Rational (moral) conduct necessitates three principles, namely universality, treating others as ends in themselves, and acting autonomously.[24] The first principle, that of universality, suggests that moral conduct is not as finite as the boundaries of the individual's specific society or state, but must be defined as having universal applicability. Furthermore, to act morally is to "Act in such a way that you always treat humanity, whether in your person or in the person of any other, never simply as a means, but always at the same time as an end."[25] Kant's individual is an autonomous being whose will, as rational being, is that which makes universal law. Kant's constructivism is illustrated in the statement that "a rational being belongs to the kingdom of ends [moral community] as a member, when, although he makes its universal laws, he is also himself subject to these laws. He belongs to it as its head, when as the maker of the laws he is himself subject to the will of no other."[26]

Individuals, according to Kant, make society since, as moral or autonomous agents, they seek to act in accordance with rational principles which have universal applicability reinforced by the sanction of law. Such universalism is not only applicable to relations between individuals within domestic society, but is also relevant to the international system, where a "unanimity of principles" evolves to make possible that condition which is "perpetual peace".[27]

The ethical universalism of Kant is based on an ontological vision where individuality is defined in terms of a rational will that is moral, in that it is above natural inclination. The free will "is the one sole and original right that belongs to every human being by virtue of his humanity".[28] The right of every individual is to be treated as an end rather than a means towards an end defined by others. While individuals exist within societies having distinctive linguistic, religious or cultural attributes, what these share is a humanity based on rationalism which recognises no boundaries. War in this condition comes to violate the universalism which Kant advocates.

For Kant, a state of peace, or "perpetual peace" is a possibility, but must be created through human reason:

> A state of peace among men living together is not the same as the state of nature, which is rather a state of war. For even if it does not involve active hostilities, it involves a constant threat of their breaking out. Thus the state of peace must be formally instituted, for a suspension of hostilities is not in itself a guarantee of peace.[29]

Kant recognises all too clearly that peace must be made or created from conditions which have historically been dominated by hostilities among states. In his *Idea for a Universal History with a Cosmopolitan Purpose* (1784), he states that "Nature has willed that man should produce entirely by his own initiative everything which goes beyond the mechanical ordering of his animal existence, and that he should not partake of any other happiness or perfection than that which he has procured for himself without instinct and by his own reason."[30] It is, therefore, through reason that a "perfect civil constitution" must be created and this in itself must be seen as "subordinate to the problem of a law-governed external relationship with other states"[31] which must also be a creation of reason.

The creation of perpetual peace is, therefore, dependent on a number of prerequisites or "definitive articles" which must be met if the conditions which have given rise to perpetual war are to be transformed. Kant suggests that whilst war may benefit the rulers, it cannot be in the interests of free citizens living within a republic for they would have "great hesitation in embarking on so dangerous an enterprise. For this would mean calling down on themselves all the miseries of war, such as doing the fighting themselves, supplying the costs of the war from their own resources, painfully making good the ensuing devastation, and, as the crowning evil, having to take upon themselves a burden of debt which will embitter peace itself and which can never be paid off on account of the constant threat of new wars."[32] Reason can, however, also be the basis of peace between states for "reason, as the highest legislative moral power, absolutely condemns war as a test of rights and sets up peace as an immediate duty".[33] For peace to be secure, a "pacific federation" would have to be established which would secure the rights and freedom of each of the contracting parties.

Kant's views of war have been criticised on a number of counts. Primary among these is his assertion that while war may benefit rulers, it could not be in the interests of free citizens. Gallie points out, "It is as if Kant had never heard of mass invasions, of wars of whole peoples or cities, driven to exterminate or enslave one another by economic, demographic, religious or ethnic causes."[34] However, for Kant, all wars stand condemned for violating reason and a universal morality. His condemnation of war derives directly from his views on human rationality and a cosmopolitan moral order. Thus, far from conceiving war as a constitutive element of social formation, he sees it as an aberration of human reason and the requisite legality that underpins free societies.

Hegel's critique of Kant is that his concept of a rational will, through its formalism, lacks substantiality which is only derivable from a conception which places the individual firmly within the realm of society. The central relationship that is of interest to the present study is that which locates the individual within society or the wider community. It is to frame war within an ontological relationship between the individual and society and to ask the question: what role does war play in this mutual constitution?

Where Kant's individual is a free-standing autonomous agent whose morality derives from his or her reason, Hegel's is constituted by the society of which he or she is part. Where Kant's individual is a social being in a universalist sense, Hegel's is a social being in a specific communitarian sense. Identity and loyalty become a central focal point in Hegel's understanding of war as a peculiarly human condition.

To suggest that societies make individuals is to view dominant institutions and discursive practices as part of the constitutional make-up of the individual. This constitutive position would legitimately start with Hegel's representation of the relationship between individual and society. A full account of Hegel's thought would be beyond the scope of this book and is best left to works, both in moral philosophy and international relations, specifically devoted to the task. What is essential in the present context, however, is to draw out aspects of Hegel's writing, primarily in his *Philosophy of Right*, which elaborate on the relationship between individual and society and, more importantly in the present context, between the individual's loyalty to the community and war.

Hegel's philosophy provides a representation of the individual as a social being or a member of a community through which that individual's self-definition is constructed. The Kantian notion of a free-standing, cosmopolitan individual existing within a society of free individuals whose purpose is the protection of the free rational will is rejected in favour of the notion that individuals as self-knowledgeable agents can only be so through their society/community/state. This is of central importance in our understanding of group identity and of war as a spatial and temporal continuity. It suggests a reification of the local and the specific, whose individuality and autonomy must be preserved if freedom is to be the ultimate goal. The freedom of the self is thus defined in terms of the freedom of the community within which that self belongs. Such is the view expressed in the statement that "sacrifice on behalf of the individuality of the state is the substantial tie between the state and all its members and so is a universal duty".[35] "Sacrifice" and "courage" are represented not as individual acts, but as emanating from the community as a "display of freedom by radical abstraction from all particular ends, possessions, pleasure, and life".[36] For Hegel, the state does not exist for the purpose of protecting the freedom of the individual rational will, but is conceived as "the actuality of the ethical idea".[37] Hegel's primary criticism of Kant's ontology was what he saw as the empty formalism which confused the individual's morality with the ethical life. Hegel's distinction between civil society and the state is formulated precisely to fit his ontological vision as is expressed in the following statement:

> If the state is confused with civil society, and if its specific end is laid down as the security and protection of property and personal freedom, then the interest of the individuals as such becomes the ultimate end of their association, and it follows that membership of the state is something optional. But the state's relation to the individual is something different from this. Since the state is mind objectified, it is only as one of its members that the individual himself has objectively genuine individuality, and an ethical life.[38]

The individuality of the state is defined in terms of its sovereignty and "the work of courage is to actualize this final end, and the means to this end is the sacrifice of personal actuality".[39]

Discourses on war which start from the individual seem to neglect the fact that conflict and war are ultimately social processes. They are part of the social world within which the relationship between self and society is most explicitly stated. The individual is neither a carrier of instinctual drives nor a free-standing agent in time of war. The individual's actions and attitudes in such times are manifestly part of a wider whole; his/her social environment. The will to sacrifice is not situated within the instinctual realm of the "natural" self, but derives from a social constitution built upon discursive continuities which reify and reward such actions taken by the individual in the name of the state. It is the social world, that "framework of the central institutions and practices of social and political life"[40] which creates such constructions as courage, sacrifice, honour and prestige associated with individual conduct in that most social of human practices, war.

It is the social world, according to Hegel, which constitutes the individual agent. Human beings are conceived as self-knowing or self-interpreting beings who can actualise themselves as spiritual beings only through their membership of a wider community. For Kant, individuality is constructed through the rational will. For Hegel, the individual's "Geist" or spirituality derives from his social or cultural membership.

The ontological conflict between Kant and Hegel is based on the question of whether the individual can be prior to society. Hegel's ontological vision was to place the individual within the social institutions which formed the individual's environment in what Hardimon calls his "project of reconciliation". Individuality, according to Hegel, is defined in terms of the self as bearer of separate and particular interests, as possessor of individual rights within the polity, and as subject of conscience. Individuality derives from selfhood in that an individual must be capable of separating himself from the social role he/she occupies. The individual is seen as having a reflective relationship with the values and norms associated with the social roles occupied.[41] It is clear that Hegel has a strong conception of individuality where the agent is a reflective self within the wider community. It is also clear that the actuality of the self is only possible through membership of the wider society and its institutions, which, for Hegel, were the family, civil society and the state.

How does this conception of the relationship between the individual and society point to an understanding of war as a social institution? Hegel's answer lies in his conception of the state as the social institution which represents the common good of the community with universal interests that move beyond the particular ends of the individual citizens. The state is taken to be the community, and citizenship is the absolute expression of individuality. Where for Kant, every individual is an end, for Hegel, the state and its sovereignty are ends which form the ethical basis of the community. The reification of the state, in whose name violence may be committed, is apparent in the following representation:

The state is the actuality of the ethical idea. It is ethical *qua* the substantial will manifest and revealed to itself, knowing and thinking itself, accomplishing what it knows and in so far as it knows it. The state exists immediately in custom, mediately in individual self-consciousness, knowledge, and activity, while self-consciousness in virtue of its sentiment towards the state finds in the state, as its essence and the end and product of its activity, its substantive freedom.[42]

Where civil society may contain and accommodate conflicting particularities, the state represents a universal rationality which is ontologically independent of its individual members. An individual's identity is seen to be constituted through the state:

Patriotism is often understood to mean only a readiness for exceptional sacrifices and actions. Essentially, however, it is the sentiment which, in the relationships of our daily life and under ordinary conditions, habitually recognises that the community is one's substantive groundwork and end. It is out of this consciousness, which during life's daily round stands the test in all circumstances, that there subsequently also arises the readiness for extraordinary exertions.[43]

Here we find a link between Hegel's ontological vision and his view of war. An individual's highest actuality is in the state, and the individual's everyday notion of identity with the state culminates in his willingness for sacrifice in the extraordinary time of war when the state (and by implication the actuality of the individual) is threatened. In a world of sovereign, self-determining states, the idea of a "league of peace" as proposed by Kant is not merely unworkable, but is also undesirable in that "just as the blowing of the winds preserves the sea from the foulness which would be the result of a prolonged calm, so also corruption in nations would be the product of a prolonged, let alone 'perpetual' peace".[44] Just as war prevents stagnation, it also ensures the preservation of the state's individuality in distinction to other states. The "ethical moment in war" reflects the permanence of the state while the "rights and interests of individuals are established as a passing phase" affirming the state's substantive individuality.[45] War is, therefore, seen as constitutive of the state, which is itself the highest actuality of the individual. War makes states just as states make individuals. Just as the self-consciousness of the state comes into being in time of confrontation with another state, so too the self-knowledge of the individual whose constitution is dependent on the state.[46]

Where Kant makes a clear distinction between the leaders of a state and the mass of the public whose rationality would suggest that a citizen body involved in decisions about warfare would be loath to commit itself to taking part in "all the miseries of war",[47] Hegel's citizen is a willing participant. The relationship between those taking the decision, either on behalf of a state or on behalf of the community group, to utilise violence in time of political conflict, and those in whose name such decisions are made is of central importance to framing a theory of conflict. Representations of "the mass" become centrally important in any discourse on the relationship between identity and conflict and between the individual and social membership. Such constructions as "patriotism" and "jingoism" suggest or point to manifestations of mass attitudes forming a self-image that is distinct from that of a defined "other". Where such distinctions may, as has already been mentioned, form part of the everyday, they are magnified in time of war so that the perceived enemy is dehumanised to the extent of being deserving of destruction. Behaviour seen as unacceptable in the everyday is, in time of war, valorised, encouraged, and rewarded. The enemy is not perceived as a collection of separate individuals possessing private lives and concerns, but becomes a monolithic entity where the leaders and led form one indistinguishable mass.

The gendered self and war

War is historically associated with the making of masculinity. Behavioural attributes associated with war, namely courage, chivalry and the will to sacrifice in the name of the nation, are constituted in terms of all that which is masculine. The public domain, that world of war, politics and the life of the state, is a realm of being open to the male of the species. The private world of the home is the location of women whose contribution to society is represented as their capacity to reproduce future individuals/fighters. The symbolic world of war repeats this dichotomy where, as was evident during the mobilisation effort for the First World War, propaganda posters presented men with the option of joining the brave world of the uniform or remaining behind in the private, feminine domain of the home containing women and children.[48]

Nowhere is the association of war with masculinity more clearly stated than in Clausewitz's *On War* where he suggests:

> Now in our days there is hardly any other means of educating the spirit of a people in this respect, except by War, and that too under bold Generals. By it alone can that effeminacy of feeling be counteracted, that propensity to seek for the enjoyment of comfort, which cause degeneracy in a people rising in prosperity and immersed in an extremely busy commerce.[49]

That which is degenerate and self-seeking is feminine while "a people" can only come to recognise itself in the masculine world of war. As Pick points out, in Clausewitz, "Femininity and degeneracy are linked. War channels desire away from 'effeminate' pursuits. Energy flows from the feminine to the masculine principle."[50] War is not only a masculine pursuit, it is also represented, as Pick points out, in imagery which evokes a male sexual drive evident in the following statement:

> it is not an extreme thing which expends itself at one single discharge; it is the operation of powers which do not develop themselves completely in the same manner and in the same measure, but which at one time expand sufficiently to overcome the resistance opposed by inertia or friction, while at another they are too weak to produce an effect; it is therefore, in a certain measure, a pulsation of violent force more or less vehement, consequently making its discharges and exhausting its powers more or less quickly – in other words, conducting more or less quickly to the aim, but always lasting long enough to admit of influence being exerted on it in its course, so as to give it this or that direction, in short, to be subject to the will of a guiding intelligence.[51]

War in this text is not merely a product of instrumental reason, but is a constitutive element of Clausewitz's notion of the masculine self. There is here an ontological commitment where "war is a major aspect of *being*; it emerges as a production, maintenance, and reproduction of the virtuous self, a way (for men) to achieve an ideal form of subjectivity".[52]

Hegel's conception of strong individuality is similarly male. Women are excluded from the public institutions of the modern social world, namely civil society and the state, but find their "substantial vocation" within the family:

> man has his actual substantive life in the state, in learning, and so forth, as well as in labour and struggle with the external world and with himself so that it is only out of his diremption that he fights his way to self-subsistent unity with himself . . . Woman, on the other hand, has her substantive destiny in the family, and to be imbued with family piety is her ethical frame of mind.[53]

Man's participation in war in the name of the state is his highest actuality where for woman, duty is conceived in term of service, loyalty and sacrifice within the family.[54] In Hegel's framework, the constitution of women's individuality is mediated through the family and since in his view "civil society is that sphere within which alone it is possible for people to realize themselves as individuals in the strong sense"[55] women's individuality cannot be equal to that of men.

The gendered nature of the public/private dichotomy is a dominant theme within Western political thought and informs dualisms which privilege the male element over that of the female. As pointed out by Susan Heckman, "In each of the dualisms on which Enlightenment thought rests, rational/irrational, subject/object, and culture/nature, the male is associated with the first element, the female with the second. And in each case the male element is privileged over the female."[56] The gendered dualism that forms the basis of Enlightenment epistemology informs ideas on the place of women in relation to the public domain and to war specifically. Western political thought, including feminist discourses on war, associates woman with peace and the world of procreation and man with war and destruction in the name of the state and nation. Jean Elshtain shows us to be "the heirs of a tradition that assumes an affinity between women and peace, between men and war, a tradition that consists of culturally constructed and transmitted myths and memories".[57] According to Elshtain, feminists who seek to privilege the female over the male, who associate "female nature" with nurturing, relatedness and community, seem to be complicit in the "paradigmatic linkages" that "dangerously overshadow other voices, other stories: of pacific males; of bellicose women; of cruelty incompatible with just-war fighting; of martial fervour at odds – or so we choose to believe – with maternalism in women".[58]

The question of gender in war is nowhere more clearly evoked than in Virginia Woolf's writings where she explores the nature of war and its impact on wider social relations, and where she overcomes the dualisms represented above by uncovering connections between private and public violence and between patriarchal institutions and the perpetuation of war itself as a social reality. In her two celebrated feminist essays, *A Room of One's Own* and *Three Guineas*, as well as in her fiction, Virginia Woolf shows an awareness of the genesis of war as situated in wider social relations, and the consequences of war for combatants and those left behind.

A first reading of Virginia Woolf's *Three Guineas* may suggest her belief in the male/female dualisms which underpin Hegel's view of the gendered self. While she states that "war is a profession; a source of happiness and excitement; and it is also an outlet for manly qualities, without which men would deteriorate", she recognises the minority position of pacific men whose views of war are similar to hers.[59] Woolf situates support for war in "patriotism" but sees its expression as being constituted through the gendering of social relations such that perceptions of identity with the state and the will to sacrifice in the name of the state are implicated in the social construction of masculinity. The self, for Virginia Woolf, is a situated or historically positioned being so that "history is not without its effect upon mind and body".[60] The worlds of meaning and practice are, therefore, experientially situated in gendered social relations:

> It would seem to follow then as an indisputable fact that "we" – meaning by "we" a whole made trained and are so differently influenced by memory and tradition – must still differ in some essential respects from "you", whose body, brain and spirit have been so differently trained and are so differently influenced by memory and tradition.[61]

Women's view of war differs from that of men, not for biological reasons, but because the former's view historically derives "from the bridge which connects the private house with the world of public life".[62] However, the two domains are "inseparably connected" such that "the tyrannies and servilities of the one are the tyrannies and servilities of the other".[63] A full understanding of war can only derive from a recognition of the relationship and mutual constitution of patriarchal structures in the family and civil society and the particularist patriotism that is the basis of the valorisation of war.

The inseparable connection between the private and public is a theme that runs throughout Virginia Woolf's fiction. Her achievement here is to "move beyond the exceptional, marked event, which takes place on a specifically militarized front or in public and institutionally defined areas, to include the private domain and the landscape of the mind".[64] As indicated by Bazin and Lauter,[65] this is nowhere more clearly invoked than in her three novels, *Jacob's Room*, *Mrs Dalloway* and *To the Lighthouse*. The first vividly contrasts the impersonal nature of war with the depth of emotion felt by a mother whose son is sacrificed in the name of war while the second concentrates on the shell-shocked combatant as victim of war. The third, *To The Lighthouse*, deals directly with the causes of war and places these firmly within the domain of patriarchal attitudes in the private realm of the home and those which generate support for war within the patriarchal nation.

The split between the public and the private is at the heart of the relationship between gender and war and is central to feminist contributions to moral philosophy. Seyla Benhabib identifies the principal constituent elements of feminist theorising:

> for feminist theory the gender-sex system is not a contingent but an essential way in which social reality is organized, symbolically divided and lived through experientially. By the "gender-sex" system I understand the social-historical, symbolic constitution, and interpretation of the anatomical differences of the sexes. The gender-sex system is the grid through which the self develops an *embodied* identity, a certain mode of being in one's body and of living the body. The self becomes an I in that it appropriates from the human community a mode of psychically, socially and symbolically experiencing its bodily identity. The gender-sex system is the grid through which societies and cultures reproduce embodied individuals.[66]

The self is, therefore, constituted through the gender-sex system which defines society and which is at the core of the oppression and exploitation of women. It is also the system which informs the split between the public and the private, situating male experiences, including war-making, in the former, and female experience, including nurturing and care, in the latter. The aim of feminist moral philosophy has been not only to uncover the binary systems of representation, but to critically unravel universalist moral theories whose ideal of moral autonomy identifies the "experiences of a specific group of subjects as the paradigmatic case of the human as such".[67]

The "self" is, therefore, a gendered being in our constructions of the social world. As we will see later in this discourse, male and female identities are multiple and have unsettling (dis)locations. War is part of the social world we construct and that world is the realm of human activity, in the form of specific interactions, material exchanges, communication, theoretical discourses within the sciences and the social sciences, art and religion which constitute society and the human beings within it. This mutually constitutive relationship is the basis of the linkage between that which forms the "everyday" and the seemingly "extraordinary" time of war, where "we" participate as decision-makers, combatants, passive onlookers, active supporters, and dissident objectors. Where we locate ourselves as individuals is part of that multiple world of identities which forms each of our constitutions.

The above discourses do not simply represent an epistemological concern with war as a product of instrumental reason. War is recognised as a response to external conditions, but it is also ontologically situated in the making of the self. This is especially apparent in reading Clausewitzian and Hegelian texts which see the (masculine) self as instantiated in social membership. War is also considered to be constitutive of society, which is defined in terms of the "nation" or the "state". Such discourses see the primary duty of the citizen to the state, the sovereignty or individuality of which is fulfilled through war. Chapter three develops a structurationist theory of violent conflict which defines the ontological relationship between self and society and the place of war therein. Central to this discourse is an analysis of action which sees a mutually constitutive relationship between agency and structure.

Notes

1. M. Shaw, *Dialectics of War* (Pluto Press, London, 1988), p. 11.
2. *Ibid.*, p. 14.

3. H. Caygill, "Violence, Civility, and the Predicaments of Philosophy", in D. Campbell and M. Dillon (eds), *The Political Subject of Violence* (Manchester University Press, Manchester, 1993), p. 53.

4. Burton's human needs theory also postulates this connection between need fulfilment and the onset of conflict. See J. W. Burton, *Deviance, Terrorism and War* (Martin Robertson, Oxford, 1979).

5. N. Machiavelli, "Discourses on the First Ten Books of Titus Livius", in *The Prince and the Discourses* (Modern Library, New York, 1950), p. 302. For an analysis of the element of desire in Machiavelli's writings, see J. Chanteur, *From War to Peace* (Westview Press, Boulder, CO, 1992), p. 29.

6. *Ibid.*, p. 30.

7. N. Machiavelli, *The Prince* (Penguin Classics, London, 1981), p. 87.

8. T. Hobbes, *Leviathan* (Penguin Classics, Harmondsworth, 1985), p. 190.

9. *Ibid.*, p. 161.

10. *Ibid.*, p. 185.

11. *Ibid.*, p. 186.

12. J. Der Derian, "The Value of Security: Hobbes, Marx, Nietzsche and Baudrillard", in Campbell and Dillon, *op. cit.*, p. 98.

13. *Ibid.*, p. 99.

14. D. Campbell and M. Dillon, "The End of Philosophy and the End of International Relations", in Campbell and Dillon, *op. cit.*, p. 31.

15. Chanteur, *op. cit.*, p. 105.

16. J.-J. Rousseau, *On the Social Contract*, trans. Donald Cress (Hackett Publishing, Indiana, 1983), p. 115.

17. See Chanteur, *op. cit.*, pp. 110–112, and G.G. Roosevelt, *Reading Rousseau in the Nuclear Age* (Temple University Press, Philadelphia, 1990).

18. See Chanteur, *op. cit.*, pp. 121–122.

19. Rousseau, *op. cit.*, p. 26.

20. *Ibid.*, p. 21.

21. See M. Howard, *War and the Liberal Conscience* (Temple Smith, London, 1978), pp. 22–23.

22. A. Linklater, *Men and Citizens in the Theory of International Relations* (Macmillan, London, 1990), p. 97–98.

23. I. Kant, *Political Writings*, ed. H. Reiss (Cambridge University Press, Cambridge, 1991), p. 17.

24. Linklater, *op. cit.*, p. 100.

25. From Linklater, *op. cit.*, p. 101, quoting Kant, *The Moral Law*, trans. H.J. Paton (London, 1961).

26. Linklater, *op. cit.*, p. 103. But see J. Rawls, "Kantian Constructivism in Moral Theory", *Journal of Philosophy*, Vol. 27 (1980), pp. 409–425.

27. Kant, "Perpetual Peace", in Kant, *op. cit.*, pp. 93–130.
28. Linklater, *op. cit.*, p. 112, quoting Kant, *The Metaphysical Elements of Justice*, pp. 43–44.
29. Kant, "Perpetual Peace", in Kant, *op. cit.*, p. 98.
30. Kant, "Idea for a Universal History with a Cosmopolitan Purpose", in Kant, *op. cit.*, p. 43.
31. *Ibid.*, p. 47.
32. Kant, "Perpetual Peace", in Kant, *op. cit.*, p. 100.
33. *Ibid.*, p. 104.
34. W.B. Gallie, *Philosophers of Peace and War* (Cambridge University Press, Cambridge, 1989), p. 29.
35. G.W.F. Hegel, *The Philosophy of Right*, trans. T.M. Knox (Oxford University Press, Oxford, 1942), para. 325, p. 210.
36. *Ibid.*, para. 327, p. 211.
37. *Ibid.*, p. 155.
38. *Ibid.*, p. 156.
39. *Ibid.*, para. 328, p. 211.
40. M.O. Hardimon, *Hegel's Social Philosophy: The Project of Reconciliation* (Cambridge University Press, Cambridge, 1994), p. 16.
41. *Ibid.*, p. 148.
42. Hegel, *op. cit.*, para. 257, p. 155.
43. *Ibid.*, para. 268, p. 164.
44. *Ibid.*, para. 324, p. 210.
45. *Ibid.*, para. 324, p. 209.
46. See D.P. Verene, "Hegel's Account of War", in Z.A. Pelczynski (ed.), *Hegel's Political Philosophy* (Cambridge University Press, Cambridge, 1971).
47. Kant, "Perpetual Peace", in Kant, *op. cit.*, p. 100.
48. Two posters produced during the recruitment drive of the First World War are especially evocative of the gendered basis of the public/private dualism. The first was produced in Great Britain in 1915 entitled "Women of Britain Say – 'Go'" in which the framing device of a window separates the private realm of women and children from the public sphere of active, soldierly manhood. Women are, however, portrayed as supportive of the war effort in their responsibility for ordering their men into war. In another recruitment poster produced in the United States in 1917 entitled "Enlist – On Which Side of the Window are YOU?" the framing device of the window is again used to depict the preferred public side of waving flags and marching soldiers and the effeminate world of the private. See P. Paret, B.I. Lewis and P. Paret, *Persuasive Images: Posters of War and Revolution* (Princeton University Press, Princeton, NJ, 1992), pp. 52–56.

49. C.von Clausewitz, *On War*, ed. and trans. M. Howard and P. Paret (Princeton University Press, Princeton, NJ, 1976), p. 262.
50. D. Pick, *War Machine: The Rationalisation of Slaughter in the Modern Age* (Yale University Press, New Haven, CT, and London, 1993), p. 31.
51. Clausewitz, *op. cit.*, pp. 118–190, quoted in Pick, *op. cit.*, p. 34.
52. M.J. Shapiro, "That Obscure Object of Violence: Logistics and Desire in the Gulf War", in Campbell and Dillon, *op. cit.*, p. 121.
53. Hegel, *op. cit.*, para. 166, p. 114.
54. A woman's citizenship as conferred by sacrifice is nowhere more clearly evoked than in Rousseau's *Emile*, where he tells the story of the Spartan mother who is told of the death in battle of all five of her sons and hurries to the temple to give thanks. For Rousseau's conception of the relationship between the individual and the body politic, this is a primary example of citizenship. Margaret Canovan refers to this in her discussion of Hanna Arendt's conception of public space. See M. Canovan, *Hannah Arendt: A Reinterpretation of Her Political Thought* (Cambridge University Press, Cambridge, 1992), p. 224.
55. Hardimon, *op. cit.*, p. 186.
56. S.J. Heckman, *Gender and Knowledge: Elements of a Postmodern Feminism* (Polity Press, Cambridge, 1990), p. 5.
57. J.B. Elshtain, *Women and War* (Harvester Press, Brighton, 1987), p. 4.
58. *Ibid.*, p. 4.
59. V. Woolf, *Three Guineas* (Penguin, Harmondsworth, 1977), pp. 10–11 (1st pub. The Hogarth Press, London, 1938).
60. *Ibid.*, p. 12.
61. *Ibid.*, p. 22.
62. *Ibid.*
63. *Ibid.*, p. 162.
64. M.R. Higonnet and P.L.R. Higonnet, "The Double Helix", in M.R. Higonnet, J. Jenson, S. Michel and M.C. Weitz (eds), *Behind the Lines: Gender and the Two World Wars* (Yale University Press, New Haven, CT, 1987), p. 47; quoted in M. Hussey (ed.), *Virginia Woolf and War: Fiction, Reality and Myth* (Syracuse University Press, Syracuse, NY, 1992), p. 4.
65. N.T. Bazin and J.H. Lauter, "Virginia Woolf's Keen Sensitivity to War: Its Roots and its Impact on Her Novels", in Hussey, *op. cit.*, p. 19.
66. S. Benhabib, *Situating the Self: Gender, Community, and Postmodernism in Contemporary Ethics* (Polity Press, Cambridge, 1992), p. 152.
67. *Ibid.*, p. 153.

Chapter three

A structurationist theory of conflict

White shall not neutralise black, nor good
Compensate bad in man, absolve him so:
Life's business being just the terrible choice.
    Robert Browning, 'The Pope', *The King and the Book* (1868–9)

The aim in this chapter is to use Giddens's theory of structuration in the development and definition of a framework for understanding violent human conflict. The underlying assumption of the analytic framework suggested here is that there are discursive and institutional continuities which legitimate and enable war as a form of human conduct and which are drawn upon and reproduced by actors in strategic interaction. In seeking to reconcile action with social structure, the relevance of Giddens's theory of structuration for the study of conflict is that it is centrally concerned with the reproduction of institutional practices or social continuities ordered across time and space.

The problem addressed by the theory of structuration is the ontological relationship between agency and structure and its implication in the reproduction of social practices. The social practice that is of concern to this particular study is war or violent human conflict. The problematic for this study is not so much the decision to utilise violence in specific instances or situations of conflict, but war as a social continuity having a historically central location in the constitution of society. War is an option that has a perpetual presence in social and political life and that is continually reproduced or reinforced through shared inter-subjective meanings and images as well as social institutions which serve a war-making machinery and its legitimation.

The orthodoxy in conflict and peace research is the empirical study of conflict. Its focus is on the discovery of regularities across a number of cases of conflict such that general explanations may be formulated of all aspects of the life cycle of a conflict. The objective is to investigate the causes of various types of conflicts, the manner in which they emerge and escalate, the factors that maintain and protract them and the various means by which conflicts are managed or resolved so that general theories related to these aspects of conflict may be formulated.

The contention made in this book is that such investigations, while useful as empirical case studies, do not provide an understanding of war as a social continuity. The use and legitimation of violence as a mode of conflict behaviour is not confined to the level of leadership, either of governments representing sovereign states or of leaders of factions and community groups. The aim in this book is to understand war or violent conflict as a form of human action centrally implicated in the relationship between self and society. This chapter is, therefore, devoted to the use of the literature on human action as a baseline from which a structurationist theory of violent conflict may be defined. The study is not, therefore, concerned with the empirical observation of regularities discernable in time of conflict, but with the nature of human action, social reproduction and transformation, and the place of war therein.

The problem defined

The orthodoxy in conflict studies is to regard the individual decision-maker, whether that individual stands alone or as representative of a collectivity, as the primary unit of analysis in investigations of processes of conflict, including violent conflict behaviour. The individual actor as purposive agent is, according to one school of thought, seen as an objective utility maximiser where the decision-maker specifies a set of preferences for outcomes, the probability of achieving each desired alternative, and a calculated utility for each outcome. The basis of the decision-maker's preferences and utility calculations is not the focus of inquiry. The elements of the equation defining utility calculations are accepted as given. If action with the highest expected utility is chosen, including the decision to go to war, the actor has maximised or acted according to the principles of rationality. In having a set of possible courses of action, the actor or decision-maker relates the utility and probability calculations and chooses that which has the highest expected utility. In one of the most comprehensive investigations of the rationalist approach to the study of conflict, Nicholson points to the domination of this approach in stating,

> The subject of "international relations" is often regarded as an account of rational actors interacting with each other. In some views of the discipline, states are held to be the primary rational actors, and their interaction is all that is of significance, certainly when it comes to the issue of peace and war. Even if we extend the number of actors to include multinational corporations, religious organisations and other actors on the scene, the basic principle is still there – for the most part an account of international relations is an account of actors rationally pursuing goals.[1]

One of the foremost conflict theorists adopting an "objectivist" utility maximisation approach is Bueno de Mesquita, whose deductive expected utility model has generated a number of critical responses in journals concerned with the analysis of conflict. First published in 1980 as an "expected utility theory" of conflict in the *American Political Science Review* and later expanded in *The War Trap*,[2] the theory of Bueno de Mesquita and his colleagues is constructed upon the premise that rational choice underlies the onset of war. For a chosen course of action to be rational, the actor compares the attraction of alternatives and chooses that which best maximises utility. In a situation of crisis, actors make choices on the course of action they believe will best suit them. In *The War Trap*, actors (assumed to be unitary) have two options, war and non-war. War is likely to emerge when both sides, in an assumed dyadic situation, have a positive expected utility for war where both sides expect to be recipients of net benefits. Logically, if both sides expect to win a war, a negotiated settlement, which implies compromise, seems to be an unlikely choice or even an irrational one in that it suggests that the actors did not pursue maximum utility. In summarising his approach, Bueno de Mesquita writes: "The broadest and seemingly obvious generalization that emerges from the theory is the expectation that wars (or other conflicts) will be initiated only when the initiator believes the war will yield positive expected utility."[3]

Bueno de Mesquita sees a positive expected utility as a necessary but not sufficient condition for the initiation of war, but suggests that "the set of necessary conditions may be small enough to be specified and encompassing enough to prove useful in discriminating between candidates for war and candidates for peace".[4] The central organising principle in de Mesquita's theory is, therefore, that war cannot start in the absence of a positive expected utility calculation on the part of an actor assumed to be unitary and, above all, whose judgement of preferences and capabilities is not subject to scrutiny. Actors, who may be individuals, groups or states, are unitary objective utility maximisers whose behaviour is consistent and goal-directed.

The second approach in conflict studies, often referred to in terms of "cognitive rationality",[5] is again individualist in orientation, but takes into account the nature of preferences that parties in conflict express, the dynamic processes involved in changes of preference orderings and the interactive nature of the life cycle of a conflict. Where formal rationalist approaches assume predictable decision-making having precise calculations of benefits, costs, and probabilities, this second individualist approach takes into account the complexities of conflict situations. Conflicts are seen as highly stressful, unpredictable occasions, where actors, far from being unitary, are constantly bedevilled with factional infighting, and the scope for the interference of rather messy and incalculable psychological processes produces such "non-rational" perceptions as over-confidence, misinterpreted signals, and "groupthink".[6] This second approach looks to the individual decision-maker, either in isolation or as a member of a larger group, and points to various cognitive constraints that come into play in situations of conflict, be they sudden crises or protracted conflicts. Attitudinal and perceptual elements are seen as explaining the observed gap between rationality as portrayed in formalised/mathematical models of decision-making and the actual dynamic process of conflict. The potential rationality of the individual, whether in isolation or as a member of a larger collectivity, is distorted by a psychological tendency to seek cognitive means by which to deal with the stresses and complexities of conflict situations. The emphasis of this second and most prolific approach is on perceptions of the self and the enemy, on information processing, and on the impact of cognitive dissonance. The aim of the approach, as stated by Ole Holsti, is to recognise that

Cognitive constraints on rationality include limits on the individual's capacity to receive, process, and assimilate information about the situation; an inability to generate the entire set of policy alternatives; fragmentary knowledge about the consequences of each option; and an inability to order preferences for all possible consequences on a single utility scale.[7]

Other contributory factors to the intensification of conflict, such as enhanced group loyalty, selective perception of mutual histories, and the dehumanisation of the enemy, seem to be the cause of deadly and protracted conflicts and tend to distort the potential of rational decision-making and calculative clarity.[8] The central focus of inquiry in this second individualist approach relates to how actors make choices in specific situations of stress, disrupted communication, and complex or conflicting information inputs. These are seen as elements of the dynamics of conflict which disrupt the calculated precision of orthodox approaches to rationality.

The two models surveyed above have primarily been applied in empirical investigations of decision-making at the level of leaderships. We may also consider their applicability to explanations of why non-decision-making elites participate in violent conflict such as situations of internal strife which seek a change in governmental structures, personnel and/or policy. Rational individuals will, in such circumstances, compare the costs and benefits of active involvement against non-participation and distant support for those directly involved in combat. The question for rational choice theory is why private individuals risk personal welfare when they could potentially reap the benefits of collective action through being inactive "free riders". One approach is to suggest that participation attracts personal material or entertainment rewards as well as allowing for a realisation of a sense of duty to class, nation, state and so on. Another variant of rational choice theory is to suggest that public goods, where the individual considers that which would be collectively rational, as opposed to private interest underpin participation in collective action.[9] Such an individualist orientation to collective action is nowhere more clearly stated than in Popkin's analysis of peasant revolutionary action. Individuals, for Popkin, are self-interested utility maximisers, and participate in collective action, such as violent revolution, purely in order to improve their own future positions. Social change, therefore, is a product of the summation of individual action aimed at the maximisation of self-interest where individuals "evaluate the possible outcomes associated with their choices in accordance with their preferences and values".[10] Self-interest derives from selective incentives accrued to participants, a belief that public goods will result in individual benefits, and the perception that a personal contribution would be critical for a successful outcome of the collective action.

What is evident from the above brief survey is that both formal and cognitive models of decision-making applied to elite decision-makers as well as rationality models applied to non-elite participation in collective action share a baseline assumption related to the concept of instrumental rationality. While formal models are characterised by calculative precision, cognitive approaches seek to uncover the input of cognitive processes in the distortion of such precision. Both share an epistemological orientation based on individual intentions and frames of reference which generate conduct, including violent action. Their value in our understanding of violent conflict must, therefore, rest on an examination of human action and how this may relate to social reproduction and transformation. The individualist orientation must, however, be juxtaposed with structuralist approaches which see social formations as conditioning or determining the actions of human agents and their outcomes.

Structuralist approaches to the study of conflict emphasise the influence of objective conditions in the generation of conflict. Social structure is thereby seen as causally related to the emergence of conflict. In his conceptual construct of "structural violence", Galtung points to the material conditions of social life which constrain the development of human potentiality as the cause of conflict. His use of the term "violence" in this context rather than, for example, exploitation, injustice or inequality, is located in his supposition that while direct violence may be the visible manifestation of conflict, structural conditions may be as injurious to the person if not more so. Reference to such conditions as "violent" also points to Galtung's wish to widen the agenda of conflict and peace studies to incorporate investigations of underlying conditions which generate conflict.[11] Galtung does not, however, provide an explanation of the processes and conditions involved in the transformation of structural into direct forms of violence.

Ross suggests that "Social structural conflict theory does not seek to explain the outbreak of any particular incident of violence

or conflict; rather, it directs attention to forces which make a society more or less prone than another to particular levels and forms
of conflict and violence."[12] The focus of structural approaches to
conflict centres on conflicts of interest deriving from and inherent
within particular social formations. Neo-Marxist interpretations of
conflict point to the relationship between the mode of production
and emerging social structures containing conflicts of interest
which ultimately become manifest in behaviour. Hechter's early
analysis of nationalist conflict centres on "internal colonialism" as
a product of the capitalist mode of production and as the underlying
cause of conflict in English-Scottish relations.[13]

At the international level,[14] Wallerstein argues that social formations such as households, ethno-national status groups, classes
and states are effects, or products, of the capitalist structure of the
world system.[15] Any inter-state or inter-class conflicts which arise
are, in turn, products of the structural properties of the world
system. Thus, state machineries are strengthened both internally
and externally in order to subdue class conflict within and gain
primacy in markets without. Internal conflict is similarly a product
of the structure of the world capitalist system. Wallerstein's structuralist approach to conflict is evident in the following statement:

> The creation of classes is matched by the creation and recre-
> ation of the multitude of status groups (whether the lines are
> national, ethnic, racial, religious, or linguistic) as a mode by
> which sectors of the bourgeoisie and of the proletariat assert
> short-run interests amidst the cyclical rhythms of the world
> economy.[16]

The capitalist structure thus produces social formations just as
the cyclical exigencies of this structure produce relations based on
conflicts of interest. The functional overtones of this approach seem
to highlight the assumed passivity of states, classes and social
movements whose behaviour is determined by the capitalist structure within which they emerge. Wallerstein does, however, recognise the role of agency in his conception of "anti-systemic" social
movements, which are seen as having a potential for transforming
"not primarily the economics but rather the politics of the capitalist
world economy".[17] The problem remains, however, as Wendt
points out, that,

> The existence and identity of agents as agents, and therefore

of their causal powers and real interests, is produced, and therefore explained, by their relation to the totality of the capitalist world system. Thus, state agents are *effects* of the structure of the world system in much the same sense that capitalists are effects of the structure of the capitalist mode of production, or slaves are effects of the structure of master-slave relations.[18]

In terms of the usefulness of Wallerstein's structuralist interpretation of the world system for our understanding of conflict, a number of problems may be highlighted. While the approach provides an indication of the contingency of social relations and an indication of the constraining impact of the capitalist structure on action, it fails to suggest a conception of individual consciousness and the relationship between the individual and social collectivity. Furthermore, while it points to social contradiction emerging through the workings of the capitalist system, it does not explain the transmutation of contradiction into manifest violent conflict. It also fails to provide an ontological conception of structure which may be useful in the development of a theory of action that may be utilised in understanding violent conflict as a continuity.

The limitations of structuralist approaches to developing an understanding of violent conflict may thus be summarised along the following line:

1   They have not provided an ontological conception of social structure and its relation to social action.

2   They have not provided an ontological conception of agency, individual consciousness and its relation to violent conflict.

3   They fail to account for the primacy of some interests over others and the processes through which structurally defined interests develop into group consciousness.

4   As a result of the above, they do not uncover the discursive and institutional continuities which are implicated in violent human conflict and reproduced through every instance of such conflict.

Individualist and structuralist approaches to conflict identify the epistemological debate within the social sciences, reflecting a division between conceptual orientations which prioritise individual agency and those which conceptualise individual action as being a product of structural constraint. The present chapter seeks to define a framework for understanding human action which incorporates both agency and structure with a view to investigating how individual decisions and actions relating to violence may interrelate with structure, enablement, and constraint.

Rational choice and human action

As pointed out by Elster, "Rational choice theory aims at explaining human behaviour. To achieve this, it must, in any given case, proceed in two steps. The first step is to determine what a rational person would do in the circumstances. The second step is to ascertain whether this is what the person actually did."[19] Central to rational choice theory is the notion that to explain an action intentionally is to point to a future state it was intended to achieve. Explanations of action must account for the actor's goals and desires as well as her/his beliefs. An intentional agent chooses an action that she or he believes will be a means to her or his goal. This belief does not arise on an ad hoc basis, but derives from various perceptions about factual matters, or the material world, and about relations between means and ends. Intentional explanation, therefore, implies a triadic relationship as shown in Figure 1 below.

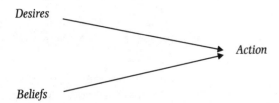

Figure 1: Elements of intentional behaviour

According to Elster, the "thin theory of rationality" leaves unexamined the origins of the desires and beliefs which form the reasons for the actions whose rationality is being assessed. The focus of investigation is "how" an actor best achieves her or his goals irrespective of the origins or merit of these goals. It does not attempt to uncover "why" that actor held the goal preferences she or he did nor does it question the beliefs underlying her or his choice of action. Bueno de Mesquita's theory of conflict is just such a theory in that it is strictly centred around a formula based on "objective" rationality where the origins of desires and beliefs are seen as idiosyncratic and, therefore, beyond the realm of "scientific" investigation.

A thin theory of rationality cannot be adequate in developing an understanding of war or violent conflict, in that to uncover the causes and origins of conflict requires investigations of the issues and preferences which lead to incompatibility between actors. It also requires an understanding of the salience of some issues over others and perceptions not only of the utility of particular courses of action but also of the legitimacy of these actions. What Elster refers to as a "broad theory of rationality"[20] seeks to inquire into the genesis of desires and beliefs and incorporates within its framework both psychological and operational processes within a decision-making model that is more broadly conceived.

Within a broad theory of rationality, the actor or party to a conflict is a situated entity, involved in a conflictual or mutually incompatible relationship with another entity and where ongoing antagonistic actions and reactions produce new elements to the conflict as it continues through its life cycle. It is an interactive situation where the desires and actions of one have implications for the other. The parties to the conflict are by no means monolithic units, but may incorporate factions and internal constituency groups possessing their own idiosyncratic agendas and attempting throughout the conflict to promote interests which may differ from that of the leadership. A broad theory of rationality takes into account the combination of both external and internal factors leading to a conflict spiral where increasing intractability, an intensification of conflict actions, and gradually ossifying psychological hostility are likely to result in violent conflict. However, as Vasquez points out, "there are a number of different paths that can lead to war"[21] and the multicausality of war suggests that while we may be incapable of defining the necessary conditions for the onset of war, we could point to any number of sufficient conditions which result in specific wars. The notion of "sufficient condition" implies that "when it is present there is a high probability that war will follow; it does not require that this condition be present prior to every known war".[22] In attempts to explain war, the methodology in conflict studies has concentrated on the decision-making process of governments and/or non-state actors leading to the onset of war. This decision-making process is broken down into several interrelated stages, including the initial definition of incompatible goals, the options deemed available for the achievement of desired outcomes, the distribution of capabilities and opportunity costs, calculations of costs and benefits associated with each tactic, and ultimately the probabilities of success. The complexity of an interactive decision-making process suggests that governments may proceed through a number of informational and analytic loops prior to the decision to go to war. The complexity of an analytic task aimed at the reconstruction of a decision-making process is furthered by the well-documented impact of bureaucratic processes which may produce conflicting analyses and information depending on the decision-maker's location within the bureaucratic framework.

Advocates of the individualist approach suggest that the notion of a purposeful agent determining action could be retrieved if it is recognised that rationality is bounded by norms and institutions. Actors' perceptions of a course of action, their preferences for outcomes, and even their perceptions of relative capabilities across the conflict divide may be influenced by the position which they hold within the decision-making structure. An illustrative example is the discrepancy shown, during the Falklands/Malvinas conflict, between the then Prime Minister, Margaret Thatcher, and the then Foreign Secretary, Lord Carrington. Where the latter perceived a negotiated settlement as an achievable and desirable outcome, the former was committed, from the outset, to the option of war as the only effective means of ensuring a return to the *status quo ante*, namely the re-establishment of British sovereignty over the islands. The two personalities differed in their interpretation of the significance of the situation as well as in their preferences for outcomes. The Foreign and Commonwealth Office is generally thought to be more cognisant of the potential merits of diplomatic procedure and the possibility of negotiated outcomes. This view was, however, rejected by Prime Minister Thatcher who, supported by the Minister of Defence, saw military action as not only enhancing her own image as "iron lady", but also as a vehicle for placing the United Kingdom firmly back within the military order.

It would seem, therefore, that both institutional role and personal inclination influence rationality and become highly significant variables in considering decision-making processes which lead to the use of force as a form of conflict behaviour. As pointed out by Nicholson, "different people's perceptions and values about a situation are deeply influenced by the role they play in the government, and they will look at any particular problem from their own perspective".[23] The impact of role differentiation is also evident in non-governmental or non-state actors involved in conflict, where the leaders of their military wings seem to be more prone to prefer the use of force in situations where a compromise outcome is perceived as a likely possibility by the "political" leadership.[24]

What is evident from the above is that war is (a) a multicausal phenomenon, where different causal sequences may apply to different conflict situations, and (b) a result of decision-making paths which, far from suggesting rationality as defined by strict criteria of consistency, point to the view that rationality is bounded by institutional roles and established norms which impact upon the informational and analytic loops which actors may go through prior to the onset of war. Both features present a problem for empirical investigations of war attempting to uncover patterns which could explain the onset of war, namely that while conflicts may share phenomena, causal patterns may not always apply. The second problem is that each war in such analyses is seen as a phenomenon resulting from the breakdown of social and political processes rather than as a constitutive part of these processes. However, since the assumption in this book is that each particular war contributes to the institutionalisation of war as a social continuity, it is important to build within the framework elements which constitute human action, including the decision to initiate war. The following section will, therefore, consider the impact of institutional roles on rational decision-making.

Institutional roles and the decision for war

One of the problems associated with rational choice theory is that it assumes unitary decision-makers whereas, in practice, governmental decision-making, especially within pluralist societies, tends to involve a number of bureaucracies and agencies of state. Even where the number of decision-makers involved is streamlined in time of crisis to a small group, it can safely be assumed that the different individuals comprising the group may have highly divergent evaluations of the situation based on variable desires and beliefs. Role theorists argue that any theory of action must incorporate the notion of role if it is to provide an understanding of human behaviour.

Perspectives which centralise role do not make universalist claims relating to all-encompassing criteria for rationality. The concern is to point to conditions under which contingent actors formulate their preferences and belief systems. In situations of conflict, it becomes imperative that the identity of the parties in conflict incorporate the specific roles occupied by individuals within the leadership group. This approach presupposes that the role held by decision-makers influences definitions of grievances, perceptions of the enemy, preferences for outcomes, as well as calculations of the distribution of advantage. To understand a particular action, therefore, requires that we situate the party within its identifiable social and institutional position. It also requires that we know or understand the normative expectations associated with each of these positions. As one of the foremost theorists of human action, Martin Hollis, states

> Think of each policy-maker at the crucial moments of collective decision as having an institutional position which accounts for his presence. Think of each position as laying normative expectations on whoever occupies it, thus giving him rules to follow, tasks to perform and demands to fulfil. Think of each actor as obedient to the demands of his position. In brief, think of the actors as role players and of the role as the normative expectations attaching to an official position.[25]

The observer requires knowledge of the normative expectations associated with each role and whether these are likely to be fulfilled. Any preference orderings and cost and benefit evaluations of the rational actor may have "bureaucratic source and shape".[26]

The concept of role has significant implications for the analysis of conflict and our understanding of war. One impact of role is "framing",[27] where an actor's judgement of issues in conflict as well as his/her perceptions of the enemy's motives and capabilities are influenced by a set of pre-existing perceptual formats and prejudices. As Hollis points out, "The information component of microeconomic decision-making includes the agent's perceptions, stock of generalisations and, wherever inferences are not a matter

of simple deductive logic, tendencies to favour some sorts of conclusions over others."[28] The framing process is itself influenced by
the role and social position of an actor, by the norms and values
which shape that actor's society and its history. An understanding
of an actor's response to an emergent conflict situation must, therefore, incorporate the actor's frame of reference. As indicated above,
one input into this frame of reference is the actor's role within the
institutional make-up of the party in conflict. The role occupied by
a decision-maker not only impacts upon the decision-maker's
judgement, but usefully provides "legitimating reasons"[29] to justify
decisions taken in accordance with expectations associated with
the role. The scheme portraying action illustrated in Figure 1 may
now be modified to take into account the impact of an agent's role
in the production of action. This modification is illustrated in
Figure 2.

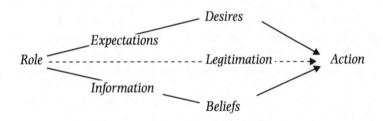

Figure 2: The impact of role on decision-making

Figure 2 shows that an actor's response to a situation, which may
be an emerging conflict with another party, is first defined by that
actor's desires and beliefs. These are in themselves influenced by
the normative expectations and processes of information gathering
associated with the institutional role that actor holds. The actor's
role in itself provides legitimating reasons for the particular action
or response adopted. The rational decision-making process is
here seen to be bounded by the influence of an actor's role in
society and the leadership of a party involved in an emergent
conflict situation. Under this scheme, the contingent actor's subjective evaluations seem to be shaped by that actor's institutional
setting. The actor is still acknowledged to be a purposeful agent
capable of rational decision-making, but that actor's evaluations

and perceptions of the costs and benefits associated with particular options may be influenced by the normative expectations associated with his or her role. There is, therefore, an interplay between personal and bureaucratic preferences.

It is evident from the above account of the impact of role on decision-making that a further factor which must be incorporated within our decision-making scheme is that of the relative distribution of influence between individual decision-makers within the leadership group. Any conflict within the decision-making body must ultimately be resolved either through a process of consensus-building or through the prevalence of one voice over others. The construction of the political agenda as well as the means to carry out policy must be assumed to depend on the distribution of influence within an organisation. As pointed out by Lukes in his three-dimensional analysis of power, the ability to influence a political agenda such that the competing party's concerns do not reach the moment of overt conflict is an important dimension of power and one that is often ignored in pluralist conceptions of power.[30] As indicated by Hollis, the ability to influence a political agenda is here defined in terms of winning "in covert, pre-agenda conflict" and "the ability to adjust the rules of the game in one's favour before the game starts".[31] This ability can reside with the individual's own resources or may derive from the role or social position held by that individual. The behavioural focus of this conception of power is that "it allows for consideration of the ways in which *decisions* are prevented from being taken on potential *issues* over which there is an observable *conflict* of (subjective) *interests*, seen as embodied in express policy preferences and sub-political grievances".[32] Here one could argue that in times of intense conflict with an already identified adversary, the preference for a violent response could be so prevalent as to exclude those whose adherence is to non-violent tactics or negotiated settlements. The political agenda in times of intense conflict is so saturated with one frame of reference relating to the adversary that any opposition to the use of force will be either deliberately excluded from the political process or openly ostracised and vilified as appeasement, treachery or cowardice. Institutional role occupants can have differential capacity to draw upon institutional resources in the control of information, in the processing of information, and in the manipulation of rules and normative expectations such that there emerges one dominant voice whose preferences for responses to a conflict prevail and ultimately become widely accepted.

Actors are role occupants and the question of whose choices prevail is dependent on the resources they have as individuals and as role players. Roles contain elements which are both constraining and enabling. The constraining elements derive from the normative expectations associated with every role. A Defence Secretary's role is constituted in terms of the military machinery of the state, and concerns decisions related to the upkeep as well as the potential use of the armed services in time of conflict. This does not, however, mean that a Defence Secretary's preference is always in favour of the utilisation of force. It could be argued that her or his greater familiarity with the military capabilities of the state would suggest that caution rather than adventure prevails. On the other hand, it may mean that a Defence Secretary's reputation may be tied with, for example, an enhanced reputation for the military forces or armed services of the state. Roles are, therefore, also enabling, in that they provide decision-makers with legitimating reasons for their preferences in situations of conflict with external parties. Legitimating reasons are not, however, real reasons, and both must be taken into account in understanding the meaning of an action. Hollis suggests a four-fold structure for the understanding of action, which is useful in our developing scheme for understanding the choice of violence in response to conflict. This four-fold structure incorporates the conventions associated with a particular role as well as the actor's intentions, legitimating and real reasons for the choice of action taken. This structure is represented in Figure 3.

	Action's meaning	Actor's meaning
What?	conventions	intentions
Why?	legitimating reasons	real reasons

Figure 3: Understanding action[33]

The decision-maker is, according to this scheme, firmly placed within an institutional context where there is an interplay between the decision-maker's preferences and all that constitutes that decision-maker's role. The balance between institutional framework and individual intentions differs from role to role and from individual to individual.

Structuralist analyses of role occupancy argue that roles are constructs maintained by institutions independent of the actors which occupy them. Primacy is given to the institution whose normative expectations shape the role player's desires and beliefs. However, the fact that role occupancy brings with it a set of pre-defined expectations where compliance acquires high salience does not negate the possibility of variation in conformity depending on the role and the specific individual which occupies that role. Even the highest degree of conformity to expectations implies purposeful actors making active decisions to obey the rules, whether these are formal or informal.[34] This individualist approach argues that in-stitutional roles are "cognitively mediated"[35] through and by the actors which occupy them. Even where the pressure to conform is great, as is the case within the military establishment, the individ-ual role occupant remains an active decision-maker potentially capable of nonconformity even where the cost is censure or even loss of life. The duality of this individualist/motivational approach is expressed by Searing in stating that "the roles of politicians are embedded in institutional contexts while at the same time treating the role players as purposive actors with independent standpoints. This integration of sociological and economic perspectives reflects, therefore, a recognition that political roles both constrain their actors and enable them."[36]

For the purposes of understanding the choice of war as a means of handling conflict, the above analysis suggests that while individ-ual decision-makers may be considered purposive actors, they are also role occupants acting within a framework of institutions which enable and constrain, as well as legitimate decisions depending upon the contingent dynamics of the situation. The institutionalis-ation of war-making also suggests the existence of rules which confer not only meaning on particular acts but also a defined appropriateness which comes to form part of society's accepted normative and discursive structures. As March and Olsen argue, behaviour is primarily "rule-governed" rather than consequence-governed such that "Politics is organised by a logic of appropriate-ness. Political institutions are collections of interrelated rules and routines that define appropriate action in terms of relations between roles and situations."[37] To do that which is "appropriate" suggests some element other than mere cost-benefit evaluation of options in time of conflict. It suggests that as well as role expectations, such continuities as social norms and cultural values must be taken into account. There is, therefore, an interrelationship between purposive agency, institutional frameworks, and the wider normative and discursive continuities which confer meaning on particular acts and situate these in the historical reproduction of society and its institutions.

Rules, roles, and reason

The above analysis suggested that decisions are taken within a wider framework of institutions which impact upon the emergence of conflict, the framing of salient issues, perceptions of the enemy, as well as preferences for particular courses of action in response to the conflict. Institutions are, however, "containers" of rules which govern behaviour in a regulative sense. On the other hand, rules may be conceived as constitutive of behaviour's meaning.

Both conceptualisations assume that rules form an element of the *structure* of social life.[38] In order to incorporate the concept of rule within the framework of action defined here, we require a conceptualisation of the nature of the dynamic interplay between purposive behaviour and social structure defined in terms of rules. We are concerned with the extent to which rules govern social action and specifically for our present purposes, what rules of social life may be implicated in the choice of violent conflict.

It must immediately be recognised that the notion of rules as defining social structure implies that they constitute the continuities of social life in the form of its institutions and dominant discourses. Conflict, and especially violent conflict, implies a breakdown of some rules and the generation of others. The relationship between rules and conflict may be conceived in terms of three possibilities, namely:

- that specific rules generate the conflict itself, where they are the matter for contention;
- that the rules of social life, as historical continuities, enable the choice of violence as an acceptable mode of conflict behaviour;
- that conflict generates its own set of rules quite distinct

from those governing society prior to the onset of violent conflict so that behaviours considered taboo in peacetime are glorified in time of war.

The third element is dependent on the second. It situates conflict firmly within the institutional and discursive continuities which define society. The first suggests that the rules in themselves become the issues for contention. If rules are conceived as "regulative" of social life, they may either allow or disallow particular courses of action carried out by specific individuals or collectivities. Conflict may arise from varying interpretations of regulative rules or in the contestation of their differential application. Social norms, both domestic and international, are a form of regulative rule defining at one and the same time guides for action and the possibility of penalty or reward. As Goffman points out,

> A social norm is that kind of guide for action which is supported by social sanctions, negative ones providing penalties for infraction, positive ones providing rewards for exemplary compliance. The significance of these rewards and penalties is not meant to lie in their intrinsic, substantive worth but in what they proclaim about the actor. Social sanctions themselves are norms about norm – techniques for ensuring conformance that are themselves approved.[39]

That norms can be a basis of conflict is immediately evident when we consider that "a norm is a rule for behaviour, the violation of which can be cited, and acceptably so, in justifying a sanction".[40] Rule violations may incur hostile reactions which are themselves justified in terms of the violated rules. Conflict could arise where regulative rules are broken or where they are seen as being asymmetrically applied. However, the fact that rule violation may generate conflict does not specify the nature of the response and whether this is violent or non-violent. Regulative rules "derive their character from their relation to sanctions"[41] and are therefore an aspect of social relations. The form of sanction applied is determined by the contingencies of the relationship experiencing breakdown.

Regulative rules have been distinguished from constitutive rules. Where the former are defined in terms of their influence on behaviour, the latter are constitutive of behaviour. A form of behaviour is only recognisable through its constitutive rules. A game of chess, for example, has specific defining rules which distinguish it from other board games. If constitutive rules define an activity, then their violation would imply that the named activity is no longer being performed. According to Von Wright, constitutive rules

> play no characteristic or important role in the explanation of behaviour. This is because they are not mechanisms for making people do things. But they are of fundamental importance to understanding behaviour, and therefore to the descriptions which anthropologists and social scientists give of the communities which are the objects of their study.[42]

Von Wright's statement implies that constitutive rules cannot be treated as "causes" of action but as inferences of behaviour's meaning where they enable communication through a shared understanding of the nature of the "game" being played. That the "meaning" of social action is related to communication points to the central role of language, as a rule-governed activity, in understanding the relationship between rules and social conflict.

Conflict is a communicative act relying for its emergence on signals which are context-specific and subject to appropriate interpretation. The expression of grievance implies to another actor, perceived as the "cause" of that grievance, the existence of conflict or the inference that an existing condition is recognised as harmful or unacceptable. Similarly, the use of the term "alarming" with reference to an action or a condition conveys the message that an action or condition is perceived as constituting a threat to the speaker's well-being, survival, belief systems and so on. Conflict, therefore, contains "communicative acts" or "action words"[43] to further or achieve specific goals in the context of social interaction containing rules of meaning which render understanding possible. Conflictual communicative acts such as the use of threats may, at first sight, imply the breakdown of rules, but are themselves rule-governed activities the effectiveness of which depends on a shared normative understanding. As clearly pointed out by Kratochwil,

> there does not seem to be a prima facie contradiction in claiming that the making of threats is rule-governed . . . while at the same time holding that any particular threat itself might violate fundamental norms. The first set of norms or rules concerns the conditions under which communication is effective; the second set deals with the issue whether the utilization

of the practice of threats or promises, etc., is allowed or enjoined by a normative order.[44]

The effectiveness of communicative acts such as threats, complaints or warnings, is dependent on constitutive rules which render these acts meaningful while the question of whether such acts are acceptable relies on the existence of regulative rules which define the contingent normative structure of a particular social situation. The absence of a shared normative structure will, therefore, have implications for the effectiveness of communicative acts at the outset of a conflict as well as during any attempts at conflict resolution.[45] It is important to recognise that rules and norms are both constraining and enabling. As pointed out by Kratochwil, "Actors are not only programmed by rules and norms, but they reproduce and change by their practice the normative structures by which they are able to act, share meanings, communicate intentions, criticize claims, and justify choices."[46] Human conduct is, therefore, both constitutive and transformative of the normative structures which render conduct and social interaction meaningful. Rules do not so much "cause" an action or a form of conduct but constitute the social continuities which situate the acting self within the wider realm of society.

Society is structured through its rules and normative structures which are constitutive of its members' identities while, at the same time, allowing them to "go on" in everyday interaction. Violent conflict is, however, an extraordinary time where the rules or the taboos which structure the everyday are directly broken and violated. To conceive of conflict as a breakdown of rules would, however, limit our conceptualisation of rules to imply constraint. Violent conflict would, in this case, indicate the breakdown of constraint. As indicated earlier, rules are also enabling in that they are guides for action as well as conferring meaning in the process of interaction. It is, therefore, important to recognise that the rules of social life, in its "everyday" sense, also contain within them those aspects which enable the expression or emergence of conflict, in its violent or non-violent modes. These are drawn upon by actors in, for example, the expression of grievances and warnings, as well as the resort to violence as a mode of conflict behaviour. Furthermore, a conflictual relationship, even a violent one, generates its own rules of conduct such that, as indicated earlier, that which was considered taboo in peacetime could be glorified in time of war.

The assertion that the normative structures which mediate between self and society also contain the enablement of conflict and violence requires an examination of the institutional and discursive continuities which legitimate the use of violence in time of conflict. Furthermore, it requires elaboration of the interplay between decision-making, institutional frameworks, and the choice of violence as a mode of conflict behaviour. The above analysis indicates that decisions may be framed by a set of normative expectations associated with particular institutional roles and by wider rules which constitute social structure. Such rules may be the basis of conflict, or they may enable or legitimate the use of violence in times of conflict. However, what are the institutional and discursive continuities which render war itself a social continuity and how are these implicated in behaviour?

The relationship between individual behaviour and social structure is one that is central to social and political theory. The relationship between self and society, or self and social collectivity, must be the focus of any attempt at understanding support for war and the individual's willingness to sacrifice life in the name of a cause. The relationship between individual behaviour and the continuities of social life is also central for understanding the reproduction of social relations, including war as a social institution. The following section looks to "structuration theory" as defined by Anthony Giddens as an analytic device which we may utilise in order to understand the place of war in the constitution of self and society.

Theory of structuration

One of the central claims made in this book is that war and support for war are practices which derive from purposive human conduct situated within deeply embedded institutional frameworks. War is taken to be a social continuity, institutionalised over time and across space, both in the development of war-making or war-fighting as well as in the identity-forming discourses which contribute to the legitimation of violence as an approach to the handling of political conflict.

Debate within conflict studies has centred around the epistemological divide between subjectivist and objectivist perspectives, where the former emphasises behaviour as conscious and purposive while the latter approaches social problems, including conflict, in terms of institutionalised inequality and exploitation as sources of "structural violence". If, however, we assume that both purposive agents and social structures are implicated in the emergence and generation of violent conflict, it is important to develop an understanding of the ways in which agents and social structure relate to one another in the production and reproduction of human conduct. What is termed the "agent-structure" problem emerges, as Alexander Wendt points out,

> in two truisms about social life which underlie most social scientific inquiry: 1) human beings and their organisations are purposeful actors whose actions help reproduce or transform the society in which they live; and 2) society is made up of social relationships, which structure the interaction between these purposeful actors.[47]

The problem is to bridge the assumed ontological gap between individualist orientations[48] and those which perceive social structure as determining behaviour. Social theory is often presented in terms of this opposition or dualism where "like Carthage and Rome, it is the war of the whale and the elephant".[49] The problem is to see both agency and structure as implicated in the production and reproduction of social systems.

In suggesting that agency and structure are implicated in the emergence and reproduction of violent human conflict, the framework developed in this chapter requires a conceptualisation of the nature of agents and structures and how they are interrelated or mutually implicated in the reproduction of social life. While individualism and structuralism respectively place agency and structure as ontologically prior entities, a structurationist approach problematises agents and structures in seeing them as mutually constitutive entities. Also, rather than being concerned with the "substance" of the social world, structuration theory is concerned with the "ontological conceptualisations of fundamental entities or mechanisms" where the primary concern is with the "constitutive potentials of social life: the generic human capacities and fundamental conditions through which the course and outcomes of social processes and events are generated and shaped in the manifold ways in which this can occur".[50]

In proposing what he terms a "theory of structuration", the domain of study for Giddens is "social practice ordered across time and space".[51] The aim of social theory is for "providing conceptions of the nature of human social activity and of the human agent which can be placed in the service of empirical work".[52] The aim in this book is to show the applicability of such social theory precisely in aiding our understanding of political violence as a form of social continuity. The battles of the social sciences, represented in terms of the epistemological conflict between the individual and social structure, are seen by Giddens as ontological:

> What is at issue is how the concepts of action, meaning and subjectivity should be specified and how they might relate to notions of structure and constraint. If interpretative sociologies are founded, as it were, upon an imperialism of the subject, functionalism and structuralism propose an imperialism of the social object.[53]

The implications of the ontological project which underlies structuration theory are clear for our present analysis. As it is a conceptual rather a substantive theory, the ontological conceptualisations provided in structuration theory are not subject to refutation on empirical grounds but require substantive research on particular social phenomena such as human conflict to "determine how these processes and properties operate and appear in any given context".[54] In developing an understanding of violent conflict, therefore, it is not sufficient simply to isolate one or one hundred case studies of conflict to discern regularities in decision-making calculations at elite levels. It means a recognition that decision-making and practice in one specific conflict is situated in time and in space such that language, meaning, perceptions and societal institutions are implicated, or drawn upon by actors involved in conflictual interactions.

Giddens starts with a rejection of structuralism and its insistence on the primacy of social structure as determinant of behaviour. He similarly rejects individualist approaches which seem to deny a role for the structural continuities which constitute society. In seeking to bridge the ontological gap between these two contending approaches, he suggests that in place of the dualisms (individualist/collectivist; voluntarist/determinist) which have preoccupied social science, the notion of a "duality of structure" which "expresses the mutual dependence of structure and agency"[55] is seen as recognising that "the structural properties of social systems are both the medium and the outcome of the practices that constitute those systems".[56] Another structurationist theorist, Roy Bhaskar, similarly recognises the mutual ontological dependence of agency and structure when he states:

> Society is both the ever-present *condition* and the continually reproduced *outcome* of human agency. And praxis is both work, that is, conscious *production*, and (normally unconscious) *reproduction* of the conditions of production, that is society. One could refer to the former as the duality of *structure*, and the latter as the duality of *praxis*.[57]

The aim of the theory of structuration is to show how agency and structure are mutually constitutive such that action is only meaningful in terms of its relationship to structure and the latter only exists as such in terms of human behaviour.

The first element of the theory of structuration relevant for our purposes is that human beings are "knowledgeable agents" in that they exhibit a familiarity with the rules of social life. Actors for Giddens are "positioned" or "situated" in time-space such that their activities reproduce the conditions that render those activities meaningful. Human knowledgeability is "reflexive" in that it is situated within the continuities of social life which itself has a "recursive character" in that every action adopted by human agents reproduces the structures which render those actions possible. As emphasised by Giddens, human acts cannot be thought of as "an aggregate or series of separate intentions, reasons and motives"[58] or as separate isolated incidents which could be subject to analysis devoid of the historical context which enables those particular acts along with others like them. Rather, the reflexivity of human conduct suggests that it occurs as a "duree" or continuous flow of conduct where the acting agent has reasons for his or her activities and is capable of elaborating discursively upon these. The central element in what Giddens refers to as his "stratification model of action"[59] is that human conduct is situated historically so that conditions which define the contextual framework of action are drawn upon reflexively and are reproduced intentionally or unintentionally through the process of interaction. Human action is, therefore, bounded by the "unacknowledged conditions of action" and by "unintended consequences of action", the latter becoming the conditions which render future action possible.

Giddens builds into his model of action a number of subjective processes which situate individuals as active knowledgeable agents capable of reflexively monitoring their conduct such that behaviour is conceived as purposive and as drawing upon the "stocks of knowledge" that actors have of the social world around them. The reflexive monitoring of action incorporates both a "practical consciousness", by which is meant a "tacit knowledge that is skilfully applied in the enactment of courses of conduct, but which the actor is not able to formulate discursively", and "discursive consciousness" where such knowledge is articulated. Practical consciousness implies a "routinisation" of social life which is inherent in the capability to "go on".[60] The model also incorporates actors' "rationalisation of action", which forms the grounds of their activity or conduct whereby actors, if asked, are capable of giving reasons for their actions. The rationalisation of action is distinguished from "motivations for action", which refers to the wants which prompt an action. The three elements of action defined in Giddens's stratification model are mutually interconnected and are bounded or situated in deeply layered continuities (social structures) which are drawn upon practically and discursively in social interaction. This model of action is illustrated in Figure 4.

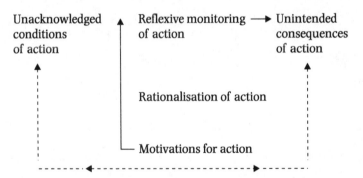

Figure 4. Giddens's "stratification model of action"

The model suggests that actors are purposive agents in that they have motives which underlie their conduct. They are capable of expressing rationalisations for their actions which, being knowledgeable agents, they reflexively monitor through both practical and discursive consciousness. Actions do not simply have intended consequences, but through their situatedness in time and space relations can have unintended consequences where the agent does not necessarily have an awareness of the full social implications of their conduct. War, for example, may be intended to produce particular outcomes within a specific conflict situation, but the choice of war in specific instances may have the unintended consequence of constituting war as a social continuity legitimised as a form of human behaviour. Similarly, the symbolism which accompanies specific national commemorations which glorify past victories in war may be said cumulatively to reproduce and perpetuate a culture of violence where identity is constituted in terms of adversity, exclusion, and violence towards past and present enemies.

As indicated earlier, any definition or understanding of war as a social phenomenon requires a conceptualisation of the individual and his or her social membership. As was seen in chapter two, social membership constitutes the self such that individual identity and individual conduct is situated in specific time and space relations. What are the elements of society or social membership which so constitute the self? How are these implicated in everyday activity? How are these elements implicated in war as a social continuity?

Collectivities constitute patterned and regulated relationships containing structural properties which are seen to "shape, channel, and facilitate system reproduction whenever it occurs by providing agents with the practical awareness of the practices, relations, and spacio-temporal settings they require in order to participate in the reproductive process".[61] Social structure is partly defined in terms of rules which "relate on the one hand to the constitution of *meaning*, and on the other to the *sanctioning* of modes of social conduct".[62] Giddens conceives of the rules of social life as "techniques or generalisable procedures applied in the enactment/reproduction of social practices".[63] An awareness of social rules enables knowledgeable agents to go on. Agents are, however, differentially situated in relation to social rules such that access to resources is also an element of constraint and enablement. Structure is, therefore, both rules and resources organised as properties of social systems defined as regularised social practices. According to

Giddens, "The structuration of social systems means studying the modes in which such systems, grounded in the activities of situated actors who draw upon rules and resources in the diversity of action contexts, are produced and reproduced in interaction."[64]

Power is a central component of all social systems and is implicated in the activities of agents in both conflictual and cooperative relationships. Power relates to the resources that agents draw upon in seeking to achieve desired outcomes. Resources that form an aspect of the structural properties of social systems may, according to Giddens, be "allocative" or "authoritative". Both are implicated in the constitution of structures of domination (to be discussed below). The first refers to control over material facilities, including means of material production/reproduction and the goods produced. The latter refers to control over the activities of human beings, their opportunities for development and self-expression, their organisation, and their mutual association.[65] These are not fixed resources, but form a continually changing aspect of different types of social formations. As will be seen later in this study, structures of domination are centrally implicated in the reproduction of war as a social continuity.

As indicated earlier, central to structuration is the idea of the "duality of structure". For Giddens,

> the structural properties of social systems are both medium and outcome of the practices they recursively organise. Structure is not "external" to individuals: as memory traces, and as instantiated in social practices, it is in a certain sense more "internal" than exterior to their activities . . . [66]

In this sense, the constitution of society is accomplished through the conduct of its knowledgeable agents but not under "conditions that are wholly intended or wholly comprehended by them".[67] The patterned regularities of social systems are, therefore, a result of an interaction between underlying structures and intentional conduct.

Interaction between agents, whether in the everyday mode or during the most violent upheavals, through the knowledgeable activities of situated actors, draws upon rules and resources in the production and reproduction of social systems. The idea of a duality of structure places the individual firmly within the context of society, each complementing the other and each constituting the other. The structural properties of social systems may be so stretched and so deeply embedded in time and space that they may be beyond the control of any individual actor, despite the fact that such properties are recursively reproduced in interaction. Furthermore, the structural properties of social systems may be so deeply embedded that actors' knowledge of these systems, through both practical and discursive consciousness, may reify specific social relations so as to naturalise historically contingent conditions. It is the production and reproduction of social systems whose structured properties are drawn upon by agents in interaction that define the continuities of social life. It is these continuities which provide the basis for everyday life and which link the everyday with the seemingly extraordinary time of conflict.

Giddens defines the means by which the interaction of knowledgeable agents draws upon and reconstitutes the rules and resources which define structure. He provides a schematic chart, illustrated in Figure 5, to illustrate the reciprocal relationship between structure and human interaction.

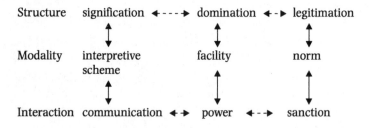

Figure 5: The association of structure and agency[68]

The two aspects of rules, constituting meaning and normative sanctions, imply firstly that actors utilise "interpretative schemes" in the reproduction of meaning or "signification". The central element of social interaction is communication and for this process to be meaningful, actors draw upon interpretative schemes which situate or typify actors' stocks of knowledge and which sustain communication. Structures of signification imply shared symbolic orders and modes of discourse which enable as well as constrain everyday interaction and situate or position actors in time and space. Structures of signification are, therefore, central to communicative interaction.

Structures of "legitimation" define that second element of the rules of social life, namely norms and the sanctions which accompany their application in social interaction. Normative expectations refer to those codes of conduct, some enshrined in law and others more informal, which legitimate some actions while censoring others. Dominant norms are central in the definition and constitution of society and can be subject to conflict at different times in the historical process. Normative sanctions as well as dominant modes of discourse also imply structures of "domination", or asymmetries in power which rely on the differential capability of different actors to mobilise allocative and authoritative resources in support of their actions. Interaction between agents draws upon these structures of signification, legitimation and domination which become institutionalised in the "long duree" of social life into political, economic, legal and symbolic orders which define societies and situate individuals in specific time and space relations. Each component of the scheme illustrated in Figure 5 is linked to the other to signify that no single aspect of the duality of structure exists apart from the other elements during the course of interaction and the reproduction of social systems.

The asymmetrical distribution of power gives rise to structures of domination which are drawn upon by contextually located actors in the conduct of their daily encounters and during the most pronounced upheavals. Social systems that have a regularised existence across time and space always exhibit forms of domination which have a defining impact on the production of dominant discourses, symbolic affiliations and normative expectations. Public space, it could be argued, is a realm of contestation for the production of dominant discourses. Such contestation draws upon the structural continuities of social systems in the reproduction or transformation of such systems. Power and domination cannot, therefore, be reduced to decisions taken in relation to specified targets. Such overt forms of power must also be seen in relation to more "hidden" forms which, for example, allow certain discourses and self-definitions while rendering others invisible and therefore beyond contestation. Such power runs silently through discursive and institutional practices and severely limits the transformative capacity of individuals and collectivities.

Contestation of structures of domination is, however, always possible, as is evident in any situation of social conflict. Where strategies of control draw upon structures of domination in seeking compliance and conformity, they also generate in their wake counter-strategies and counter-discourses which challenge the given, established order. Such is what Giddens refers to as the "dialectic of control", which points to the capacity of agents "to make a difference".[69] The structural properties of social systems are always, therefore, both enabling and constraining. Given the duality of structure in structuration theory, actors are seen to reproduce and transform social systems through drawing upon the structural continuities of these systems, just as the rules and resources which constitute structure may limit the possibilities of choice available to situated actors. The latter is especially the case with deeply-embedded social institutions which become resistant to change by any specific individual agent.[70]

One of the most important features of structuration theory for the present context is its recognition that the actors whose conduct constitutes the regularities of social systems are "positioned" or situated in time and space. A social position typifies an agent and specifies for that agent a definite identity within a network of social relations. The concept of social position is a central "mediating concept" between agency and structure. The importance of social position in structuration theory is evident in Bhaskar's statement that,

> We need a system of mediating concepts, encompassing both aspects of the duality of praxis, designating the "slots", as it were, in the social structure into which active subjects must slip in order to reproduce it; that is, a system of concepts designating the "point of contact" between human agency and social structures . . . It is clear that the mediating system we need is that of the positions (places, functions, rules, tasks, duties, rights, etc.) occupied (filled, assumed, enacted, etc.) by individuals, and of the *practices* (activities, etc.) in which, in virtue of their occupancy of these positions (and vice versa), they engage. I shall call this mediating system the position-practice system.[71]

As previously discussed in this chapter, the notion of role is central to our understanding of human action. The concept of role must, however, be distinguished from that of social position in that where the former implies an element of clarity in formalised institutional frameworks, social position is a wider concept in that it incorporates other interlocking spatial zones such as the home, the workplace, the nation-state, and global society as a whole. The concept of social position implies that all encounters are contextualised or framed by rules which sustain meaning and define normative expectations. Framing makes sense of the activities in which actors engage in that it constitutes and regulates activity within specified criteria.[72] A social position also indicates the contingent elements which constitute individual identity and its relationship to conflict and social mobilisation.

The framework developed in this chapter starts from the notion that actors are purposeful agents whose formulations of desires and beliefs define specific preferences for outcomes resulting from social interaction. Such interactions take place between situated individuals whose membership of the wider society and its institutions suggests an interplay or a duality where the individual as agent and the structured properties of social systems are mutually constitutive through the continuities of social life. Actors' motivations for conduct are not, as in classical rational theory, taken as given, but their constitution becomes central to an understanding of the situated nature of the self and the place of conflict therein. The framework utilises the notion of role in order to incorporate the impact of bounded institutional frameworks on actors' decision-making processes. The framework also argues that social systems, defined in terms of the regularities of social life, are reproduced through the interaction of agency with the structured continuities of signification, legitimation and domination. Specific actions between situated agents are, therefore, seen as forming part of the wider whole, and as implicated in the reproduction of social systems. It is this recursive/reflexive part of social life which suggests that the analysis of particular conflicts as isolated incidents cannot adequately address the question of war as a social continuity. The single conflict is, however, seen as reconstitutive of the wider realm of society and the contingent nature of its time-space instantiation. It is this continual interplay of occurrences that renders war a specifically social phenomenon having elements of continuity so deeply layered as to make it a social institution defined by its own particular rules, but enabled through the wider rules and resources of social systems.

The objective of the remainder of this book is to utilise the framework developed in this chapter to analyse or provide an understanding of violent conflict recognised as an extraordinary form of activity which is, however, situated within the institutional continuities of social life. It specifically seeks to locate violent human conflict in terms of its relationship to discursive and institutional continuities which underpin structures of signification, legitimation and domination. Chapter four analyses the discursive structures which enable and legitimate violence, while chapter five analyses the construction of identity and its relationship to conflict.

Notes

1. M. Nicholson, *Rationality and the Analysis of International Conflict* (Cambridge University Press, Cambridge, 1992), p. 45.
2. B. Bueno de Mesquita, *The War Trap* (Yale University Press, New Haven, CT, 1981).
3. *Ibid.*, p. 127.
4. *Ibid.*, pp. 4–5.
5. O. Holsti, "Crisis Management", in B. Glad (ed.), *Psychological Dimensions of Conflict* (Sage, London, 1990).
6. I.L. Janis, *Groupthink* (Houghton Mifflin, Boston, 1982); R. Jervis, *Perception and Misperception in International Politics* (Princeton University Press, Princeton, NJ, 1976); Nicholson, *op. cit.*, pp. 120–137.
7. Holsti, *op. cit.*, p. 122.
8. For detailed analyses of the psychological manifestations of international conflict, see M. Deutsch, "Subjective Features of Conflict Resolution", in R. Vayrynen (ed.), *New Directions in Conflict Theory* (Sage, London, 1991); C.R. Mitchell, *Structure of International Conflict* (Macmillan, London, 1981); R.K. White, *Nobody Wanted War: Misperception in Vietnam and Other Wars* (Doubleday/Anchor, New York, 1970); R.K. White, *Fearful Warriors: A Psychological Profile of US–Soviet Relations* (Free Press, New York, 1984).
9. E.N. Muller and K.-D. Opp, "Rational Choice and Rebellious Collective Action", *American Political Science Review*, Vol. 80, No. 2 (1986), pp. 472–487.
10. Popkin argues that it is a function of the ability of revolutionary organisations to provide the incentives necessary to persuade individuals to participate in revolutionary conduct. S. Popkin, *The Rational*

Peasant: The Political Economy of Rural Society in Vietnam (University of California Press, Berkeley, 1979), p. 31.

11. For a discussion of the debates which Galtung initiated within the field of conflict and peace studies, see chapter one.

12. M.H. Ross, *The Culture of Conflict: Interpretations and Interests in Comparative Perspective* (Yale University Press, New Haven, CT and London, 1993), p. 35.

13. M. Hechter, *Internal Colonialism: The Celtic Fringe in British National Development 1536–1966* (University of California Press, Berkeley, 1975). It is important to point to Hechter's later research, which places emphasis on rational choice as the basis of human conduct. See M. Hechter, "Rational Choice Theory and the Study of Race", in J. Rex and D. Mason (eds), *Theories of Race and Ethnic Relations* (Cambridge University Press, Cambridge, 1986).

14. Neo-realism, as a structuralist orientation to international relations, conceptualises war as a product of the anarchic international system. See chapter one for a brief review of this approach.

15. See I. Wallerstein, "The Future of the World Economy", in T.K. Hopkins and I. Wallerstein (eds), *Processes of the World System* (Sage, London, 1980); I. Wallerstein, *The Capitalist World Economy* (Cambridge University Press, Cambridge, 1979).

16. Wallerstein (1980), *op. cit.*, p. 171.

17. *Ibid.*, p. 177.

18. A.E. Wendt, "The Agent-Structure Problem in International Relations Theory", *International Organisation*, Vol. 41, No. 3 (1987), p. 346.

19. J. Elster, *Nuts and Bolts for the Social Sciences* (Cambridge University Press, Cambridge, 1989), p. 30.

20. J. Elster, *Sour Grapes: Studies in the Subversion of Rationality* (Cambridge University Press, Cambridge, 1983), pp. 15–26.

21. J.A. Vasquez, *The War Puzzle* (Cambridge University Press, Cambridge, 1993), p. 48.

22. *Ibid.*, p. 49.

23. Nicholson, *op. cit.*, p. 56.

24. Hobbes points to the war-proneness of the military when he states "all men that are ambitious of military command, are inclined to continue the causes of warre; and to stirre up trouble and sedition: for there is no honour Military but by warre; nor any such hope to mend an ill game, as by causing a new shuffle". T. Hobbes, *Leviathan* (Penguin Classics, Harmondsworth, 1985), p. 162.

25. M. Hollis, *The Cunning of Reason* (Cambridge University Press, Cambridge, 1987), p. 151.

26. *Ibid.*, p. 157.

27. See R. Nisbett and L. Ross, *Human Inference: Strategies and Short-comings of Social Judgement* (Prentice Hall, Englewood Cliffs, NJ, 1980); and A. Tversky and D. Kahneman, *Judgement Under Uncertainty: Heuristics and Biases* (Cambridge University Press, Cambridge, 1982).
28. Hollis, *op. cit.*, p. 158.
29. *Ibid.*, p. 182.
30. S. Lukes, *Power: A Radical View* (Macmillan, London, 1974).
31. Hollis, *op. cit.*, p. 161.
32. Lukes, *op. cit.*, p. 20.
33. Hollis, *op. cit.*, p. 184.
34. B.J. Biddle, "Recent Developments in Role Theory", *Annual Review of Sociology*, Vol. 12 (1987), pp. 67–92.
35. W. Carlsnaes, "The Agency-Structure Problem in Foreign Policy Analysis", *International Studies Quarterly*, Vol. 36, No. 3 (1992), p. 255.
36. D.D. Searing, "Roles, Rules, and Rationality in the New Institutionalism", *American Political Science Review*, Vol. 85, No. 4 (1991), p. 1252.
37. J.G. March and J.P. Olsen, *Rediscovering Institutions: The Organizational Basis of Politics* (Free Press, New York, 1989), p. 160.
38. Hollis defines structure as "systems of rules". Hollis, *op. cit.*, p. 136.
39. E. Goffman, *Relations in Public: Microstudies of the Public Order* (Harper and Colophon, New York, 1972), p. 95, quoted in J. Bilmes, *Discourses and Behaviour* (Plenum Press, New York, 1986), p. 173.
40. *Ibid.*
41. *Ibid.*
42. G.H. Von Wright, *Explanation and Understanding* (Cornell University Press, Ithaca, NY, 1971), p. 152.
43. F.V. Kratochwil, *Rules, Norms, and Decisions: On the Conditions of Practical and Legal Reasoning in International Relations and Domestic Affairs* (Cambridge University Press, Cambridge, 1989), p. 7. For the concept of "action words" see J.L. Austin, *How to Do Things with Words* (Harvard University Press, Cambridge, MA, 1962).
44. Kratochwil, p. 9.
45. The absence of internalised norms which are shared by actors is at the basis of the difficulties encountered in the resolution of conflicts over belief systems as opposed to conflicts centred on material resources. The "Salman Rushdie Affair" illustrates the intractability of the former type of conflict. For details of this particular conflict, see M. Ruthven, *A Satanic Affair: Salman Rushdie and the Wrath of Islam* (The Hogarth Press, London, 1991); L. Appignanesi and S. Maitland (eds), *The Rushdie File* (Fourth Estate, London, 1989).
46. Kratochwil, *op. cit.*, p. 61.

47. A.E. Wendt, *op. cit.*, pp. 337–338.
48. "Methodological individualism" assumes that "the elementary unit of social life is the individual human action. To explain social institutions and social change is to show how they arise as the result of action and interaction of individuals." J. Elster (1989), *op. cit.*, p. 13.
49. A. Collier, *Critical Realism: An Introduction to Roy Bhaskar's Philosophy* (Verso, London, 1994), p. 143.
50. I.J. Cohen, *Structuration Theory: Anthony Giddens and the Constitution of Social Life* (Macmillan, London, 1989), p. 17.
51. A. Giddens, *The Constitution of Society* (Polity Press, Cambridge, 1984), p. 2.
52. *Ibid.*, p. xvii.
53. *Ibid.*, p. 2.
54. Cohen, *op. cit.*, p. 17.
55. A. Giddens, *Central Problems in Social Theory: Action, Structure and Contradiction in Social Analysis* (Macmillan, London, 1979), p. 69.
56. *Ibid.*
57. R. Bhaskar, *The Possibility of Naturalism* (Harvester Wheatsheaf, Hemel Hempstead, 1989), pp. 34–35.
58. Giddens (1984), *op. cit.*, p. 3.
59. Giddens (1979), *op. cit.*, pp. 56–59.
60. Giddens (1984), *op. cit.*, p. 4.
61. Cohen, *op. cit.*, p. 201.
62. Giddens (1984), *op. cit.*, p. 18.
63. *Ibid.*, p. 21.
64. *Ibid.*, p. 25.
65. *Ibid.*, p. 258.
66. *Ibid.*, p. 25.
67. A. Giddens, *New Rules of Sociological Method: A Positive Critique of Interpretative Sociologies* (Hutchinson, London, 1976), p. 102.
68. Giddens (1984), *op. cit.*, p. 29.
69. A. Giddens, *The Nation-State and Violence* (Polity Press, Cambridge, 1985), p. 11.
70. For a critique of this position see A. Callinicos, "Anthony Giddens: A Contemporary Critique", *Theory and Society*, Vol. 14 (1985), pp. 133–166; and Cohen, *op. cit.*, pp. 213–228.
71. Bhaskar, *op. cit.*, pp. 40–41.
72. Giddens (1984), *op. cit.*, p. 87.

Chapter four

Legitimation and the discursive structuration of war

What, then, was war? No mere discord of flags
But an infection of the common sky
That sagged ominously upon the earth
Even when the season was the airiest May.
Robert Graves, The Oxford Book of War Poetry (1988)

This chapter has two primary objectives. The first is to uncover discourses implicated in the legitimation of war as a social continuity. Discourse analysis is used to draw attention to the linguistic resources through which the sociopolitical realm, including war as a social phenomenon, is produced and reproduced. The aim is to locate structures of signification and legitimation which are drawn upon and reproduced by actors in the structuration of war as a social continuity. The second, related, objective is to situate the discourse of war in relation to structures of domination and specifically the state as a social formation centrally implicated in the reproduction of violent political conflict.

It will be recalled from the last chapter that to conceptualise war as a social continuity requires an analysis which moves beyond the specific decision-making process leading to the use of force in a specific instance of conflict and to see such instances as occurring within discursive and institutional continuities which are drawn upon by actors in the reproduction of social systems. Using Giddens's theory of structuration which makes an ontological statement on the relationship between agency and structure, it was argued that action, including the use of force, can only be understood in terms of its relationship to structure and that the latter is instantiated through the activities of knowledgeable social agents.

The emphasis on the "duality of structure" points to an interdependent constitutive relationship between the activities of social agents and the structural properties of social systems. As pointed out by Cohen,

> Structural properties in social systems may not reproduce systems, but they shape, channel, and facilitate system reproduction whenever it occurs by providing agents with the practical awareness of the practices, relations, and spatio-temporal settings they require in order to participate in the reproductive process. In institutionalised systems, practices, relations, and articulations which are central to system reproduction may be regarded as structured processes; processes, that is, which are reproducible by an indefinite number of knowledgeable agents. Since this is the case, systems consisting of structured processes may be reproduced by succeeding cohorts or generations of agents. The systems thus endures even though agents who contribute to its existence come and go.[1]

Cohen's interpretation of Giddens's notion of the duality of structure is central to the aims articulated in this study of war as a form of continuity in social systems. The assumptions that underpin this study are firstly, that violent conflict forms an aspects of social systems. Secondly, such systems contain structural properties which are implicated in the reproduction of war as a continuity. Thirdly, these structural properties are drawn upon and reproduced through the activities and articulations of knowledgeable social agents whose decisions to use force or support such use in every instance of social conflict contribute to the reproduction of war as a social continuity.

A number of methodological issues must be considered before highlighting the nature of the structural properties which are implicated in the structuration of social systems, including war as an aspect of such systems. The first problem relates to agents' awareness of their role in the constitution of social life and in the reproduction of social systems. While agents may rationalise their conduct and be able to articulate discursively the reasons for their choice of violence in time of conflict, they are not necessarily aware of the implications of their conduct in the reproduction of social systems and war as a social continuity. The first methodological measure required here is a move from "first order analysis", which is confined to agents' articulations of their conduct, to "second order analyses" which "study aspects of the constitution of social life which cannot be grasped through concepts and tacit forms of mutual knowledge to which agents have access in their day-to-day lives".[2] Second order analyses, therefore, involve a language or discourse that is situated within the domain of the social sciences. However, the "double hermeneutic" in social theory suggests that the discourses and meta-languages of the social sciences do not remain confined to the domain of the social sciences for long, but come to permeate social life itself and the language of the everyday.[3] A second methodological issue which emerges is the temporal relationship between strategic conduct and institutional continuities.[4] The aim of structuration theory is not, however, to discern a one-to-one direct relationship between action and structure, but to analyse the properties of practices and relations which are chronically reproduced across time and space. The methodological measure undertaken here is the bracketing of the analysis of strategic conduct from "institutional analysis" while recognising the ontological relationship that is defined in the duality of structure. As pointed out by Cohen, "each instance of the reproduction of an institutionalised activity comprises an intersection between structural properties of conduct inherited from the past and the situated exercise of agency by social actors".[5]

The suggestion is that structural properties of social systems are not so much the direct cause of particular forms of conduct, but are at one and the same time both implicated and drawn upon (intentionally or unintentionally) by agents through whose actions social systems are reproduced. All social systems contain structural continuities which are reproduced through the practices of situated agents, even if such reproduction often occurs in a tacit and un-acknowledged manner.

As was indicated in the last chapter, structural properties of social systems are both constraining and enabling. According to Giddens,

> structuration theory is based on the proposition that structure is always both enabling and constraining, in virtue of the inherent relation between structure and agency (and agency and power) . . . it is true that the greater the time-space distanciation of social systems – the more their institutions bite into time and space – the more resistant they are to

manipulation or change by any individual agent. This meaning of constraint is also coupled to enablement. Time-space distanciation closes off some possibilities of human experience at the same time as it opens up others.[6]

While structural properties of social systems close off certain possibilities for situated agents, they also form a backdrop which renders action possible or meaningful. Constraint always derives from the contextuality of action; the constraining or enabling qualities of structural properties of social systems vary according to the context and the nature of any form of action or interaction.[7] As will be evident from the analysis provided below, the doctrine of just war as a deeply embedded or chronically reproduced mode of discourse restricts the utility of force while at the same time rendering it a legitimate course of action in specific circumstances. What remains for the present introduction is to identify the forms of structure which are implicated in the reproduction of social systems.

Following Giddens, three forms of structure were implicated in the reproduction of social systems, namely structures of signification, legitimation and domination. Interaction between positioned social actors is only meaningful through shared modes of discourse and symbolic orders which are reflexively drawn upon in the reproduction of structures of signification, just as structures of legitimation are reproduced through a shared understanding of normative expectations and codes of conduct. The production of dominant modes of discourse and generalised norms is itself dependent upon differential access to resources which define structures of domination. The regularities of social systems, including war as a social phenomenon, are a result of an interaction between intentional conduct and underlying structures which constitute the continuities of social and political life.

This chapter aims at uncovering the discursive continuities which are implicated in the legitimation of violent conflict. After providing an overview of the assumptions which underpin discourse analysis, the chapter evaluates militarism and the doctrine of just war in terms of their role in the reproduction of war as a social continuity. The last section of the chapter situates the language of war in relation to the state as the institutional location of violence and territoriality.

Discourse analysis

One of the central tenets of the rational actor model is consistency in the perceptions and accounts that actors give of the social world around them. The analysis of conflict is based on definitions given by actors of their grievances or the issues that underlie a conflict, their expressions of a perceived "other" whose behaviour is seen as the source of grievance, and their calculations of costs and benefits related to their choice of violence as a mode of conflict behaviour. Any distortion in the consistency of accounts actors in conflict give of the sources of their conflict or of the images they carry of the enemy is explained in terms of the psychological stresses which accompany the state of conflict and which generate misperception, miscalculation and a resultant misinformed decision-making process. This form of analysis sees language, or talk, simply as a mode of transmitting information in the process of communication. More importantly, because this form of conflict analysis concentrates on a study of decisions and forms of conduct associated with particular instances of conflict, it fails to locate the social and political continuities which are implicated in the generation and legitimation of violent modes of conflict behaviour.

A discourse analytic approach, on the other hand, sees language as a far more complex phenomenon. Actors involved in communicative interaction utilise interpretative schemes and shared worlds of meaning in the reproduction of discursive structures of signification and legitimation. Meaning or linguistic resources constitute the repertoires which are borrowed in the process of communication. Discourses are social relations represented in texts where the language contained within these texts is used to construct meaning and representation. The focus of discourse analytic research is on regularities in the construction and function of linguistic resources.[8] The questions that are pertinent to this study include the following:

1   What are the linguistic resources or regularities associated with the legitimation of war as a social continuity?

2   What are the repertoires (recurrent patterns in linguistic constructions such as terms, phrases, or metaphors) which are drawn upon by actors in their support for war?

3   Will discourse analysis point to a limited range of linguistic

resources drawn on by actors in conflict pointing to the constraining element of language?

4   Is there a possibility of constructing new forms of discourse as a means towards establishing non-violence as a norm in the resolution of conflict?

The underlying assumption of discourse analysis is that "social texts do not merely *reflect* or *mirror* objects, events and categories pre-existing in the social and natural world. Rather, they actively *construct* a version of those things. They do not just describe things, they *do* things. And being active, they have social and political implications."[9] Translated in terms of the duality of structure, the suggestion here is that social actors involved in communication draw upon pre-existing symbolic orders or modes of discourse which enable the creation of meaning but also constrain, in the limited range of linguistic resources, the potential variety of interpretations involved in the construction of social reality.[10]

To state that discourse is implicated in the construction and reproduction of social systems is to point to the centrality of the "text", as represented in talk, writing and other modes of representation, in investigations and understandings of the continuity of social and political phenomena such as war and violent conflict. As stated in earlier chapters, communication is a central aspect of the conflict process, and such communication would not be possible in the absence of a shared "symbolic representational system".[11] In our attempts to understand the resort to force as a mode of conflict behaviour where each instance of such use is implicated in the constitution of war as a social continuity, what is required is to uncover the representational systems which underpin structures of signification and legitimation surrounding war as an aspect of social systems.

Following the terms of structuration theory, discursive structures, or structures of signification and legitimation, are properties of social systems which are instantiated in the "practices and memory traces orienting the conduct of knowledgeable human agents".[12] For Giddens, the most important aspects of structure are rules and resources recursively involved in institutions. As indicated in the last chapter, actors draw upon the modalities of structuration in the reproduction of social systems and the reconstitution of their structural properties. The communication of meaning in interaction

draws upon interpretative schemes, which are "the modes of typifi-
cation incorporated within actors' stocks of knowledge, applied reflexively in the sustaining of communication".[13] The stocks of
knowledge which actors draw upon in the production and reproduction of action are the same as those which they use to give accounts or reasons for their actions. Structures of signification, seen
in their institutional order in terms of symbolic orders or modes of
discourse, are interlinked with structures of domination and legitimation. The emergence of dominant modes of discourse is related to
differentials in the distribution of power[14] where "structures of
signification are mobilised to legitimate the sectional interests of
hegemonic groups".[15] This process involves the direct manipulation
of information or communication as a form of strategic conduct to
further the interests of dominant groups within society. However,
the emergence of dominant discourses and "deeply ingrained"[16]
symbolic orders is not necessarily always apparent in strategic conduct, but is implicated in the institutional continuities of social life.
The transformation of a mode of discourse into an ideological construction is, therefore, related to structures of domination. As pointed
out by Giddens, "To study ideology from this aspect is to seek to
identify the most basic structural elements which connect signification and legitimation in such a way as to favour dominant interests"[17] where "buried" forms of ideology are reproduced through the
connection between unacknowledged conditions of action and
structural asymmetries of resources. Again, as indicated by Giddens,
"Ideological elements here are likely to be deeply sedimented in both
a psychological and an historical sense."[18] To speak of a mode of
discourse or a deeply ingrained symbolic order as ideological is to
suggest that it is implicated in the reproduction of an existing order
of domination. Ideology as a concept incorporates symbolic orders
drawn upon in furthering sectional interests.

Dominant modes of discourse and symbolic orders are not always
apparent but may conceal domination, where "power is harnessed
to conceal sectional interests on the level of strategic conduct".[19]
The means through which dominant modes of discourse are reproduced may be summarised on three levels.[20]

1   The representation of sectional interests as universal ones:
    here legitimacy is sustained through the claim to represent
    the interests of the community as a whole.

2 The denial or transmutation of contradictions: this primarily serves to prevent the translation of social contradiction into social conflict.

3 The naturalisation of the present – reification: the condition in which the interests of dominant groups are bound up with the preservation of the *status quo*. Forms of signification "naturalise" the existing state of affairs, negating the mutable, historical character of human society. It is here that modes of discourse and particular social orders are taken for granted in lived experience. They largely constitute the unacknowledged conditions of action which are continually reproduced intentionally or unintentionally through human interaction.

The language of war aims primarily at the generation of conformity within a unified social entity. The mobilisation of support for war is built upon representations of grievance as applicable to the entirety of the state or community. Nonconformity or dissent is conceived as treachery against not simply the leadership, but the community as a whole. Sectional interests come to be translated into universal interests, where any contradictions or conflicts within society are either directly prevented from reaching the political agenda or are negated in the name of a mythical solidarity against a constructed common enemy. The discourse of war is also "naturalised" in the sense that war is "naturally" seen to be the preserve of the state, either in its original formation or in its continuity as the predominant mode of social organisation.

The following two sections define militarism and the just war doctrine as dominant modes of discourse which are implicated in the reproduction of war as a continuity within social systems. The language of war, both in its instantiation in specific conflicts and in representations of war through shared interpretative schemes in specialised texts and wider political commentary, centres around two linguistic or conceptual categories, namely strategy and morality. These are drawn upon by actors in conflict and textual representations of war. Following structurationist premises, the discourse of war is interpreted as forming the basis through which war is reproduced as a continuity in social relations.

Militarism

Militarist discourse variously represents war as either a positive good or a necessary evil. The first interpretation judges war as a constitutive aspect of masculinity, individuality, nationhood and supremacy. The latter position argues that the use of force could be an effective instrument of policy within an anarchical inter-state system where military defence is seen as the prerequisite for state security.

Militarism is often represented as an extreme position held by Prussian historians and contemporary supremacists.[21] None could be more representative of the former category than the Hegelian historian Heinrich von Treitschke, who sees war as constituting a people's national identity. Hegel's views are clearly expressed in the following statement:

> We have learned to perceive the moral majesty of war through the very processes which to the superficial observer seem brutal and inhuman. The greatness of war is just what at first sight seems to be its horror – that for the sake of their country men will overcome the natural feelings of humanity, that they will slaughter their fellow men who have done them no injury, nay whom they perhaps respect as chivalrous foes. Man will not only sacrifice his life, but the natural and justified instincts of his soul; his very self he must offer up for the sake of patriotism; here we have the sublimity of war . . . War with all its brutality and sternness, weaves a bond of love between man and man, linking them together to face death, and causing all class distinctions to disappear.[22]

Treitschke sees war as not only the manifestation of individuality within the single individual, but the ultimate vehicle through which the collective personality of the nation emerges. War is here universalised in its consequences and reified to the extent that its "naturalness" is seen to deny any contradictions. Furthermore, the will to sacrifice exists within every (male) individual if he is to be a full and complete member of the nation-state, which in itself comes into existence through war. What is expressed here and by others prior to the First World War period is not only a positive conception of war but an assumed constitutive relationship between war and nationhood.[23]

One of the central themes of militarist discourse is the centrality of war in the constitution of individual identity, the cultural attributes of a society, and the underpinning of the state. In analysing nineteenth-century discourse on war, Pick finds a commonality of themes which function in the legitimation of war. Commenting on Proudhon's *War and Peace* (1861), Pick points out that the "question of war continually leads back to the question of the origin of each state. Without positing a right to war, the state (always and inevitably founded on violence) can have no moral authority."[24] Furthermore, to reject Proudhon's argument would amount to a denial of the legitimacy of the state and all organised societies, which for Proudhon would imply the acceptance of his position, namely anarchism. Pick also points to De Quincey and Ruskin who saw war not only as a mode of fulfilment for the nation, but as essentially constitutive of statehood.[25]

Contemporary militarism is a wider form of discourse which sees war and the preparation for war as a constitutive province of the state. Michael Mann recognises this wider legitimation of war in defining militarism as "an attitude and a set of institutions which regard war and the preparation for war as a normal and desirable social activity".[26] The constituent elements of militarism as a form of discourse point to a wider militarisation of society where the militarist interests of the state are generalised to the community contained within the state. The prestige attached to soldiering, the value conferred on military honours, the maintenance of armed services and related institutions point to the seemingly inextricable link between statehood and symbolic representations of violence. The legitimation of a militarist mode of discourse is also related to the concealment of social contradictions through its emphasis on conformity across the social divide and intolerance towards dissent.

While traditional militarist values emphasised valour and masculinity, contemporary militarism places emphasis on technological advancement and the efficacy of war as a means of achieving political objectives. As defined by Giddens, "Militarism today means more than anything else a proclivity on the part of those in the higher echelons of the armed forces and in other leading circles outside to look first of all for military solutions to issues which could be solved by other means; and the readiness of the lower ranks to accept such solutions unquestioningly."[27] What is observed in militarist discourse is a shift from the glorification of war towards the perception of war as an instrumentally effective tool in the pursuit of policy.

According to Ceadel militarism must be distinguished from "crusading" or "defencism", in that it "regards war both as a positive good (rather than a lesser evil) and as essential for human development".[28] Militarism, he suggests, celebrates "martial values" and the superiority of the state or society which prevails within the military arena. The "true militarist" not only believes that "war offers a unique opportunity for human fulfilment", but also requires such fulfilment to be accompanied by "hegemony" over those regarded as militarily inferior.[29] "Crusading", on the other hand, does not celebrate war as a positive good, but "resorts to coercion in the interests, as it sees them, of either order or justice and therefore also of peace . . . it is an altruistic theory".[30] A crusade may be domestically situated, as in the desire to rectify the internal conditions of a particular state, or externally oriented in order to change the behaviour of another state. Wars of national liberation, class struggles, and interventions against other states in the name of a perceived humanitarian cause, are thus labelled as crusading. The defining characteristics of a crusade include an ideological commitment to a cause, such as national liberation, and military confidence seen as essential if the crusader is to "convince himself both that he can win at acceptable cost and that he can do so without concern for his own national interests".[31] The crusader, therefore, sees military means not as a cause for celebration but as a necessary and last resort means of achieving change.

Ceadel implies that the three "theories" of militarism, defencism and crusading may be distinguished along motivational lines. All three, however, share a discourse based on the usability of military means in the prosecution of conflict. Rather than being assumed to be distinguishable, they are implicated in the constitution of a militarist discourse which places reliance on the military institutions of the state. They constitute a mode of discourse which assumes an inextricable link between political life and access to the use of violence.

Militarism has contested meanings and associations. While the concept of militarism made its appearance in the nineteenth century, its association with the military machinery of the state was textually represented in the seventeenth century. It is in this earlier period that the dualism was established between militarism and

civilian government.[32] The juxtaposition of militarism with autocratic rule and in opposition to civilianism permeates anti-militarist
discourse. This view is reflected in Vagt's assertion that militarism
is "not the opposite of pacifism: its true counterpart is civilianism".[33] As pointed out by Berghahn, the predominant view of the
pre-1914 period associated militarism with the institutions of the
military and their influence on governmental decision-making:

> By the time "militarism" became established in political lan-
> guage, two major strands can be discerned within the critique
> of military organisation and its effect upon civilian society;
> i.e. those analysts who saw it in a political and constitutional
> framework and those who examined it as a socio-economic
> problem. Both approaches shared a common vision of a pro-
> gressive movement towards an age in which armies would at
> least be closely controlled, if not abolished altogether.[34]

The dualism of militarism and civilianism is repeated by Herbert
Spencer who defined a "militant type of society" as one which
assumes that all those fit for fighting do so against other societies
and where those not involved in direct combat are mobilised indirectly towards the war effort. The mobilisation of society, according
to Spencer, is based on patriotism which Spencer defines as an
ideology which "regards the triumph of their society as the supreme
end of action".[35] Lasswell, writing in 1941, accepts the dichotomy
between militarism and civilianism, when he states that,

> If we understand by "militarism" the permeation of an entire
> society by the self-serving ideology of the officer and soldier,
> we can speak of "civilianism" as the absorption of the military
> by the multivalued orientation of a society in which violent
> coercion is deglamorized as an end in itself and is perceived
> as a regrettable concession to the persistence of variables
> whose magnitudes we have not as yet been able to control
> without paying what appears to be an excessive cost in terms
> of such autonomy as is possible under the cloud of chronic
> peril.[36]

What is evident from such dichotomous representations is the
association between militarism and autocratic rule, where the former is seen not as the opposite of peace, but rather as the opposite
of civilian control of pluralist democratic government. Rather than

permeating the entire community, the military machinery is contained as merely one aspect of the institutions which constitute the state.

Interpretations which associate militarism with martial values as expressed in nineteenth-century discourse and those which distinguish between militarism and civilianism suggest that militarism is a distinctive ideological framework which must be separated from civil society. Such dichotomous representations were, however, challenged by writings devoted to uncovering the location and influence of the "military-industrial complex". The military-industrial complex was first conceived as a coalition between the military establishment, including the armed forces and defence ministries, and arms manufacturers. The purpose of the coalition was not necessarily to wage war, but to maintain high military expenditures. It was soon recognised, however, that the military-industrial complex permeated civil society, including the education system and wider research institutions. Dieter Senghaas expands the concept by referring to the "political-ideological-military-scientific-technological-industrial complex"[37] in support of C. Wright Mills's emphasis on the penetration of militarist values into all aspects of modern industrial life.[38] Militarism is, therefore, not merely the discourse of military practitioners and historians, but has penetrated wider civilian life. This process is not, however, confined to domestic industrial society, but has had, as Giddens points out, global repercussions in the production of a "world military order" which is not merely the product of the globalisation of the capitalist system, but has emerged through the spread of the state system as a universal mode of representation:

> The nation-state is the prime vehicle of political organisation in the contemporary world, recognised as holding legitimate monopoly of the means of violence by its own subject population and by other nation-states. As the possessor of the means of waging industrialised war, in a global context of the continuing application of science to the advancement of military technology, the state participates in and furthers a generalised process of militarisation within the world system as a whole.[39]

Modern militarism is not a blatant, overt celebration of war as an assertion of nationhood, but is more of a diffuse process involving the entirety of industrial society. As stated by Michael Mann, "the principal activities of most capitalist states – preparing for, and conducting, war" have been a primary defining condition.[40] The relationship between war and the establishment of organised society is emphasised by Mann when he states "where we find socially and territorially fixed groups with states and surpluses, we find systematic killing in organised wars".[41]

Unlike the militarism of the nineteenth century which decried the industrialisation of war as a denial of chivalry, modern or contemporary militarism is inextricably associated with technological innovation and the consequent globalisation of the militarist order. The consequence is the creation of a "culture of militarism" where, as Mann points out:

> It is a necessary part of militarism to value highly whatever qualities are thought useful to military efficiency. For most of history, these qualities centred upon martial physical valour. Thus physical violence was glorified. The fact that this no longer occurs to any significant extent should not blind us to the continued existence of high regard for military efficiency. Our sports may not be dominated by chariot races, gladiatorial combat or races in full battle gear, but our culture is permeated by the desirability of team discipline, of mathematically precise logistical planning, of split second timing: all qualities which are most closely paralleled in our society by the requirements of warfare.[42]

The technological sophistication of warfare in the present era, furthermore, has rendered killing an impersonal affair where combat is carried out at a distance and where destruction of life and property is, paradoxically, distant from the combatant while being proximate to the onlooking audiences of the mass media. Modern militarism is not, therefore, the domain of the officer and soldier alone, but permeates social life through "civilian participation" in the armaments and related industries and in a legitimating discourse which is mediated through the manipulation of information in time of war.

The doctrine of just war

The notion that war may be conducted for just cause and through just means has, like militarism, a long tradition which still permeates and indeed dominates the discourse of war and its legitimation. As Jean Elshtain points out, just war is a "mode of discourse and a language of justification and evaluation".[43] The just war doctrine has evolved from being primarily a theological domain to playing a formative role in the discourses of international lawyers, military professionals, policy-makers, international relations theorists, moral philosophers and the wider public perceptions of war. It is, therefore, an aspect of the discursive structuration of war which must be analysed to situate its role in the legitimation of violence.

The just war doctrine as a mode of discourse contains essentially contested concepts which point to the centrality of interpretation and the role played by linguistic categories in political and social life. The discourse of just war, containing as it does premises relating to the justification of action, including the notion of *jus in bello*, or justice in the conduct of war, and *jus ad bellum*, or justified cause, constitute domains of contestation which point to the problematic nature of attempts to reconcile killing and destruction with human morality. By definition, the aim of the doctrine is the view, expressed first in St Augustine's *The City of God*, written in the year 427, and in the present era by such moral philosophers as Michael Walzer in *Just and Unjust Wars*,[44] that some notion of "justice" must override considerations of "peace", defined as the absence of war. Within the just war tradition, peace is not the ultimate human value. Rather, the just war doctrine suggests that in some circumstances, the resort to force is a desirable form of conduct. It is important to recognise, therefore, that unlike realist conceptions of war, which define war as the purposeful and instrumental use of force decided upon on cost/benefit grounds, war is undertaken in the name of certain specified values such as the protection of international law or the punishment of aggression. In these circumstances war, despite its consequences as a destructive force, is defined as a positive good.

The discourse of just war contains other structuring categories such as inclusion and exclusion. The decision to utilise force must be made by a legitimate authority, or the state which represents the internal community while the defined enemy is perceived as the external "other". This other is not confined to the leadership group responsible for a particular grievance, but contains all combatants, conscripted or voluntary, as well as, with some restraint, the civilian bystanders which come to form the unfortunate casualties of their leaders' actions.[45] That punishment is collective is clearly evident in St Augustine's view, quoted by Aquinas, that "Those wars are generally defined as just which avenge some wrong, when a nation or a state is to be punished for having failed to make amends for the wrong done, or to restore what has been taken unjustly."[46]

The other contested structuring category of just war discourse is the differentiation between the private morality of the individual and the public/political realm of the state. The everyday moral considerations of the individual are distinguished from her or his obligations as citizen. The Hegelian basis of this private/public dichotomy perceives a distinction between killing for private gain, which is subject to censure and condemnation, and killing on the battlefield, which, if undertaken in the name of an assumed collective just cause, is perceived as a form of moral conduct deserving of valour and glorification.

Just war as a mode of discourse draws upon interpretative schemes and linguistic frameworks based on such notions as "justification", "moderation", "control" and "legitimacy". It suggests a third dichotomy, namely that between strategy, deemed to be the preserve of realist thinkers and generals, and morality, which is seen to belong to the realms of theology, moral philosophy and international law. Both, however, constitute a "language of war".[47] Walzer, an advocate of just war, acknowledges this when he states that "moral concepts and strategic concepts reflect the real world in the same way. They are not merely normative words . . . They are descriptive terms, and without them we would have no coherent way of talking about war".[48] Michael Howard, as a realist thinker, also points to the ambiguity that exists between the two categories of strategy and morality. He recognises war as a distinctively social activity which, by definition, contains a high degree of control:

[i]t involves the reciprocal use of organized force between two or more social groups, directed according to an overall plan or series of plans for the achievement of a political object . . .

Members of belligerent armed forces normally operate according to orders transmitted through a highly structured hierarchy. They may legitimately kill members of opposing armed forces in battle unless the latter explicitly surrender, and there is a distinct risk that they will kill them even then. The persons and property of civilians in zones of military operations or within reach of military projectiles are at risk even if they are totally non-combatant.[49]

Just war, as a language of war, requires strategic calculation on the part of generals, whose responsibility or mandate is to win a war that has been "justified" by those claiming to incorporate in war an element of moral consideration. Both strategy and just war, therefore, constitute a language of justification in the decision to use force in time of emerging conflict. While Howard suggests that it is within the remits of strategy to determine "how, where, and upon whom . . . destruction is to be inflicted",[50] strategy shares with just war that element of destruction which is the constitutive, defining characteristic of war.

What modern strategy also shares with modern just war doctrine is an essential state-centred discourse. Michael Walzer's "theory of aggression" emphasises "rights of political communities" incorporating "territorial integrity and political sovereignty" which Walzer says belong to states but "derive ultimately from the rights of individuals, and from them they take their force".[51] Using a contractarian metaphor, Walzer sees the state or the community contained within the boundaries of the state as one of "association and mutuality" where the state's obligation is the protection of the community just as the obligation of the citizen is in joining in its defence against aggression. The dualism of inclusion and exclusion is evident where Walzer states that "territorial integrity is a function of national existence . . . It is the coming together of a people that establishes the integrity of a territory. Only then can a boundary be drawn the crossing of which is plausibly called aggression."[52] Walzer asserts that the rights of states for self-defence also contains an element of obligation within the domain of international society where the "citizens" are the member states of that society. Aggression challenges the order of international society and must be resisted and punished.[53]

Strategic and normative (just war) discourses on war share a number of assumptions and indeed constitute together the structuring language of war. The just war doctrine centres around the regulative aspect of the rules of war, where the emphasis on normative or moral expectations associated with the conduct of war form a central defining aspect of the international law of war. The regulation of war is expressed in a number of international conventions including the Hague conventions and the Geneva conventions.[54] The international law of war is one important element of the institutionalisation of the war process in humanity's attempts to regulate it. The constituent elements of the regulation of war include the treatment of civilians under occupation, the treatment of war prisoners, and restraint in the use of force against civilians and retreating armies. The regulative aspect of the rules of war is emphasised by just war theorists who have focused upon *jus in bello* as an aspect of justice in war, where it is asserted that there must be limits and restraints in the conduct of war.

The doctrine of just war is, however, also constitutive of war. That is, it contains constitutive rules which enable war as a form of conduct and which have, like its regulative rules, institutionalised war as a social continuity. As indicated earlier, one of the constitutive elements of war is a highly structured hierarchy of control. This assumption is shared by realist historians such as Michael Howard and just war theorists such as Michael Walzer. The latter's statement that "War is distinguishable from murder and massacre only when restrictions are established on the reach of battle"[55] suggests that the rules of war, both strategic or moral, constitute war as a social and political activity. The rules of war, including those which determine when and against whom force should be utilised, as well as those which place restraint on the conduct of war, define or constitute war as an institutionalised social activity. Indeed the institutional basis of war is structured through its regulative rules which are in themselves constitutive of war. The rules of just war constitute the normative structure of war; they do not merely render war tolerable, they enable war to take place where the constitutive element of this enablement is justification.

The above analysis suggests that the doctrine of just war as a mode of discourse constitutes a set of interpretative schemes and structuring categories which are drawn upon by policy-makers, constituents, military personnel and social theorists, in the production and reproduction of structures of signification and legitimation which constitute war as an aspect of social systems. It is in time of specific wars that such discourses are drawn upon by policy-makers and publics alike with the intention of generating support for the use of violence in time of conflict. The unintended consequence of the discourse of specific wars is the reproduction of war as an institutionalised aspect of structured social systems.

The justification and rationalisation of war form a central component of a discourse of war utilised during specific conflicts as leaderships attempt to mobilise support for action which could have costly ramifications for their wider publics. Such discourses draw upon already existing linguistic repertoires which constitute a shared world of meaning and normative social order. Kant's assertion that the public would by nature oppose war is not borne out by the widespread support for war witnessed during major wars from the First World War to the recent Gulf War and the violent breakdown of the former Yugoslavia. These conflicts witnessed the emergence of what Richardson referred to as the "war mood" where a sudden and widespread support for war takes hold of entire populations.[56] Such circumstances are framed in a language of war which draws upon existing deeply embedded discourses centred around such concepts as militarism, masculinity, identity, moral legitimacy and technological superiority. The language of war also contains structuring dualisms such as the "self" and "other", where the self is associated with courage and civilisation while the other is represented as barbaric and diabolical. The other dualism contained in the language of war is conformity versus dissent, where individuals and groups refusing to participate in the war effort are seen as treacherous to their community and therefore deserving of censure, punishment or even banishment.[57]

Wars experienced across generations share discursive repertoires framed around justification and rationalisation. The recent war in the Gulf represented Iraq as a maverick state whose leaders aimed at the domination of the entire Middle East region. Iraq was also represented as technologically a highly sophisticated society with access to destructive weapons and the willingness to use them. The technological sophistication of the allied forces was legitimised through a discourse which emphasised the technological sophistication of the enemy. The image portrayed was one of maniacal leaders, intoxicated populations, and "rampaging technology".[58]

The discourse of war submerges individual identity into a wider communal identity. Just as the self is so submerged so too the enemy is represented as one monolithic whole such that all Argentinians and all Iraqis become culprits, deserving of collective punishment.[59] The role of the media in the generation of a war mood and the creation of a "collective mind" is central in the process of linking the masses to the war process. Wartime propaganda draws on an already existing discourse and in the Gulf conflict it drew on stereotypes of the Middle East as an arena of fanaticism and irrationality. The "orientalism" of wartime discourse drew upon already existing representations generated through literary, journalistic and political commentary. As pointed out by Edward Said, such orientalism is "premised upon exteriority" where "The value, efficacy, strength, apparent veracity of a written statement about the Orient . . . relies very little, and cannot instrumentally depend, on the Orient as such."[60] Referring to the propaganda of the First World War, Pick states that it constituted a "crucial process of definition, an ideological work in progress, specifying the aims as the war proceeded, endeavouring to conjure up a sense of nation and to draw the physiognomy of the enemy".[61] Such a manipulation of communication in the construction of images was also evident in the recent Gulf war which illustrated that the language of war has two distinct phases: one drawing on justifications for war and the other carried out during the course of war. While the war aims and the issues at the basis of a conflict may be highly complex and subject to change with time, the aim of the language of war is always to simplify into discrete, often dualistic, categories. The consequence of the manipulation of communication during war is the militarisation of everyday life and the collectivisation of the war process. Despite the proximity of contemporary war made manifest through the revolution in information technology, the effects of war are paradoxically sanitised through discourse. As pointed out by Norris in writing on the Gulf war,

> what comes across most strikingly in many "first hand" (journalistic or combatant) recollections of the Gulf War is the curious sense of not really having *experienced* these events at all, but having witnessed them only at a distance remove where "reality" could scarcely get into conflict with the steady stream of images, war-game scenarios, media liaison exercises and so forth. Then there is the fact – less often mentioned – that Iraqi losses, military and civilian, may never be known

with any degree of accuracy, given the sheer destructive power of the weaponry involved and its capacity to well-nigh obliterate the evidence.[62]

The role of the discourse of this particular war was to sanitise or to "hygienically edit"[63] the effects of war by reference to "surgical strikes", or "classification errors", where an assumed "precision bombing" was not so precise in its effects. The language of justification and rationalisation of this particular war and others before it had a primary and immediate role in the generation of support for the use of violence. The language of any war, however, has deeply embedded sources which are drawn upon by actors and which are regenerated in the constitution of war as a social continuity.

War as a social continuity thus draws upon linguistic constructs and regularities based on justification and rationalisation. The construction of identity is centrally implicated in the mobilisation of support for violent conflict. As will be shown in the next chapter, social identity is constituted through deeply ingrained institutional and discursive continuities which situate the self within bounded communities, the definition of which is based on modalities of inclusion and exclusion. As is evident from the above analysis, the discursive regularities implicated in the legitimation of war are institutionalised in the structure of the state as a social formation. Both militarism and the doctrine of just war centralise the nation-state as the primary construct and principle of human organisation. As will be seen in the following section, the discourse of war must be situated in relation to the state as centrally implicated in the institutionalisation of political violence.

The state, structures of domination, and violence

From Hobbes to present-day realist interpretations of the international system, the idea of the state and the inter-state system as the primary source of war remains of central importance to theoretical and normative discourses on the subject of violence. Both idealist and realist discourses on international relations situate war as a product of an assumed anarchical inter-state system. Where the two frameworks of thought differ on questions of the regulation of the system, both share an underlying premise that the existence of a system of sovereign states coupled with the absence of enforceable law at the international level suggest that conflict, often leading to war, is inevitable.

Based on Hobbesian foundations of paradigmatic stature, the view is that states are in a condition of constant military prepared-ness against external threats. Kenneth Waltz, for example, suggests that the structure of anarchy which defines the inter-state system provides a "permissive cause"[64] of war generally. Waltz does not seek to explain the onset of particular wars, but to explain the presence of war as a systemic phenomenon within an international system where "self-help is necessarily the principle of action in an anarchic order".[65]

In Waltz's conception of the international system, states are taken as given, ahistorical entities. The state itself is not subject to analysis. As pointed out by Linklater,

> What is limited about this perspective is not its belief that the fundamental problem of international relations – the problem of war – can be overcome only by adjusting the external re-lations of states, but the supposition that this transformation might be effected while the ethical basis of the state remained uncriticised and unchallenged. Within Waltz's analysis there is no need to undertake a reconsideration of the way in which citizens organise their obligations to the state and to the re-mainder of humanity; the rights and duties of the citizen and the state are not understood to enter into the permissive causes of war.[66]

Linklater calls for a normative critique of the state as a bounded, particularist social formation implicated in the perpetuation of violence. Such a critique is made possible only by questioning the nature of the state, its contingent character, and as constituting a form of organisation historically linked to internal and external violence.

Violence is conceived as a constitutive element in the develop-ment of states as the paramount form of human organisation. Most non-Marxist orientations to the state adopt a Weberian emphasis on the institutional development of the state and particularly its territoriality and monopoly over the means of violence. Accord-ing to Weber, "A compulsory political organisation with con-tinuous operations will be called a 'state' in so far as its administrative staff successfully upholds the claim to the *monopoly* of the *legitimate* use of physical force in the enforcement of its order."[67] Michael Mann develops this definition by loosening the tie between political and military power, but retains the element of "organised physical force" which is used to back up control over a specified territorial jurisdiction. Such internal control became consolidated in the development of organised armed forces and greater specialisation and rationalisation of administrative institutions. The state's increasing rule over society was historically paralleled by the emergence of the nation-state which, according to Mann, came to represent "citizens' internal sense of community as well as emphasising the distinctness of their external interests in relation to the citizens of other states".[68] While national identity, as will be discussed in the next chapter, is an important factor in considerations of the mobilising force of the state, the important point within the present context is that increasing bureaucratisation of the civil and military institutions of the state not only enabled the modern state to consolidate structures of domination internally, but ensured successful control of bounded territories against external adversaries.[69]

The relationship between internal control and the external relations of states is emphasised by other social theorists, including Theda Skocpol, Charles Tilly and Anthony Giddens. Skocpol's analysis of peasant revolution suggests that this phenomenon emerges as a result of structural crises in the control mechanisms of the state:

> We can make sense of social revolutionary transformations only if we take the state seriously as a macro-structure. The state properly conceived is no mere arena in which socioeconomic struggles are fought out. It is, rather, a set of administrative, policing, and military organisations headed, and more or less well coordinated by, an executive authority.[70]

State organisations are not mere reflections of class interests but function within the context of both class-divided socio-economic relations and external inter-state relations. For Skocpol, conflict within the latter creates a crisis of control within the former set of relations, transforming class contradictions into manifest conflict. While Skocpol is concerned with the genesis of social revolutions within states, Charles Tilly places emphasis upon the constitutive role of violence in the emergence of states as units of human organisation. Tilly considers states as being "built on foundations of recurrent warfare and the construction of state capacities to mobilise social resources for war".[71] The constitutive relationship between "war-making" and "state-making" is, for Tilly, analogous to "protection rackets with the advantage of legitimacy". Governments have historically created threats and then charged for their reduction.[72] Furthermore, governments have historically sought to organise and monopolise violence in order to fulfil four activities, namely war-making directed against outsiders; state-making, aimed at eliminating rivals within the state; protection of clients; and extraction, which relates to "acquiring the means of carrying out the first three activities – war-making, state-making, and protection".[73]

Giddens situates his conception of the state within a wider social theory based on the structurationist premises highlighted in the last chapter. Modern states are presented as highly administered social systems defined, along Weberian lines, in terms of territoriality and violence. The concentration of allocative and authoritative resources within the state intersects all forms of social interaction including the communication of meaning and normative modes of sanctioning. The distinguishing feature of the state as political organisation is that its "administrative power" is territorially bounded and consolidated through the control of the means of violence.[74] The state is defined as the "pre-eminent power container . . . a territorially bounded, administrative unity".[75]

Giddens develops his conception of the state and its relation to violence by focusing on the question of power. The power contained within highly administered social systems, such as the modern state, is achieved through the accumulation and storage of coded information relating to individuals contained within the bounded domains of the state. Such "surveillance" constitutes one of the key attributes of the modern state and distinguishes it from traditional social formations. Giddens follows Foucault in formulating the central underpinning premise of his conception of the state and its relation to violence, namely that the sophistication of surveillance achieved within the modern state has, through time, generated a "pacification" of internal society only to relocate the direction of the state's military machinery outwards. The historical development of the modern nation-state is based on key developments in military organisation, innovation in military technology, and greater effectiveness in techniques of surveillance of internal societies leading to the near marginalisation or elimination of violence within them. A characteristic of "internal pacification" is "the withdrawal of the military from direct participation in the internal affairs of state". This withdrawal does not, however, involve "the decline of war but a concentration of military power 'pointing outwards' towards other states in the nation-state system".[76]

Two vital elements derive from the conceptualisation of the state as defined by Giddens. The first relates to state sovereignty which, as pointed out by Rosenberg, comes to be dependent on internal factors: "The (outward) political sovereignty which becomes the central organising principle of the state system is the expression of an (internal) administrative and coercive unity established at the expense of other, transnational and local, forms of political power."[77] The second related issue concerns the continuance of internal political violence based increasingly on demands for ethnic secession and calls for theocratic forms of governance. According to Giddens, the violence generated in these situations of conflict only affirms the presumption of a "norm of monopolistic state authority".[78]

Internal pacification does not, however, imply the end of militarism and military power as one of the core "institutional clusterings" of modern societies. The nation-state remains "the prime vehicle of political organisation . . . recognised as holding legitimate monopoly of the means of violence" by its own population and by other nation-states. The nation-state, furthermore, is part of a world military order in which it "participates in and furthers a generalised process of militarisation within the world system as a whole".[79]

The sociological approaches reviewed above lay stress on violence as a constitutive component of the state and militarism as centrally associated with the state and the world military order. What emerges is not a specific theory of war,[80] but a conception of violence as both constitutive of and situated within the continuities of structured social formations. The state, as an administered power system, becomes a central location of the institutionalisation of the machinery of violence. The state is also reified within militarist as well as just war discourses which, as was argued earlier in this chapter, have contributed to the legitimation of war as a form of human interaction. As the next chapter will argue, the state is not simply a power container but incorporates symbolic orders which define social identity and affiliation and which are constructed around exclusionist discourses implicated in the legitimation of violence.

Notes

1. I.J. Cohen, *Structuration Theory: Anthony Giddens and the Constitution of Social Life* (Macmillan, London, 1989), p. 201.
2. *Ibid.*, p. 204.
3. A. Giddens, *The Constitution of Society* (Polity Press, Cambridge, 1984), pp. 284–285.
4. For the temporal relationship between action and structure as a basis of critique of Giddens's structurationist assumptions, see M.S. Archer, *Culture and Agency: The Place of Culture in Social Theory* (Cambridge University Press, Cambridge, 1988); M. Taylor, "Structure, Culture and Action in the Explanation of Social Change", *Politics and Society*, Vol. 17, No. 2 (1989), pp. 115–162. For an application to foreign policy analysis, see W. Carlsnaes, "The Agency-Structure Problem in Foreign Policy Analysis", *International Studies Quarterly*, Vol. 36, No. 3 (1992), pp. 245–270.
5. Cohen, *op. cit.*, p. 207.
6. Giddens, *op. cit.*, pp. 169–171.
7. For critiques of the assertion that structure can be both constraining and enabling, see J.B. Thompson, *Studies in the Theory of Ideology* (University of California Press, Berkeley, 1984), pp. 168–170; Cohen, *op. cit.*, pp. 223–231.
8. E. Burman and I. Parker, *Discourse Analytic Research: Repertoires and Readings of Texts in Action* (Routledge, London, 1993), p. 49.
9. J. Potter and M. Whetherell, *Discourse and Social Psychology: Beyond Attitudes and Behaviour* (Sage, London, 1987), p. 6.
10. For a review of discourse analysis see T.A. Van Dijk (ed.), *Handbook of Discourse Analysis, Vols 1–4* (Academic Press, London, 1985).
11. Potter and Whetherell, *op. cit.*, p. 9.
12. Giddens, *op. cit.*, p. 17.
13. *Ibid.*, p. 29.
14. A. Giddens, *Central Problems in Social Theory* (Macmillan, London, 1979), pp. 190–193.
15. *Ibid.*, p. 188.
16. *Ibid.*, p. 190.

17. *Ibid.*, pp. 191–192.
18. *Ibid.*, p. 192.
19. *Ibid.*, p. 193.
20. *Ibid.*, pp. 193–195.
21. M. Ceadel, *Thinking about Peace and War* (Oxford University Press, Oxford, and New York, 1989).
22. Quoted in D. Pick, *War Machine: The Rationalisation of Slaughter in the Modern Age* (Yale University Press, New Haven, CT, and London, 1993), p. 85.
23. The English counterpart to Treitschke is Lieutenant-General Sir Reginald C. Hart whose "A Vindication of War" proclaims that "History proves up to the hilt that nations languish and perish under peace conditions, and it has only been by war that a people has continued to thrive and exist." Quoted in Ceadel, *op. cit.*, p. 37.
24. Pick, *op. cit.*, p. 46.
25. *Ibid.*, p. 84.
26. M. Mann, "Capitalism and Militarism", in M. Shaw (ed.), *War, State and Society* (Macmillan, London, 1984), p. 25.
27. A. Giddens, *The Nation-State and Violence* (Polity Press, Cambridge, 1985), p. 328.
28. Ceadel, *op. cit.*, p. 21.
29. *Ibid.*, p. 27.
30. *Ibid.*, p. 43.
31. *Ibid.*, p. 58.
32. Two pamphlets proclaiming an opposition to the emergence of standing armies as violations of civilian rule included John Trenchard (1697), "An Argument Showing that a Standing Army is Inconsistent with a Free Government and Absolutely Destructive to the Constitution of the English Monarchy"; and Andrew Fletcher (1697), "A Discourse Concerning Militias and Standing Armies with Relation to the Past and Present Governments of Europe and of England in Particular". See V.R. Berghahn, *Militarism: The History of an International Debate 1861–1979* (Berg Publishers, Leamington Spa, 1981).
33. A. Vagts, *A History of Militarism* (Meridian Books, New York, 1959), p. 15.
34. Berghahn, *op. cit.*, p. 10.
35. H. Spencer, *The Principles of Sociology, Vol. II* (New York and London, 1886), p. 568. Quoted in Berghahn, *op. cit.*
36. H.D. Lasswell, "The Garrison State and the Specialists on Violence", *American Journal of Sociology* (January 1941), pp. 455–468.
37. D. Senghaas, *Rustung und Militarismus* (Frankfurt, 1972), p. 14. Quoted in Berghahn, *op. cit.*, p. 87.

38. C. Wright Mills, *The Causes of World War Three* (Secker and Warburg, London, 1959) and *The Power Elite* (Oxford University Press, Oxford and New York, 1956).

39. Giddens (1985), *op. cit.*, p. 254.

40. Mann, *op. cit.*, p. 28.

41. *Ibid.*, p. 30.

42. *Ibid.*, p. 34.

43. J.B. Elshtain (ed.), *Just War Theory* (Blackwell, Oxford, 1992), p. 1.

44. R.H. Barrow (trans.), *Introduction to St. Augustine: City of God* (Faber and Faber, London, 1950); M. Walzer, *Just and Unjust Wars: A Moral Argument with Historical Illustrations* (Basic Books, New York, 1977).

45. Aquinas introduced the notion that just war must be declared by legitimate authority in his *Summa Theologia*: ". . . the authority of the ruler within whose competence it lies to declare war. A private individual may not declare war; for he can recourse to the judgement of a superior to safeguard his rights." From A.P. d'Entreves (ed.), *Aquinas: Selected Political Writings* (Blackwell, Oxford, 1965).

46. *Ibid.*

47. Walzer, *op. cit.*, p. 13.

48. *Ibid.*, p. 14.

49. M. Howard, "Temperamenta Belli: Can War be Controlled?", in Elshtain, *op. cit.*, p. 23.

50. *Ibid.*, p. 25.

51. Walzer, *op. cit.*, p. 53.

52. *Ibid.*, p. 57.

53. *Ibid.*, p. 62.

54. G. Best, *Humanity in Warfare: The Modern History of the International Law of Armed Conflicts* (Weidenfeld and Nicolson, London, 1980).

55. *Ibid.*, p. 42.

56. L.F. Richardson, "War Moods", *Psychometrica*, Vol. 13, Part 1 (1948), pp. 147–174.

57. P. Brock, *Pacifism in Europe to 1914* (Princeton University Press, Princeton, NJ, 1972); D.L. Cady, *From Warism to Pacifism: A Moral Continuum* (Temple University Press, Philadelphia, 1989).

58. See Pick, *op. cit.*, p. 110 for a description of the language utilised at the outset of the First World War.

59. Writing in the *Psychology of Jingoism* in 1901, the liberal theorist J.A. Hobson defines jingoism as an "introverted patriotism whereby the love of one's own nation is transformed into the hatred of another nation, and the fierce craving to destroy the individual members of that other nation". Quoted in Pick, *op. cit.*, p. 112.

60. E. Said, *Orientalism: Western Conceptions of the Orient* (Penguin Books, London, 1991), pp. 20–21.
61. Pick, *op. cit.*, p. 140.
62. C. Norris, *Uncritical Theory: Postmodernism, Intellectuals, and the Gulf War* (Lawrence and Wishart, London, 1992), p. 122.
63. D. Hebdige, "Bombing Logic", *Marxism Today*, (March 1991), p. 46, quoted in Norris, *op. cit.*, p. 123.
64. K. Waltz, *Man, the State and War* (Columbia University Press, New York, 1959), p. 233.
65. K.N. Waltz, *Theory of International Politics* (Addison-Wesley, Reading, MA and London, 1979), p. 111.
66. A. Linklater, *Men and Citizens in the Theory of International Relations* (Macmillan, London, 1990), p. 28.
67. M. Weber, *Economy and Society, Vol. I* (University of California Press, Berkeley, 1978), p. 56.
68. M. Mann, *The Sources of Social Power, Vol. II* (Cambridge University Press, Cambridge, 1993), p. 57.
69. *Ibid.*, p. 424.
70. T. Skocpol, *States and Social Revolutions: A Comparative Analysis of France, Russia, and China* (Cambridge University Press, Cambridge, 1979), p. 29.
71. C. Tilly, "War Making and State Making as Organized Crime", in P.B. Evans, D. Rueschemeyer, and T. Skocpol (eds), *Bringing the State Back In* (Cambridge University Press, Cambridge, 1985), p. 166.
72. *Ibid.*, p. 171.
73. *Ibid.*, p. 181.
74. Giddens (1985), *op. cit.*, pp. 19–20.
75. *Ibid.*, p. 13.
76. *Ibid.*, p. 192.
77. J. Rosenberg, "A Non-Realist Theory of Sovereignty: Giddens' *The Nation-State and Violence*", *Millennium*, Vol. 19 (1990), p. 253.
78. Giddens (1985), *op. cit.*, p. 121.
79. *Ibid.*, p. 254.
80. That Giddens does not produce such a theory is a point of critique for Martin Shaw, who suggests that Giddens especially fails to provide an explanation of why states resort to violence in particular circumstances. See M. Shaw, "War and the Nation-State in Social Theory", in D. Held and J.B. Thompson (eds), *Social Theory of Modern Societies: Anthony Giddens and His Critics* (Cambridge University Press, Cambridge, 1989), pp. 144–145.

Chapter five

The construction of identity and the discourse of violence

How should one read a book? The only advice . . . that one person can give another about reading is to take no advice, to follow your own instincts, to use your own reason, to come to your own conclusions . . . To admit authorities, however heavily furred and gowned, into our libraries and let them tell us how to read, what to read, what value to place upon what to read is to destroy the spirit of freedom, which is the breath of those sanctuaries. Everywhere else we may be bound by laws and conventions – there we have none.
                    Virginia Woolf, *The Second Common Reader* (1932)

Virginia Woolf's ideas on the reading of a book are highly pertinent to how we may formulate ideas and consider questions related to the construction of identity and the emergence of conflict. Her statement suggests that to be free is to reject the authoritative voice; to be free is to elevate individual autonomy over and above the decrees and identifications set down and promulgated by authority which attempt to define an individual's place in society and the individual's obligations bounded by a specified community. The second reading of Woolf's statement is to interpret it in terms of the resolution of conflict. Freedom, for Woolf, is also to allow others their interpretations, their identities and modes of expression. One means by which conflict resolution may be defined, therefore, is to state that this is a condition where it is recognised that each interpretation of a text, be that a poem, a novel, a painting, an interpretation of history, a myth, must be dependent on the individual drawing upon the depths of experience, which differ from individual to individual and across time and context. Conflict resolution is thus a recognition of the multiple and shifting identities of individuals all of which constitute the basis of communicative interaction.

Violent conflict does, however, arise from the individual's membership of bounded communities constituted through discursive and institutional dividing lines. The multiple identities of individuals come to be expressed in terms of one dominant identity, assumed to be inclusive of a community, whose unity is constructed upon an imagined nation. To understand the significance of identity in the present context is to unravel its construction, the basis upon which some forms of identity come to dominate others, and the means through which exclusionist identities are implicated in violent human conflict. Conflicts which prevail in the present-day world system and those which have shown intense violent conflict, such as those witnessed in the former Yugoslavia and in the African state of Rwanda, are predominantly if not solely attributable to identity differences, and more specifically to the construction of ethno-national difference. These, coupled with the rise in racist violence directed against refugee and immigrant communities across Europe and elsewhere, suggest that despite the globalising tendencies of the modern era, the reification of the local and the particular remains a central feature in the emergence of violence.

This chapter seeks to analyse the relationship between the construction of identity and the emergence and support for violent conflict. In elaborating further on the theme of this book, the chapter specifically seeks to situate social identity within the constructed boundaries of regularised social systems. It, therefore, utilises the main concepts of structuration theory in an interpretation of the nature of identity as it is implicated in the reproduction of violent conflict as a sociopolitical phenomenon. The chapter first explores "social identity theory" as a potential basis for understanding the self and moves on to argue that in order to locate the relationship between identity and conflict, what is required is a conceptualisation which reads the self as a "positioned" entity, constructed through and constitutive of the structural properties of patterned and regularised social systems.

Social identity theory and conflict research

Conflict and specifically war within the international system have been represented as involving states as actors, anthropomorphised at one and the same time into decision-maker and combatant. The state, however, contains populations whose consent, derived through democratic representation or full-scale coercion, is either taken as given or is considered outside the remits of the study of "inter-state" relations.[1] There is, moreover, an increasing acceptance of the contributions made by the study of nationalism in our understanding of the mobilisation of mass populations into support for violent conflict. In recognising the intimate relationship between nationalism and the resort to force, Mayall points out that "[T]he major wars of the twentieth century required the mobilisation of nations, their civilian populations, economic resources and productive effort, as well as their uniformed military guardians. A nation in arms fights not for narrow political advantage but for its own survival and the survival of the civilisation it represents."[2] A central aspect of the mobilisation of support for armed conflict is identity with the group, community, or state whose representatives decide on the use of force as a means of handling conflict. Identity is assumed to be the essential link between the individual and mass mobilisation for conflict. The constitutive elements of this relationship may be discerned by posing the following questions:

1 What are the processes which constitute the individual's identity?

2 How does identity come to be framed in exclusionist terms?

3 How does the inclusion-exclusion dichotomy result in the emergence of and support for violent human conflict?

Inquiries into the nature of identity and its relationship to conflict may be located along a polarity between a human needs approach which situates identity within the ontological make-up of the individual and sociological approaches which have their basis in Durkheim's notion of the "collective conscience". Social identity theory is an attempt to bridge this polarity between the individual and the collectivity.[3]

The basic premise which underpins a human needs approach is that political behaviour and political beliefs have their basis in a set of ontological needs which are universal and, therefore, shared across cultural and economic divisions. The "basic human needs" approach, as it has been termed in conflict research, defines social identity as an innate characteristic having universal application. The Hobbesian notion of humanity competing in a "state of nature" is rejected in favour of the view that human beings are somehow "programmed" to enter into social relationships. Mary Clark, an advocate of the human needs approach, suggests that "[W]hat Hobbes failed to realize – and many still do today – is that humans evolved with a desire to *belong*, not to *compete*. Biologically, we are obligatory social animals, wholly dependent on a supportive social structure, and it is in the *absence* of such a support system that destructive, 'inhuman' behaviour occurs."[4] The *biological* underpinning of the basic human needs approach is clearly evident in the writings of Clark and other advocates who seek "biological evidence" in support of their universalist assertions.[5] Such "evidence" looks to the bonding behaviour of mammals closely associated with the human species; it looks to patterns in the ovulation cycle which in evolutionary terms led to the spacing of births in order that offspring could achieve parental bonding in the absence of competition; and to the evolution of the human brain and its capacity for information gathering and communication. Other forms of evidence recurrent in the human needs literature emphasise the pathological states which result from protracted periods of isolation in infants and adults alike, arguing that violations of the basic need for identity result in psychological stress for the individual, conflict within the community, and ultimately intense violent conflicts between communities. Having their most explicit statement in Maslow's "hierarchy of needs"[6] and applied to conflict research in John Burton's *Deviance, Terrorism and War*,[7] the formative idea is that "needs represent the basic requirements of human beings for survival and development in both physical and social terms".[8]

Studies which focus on the individual as the primary unit in the analysis of conflict point to the need for identity as fundamental to the survival and well-being of the individual and the society within which that individual exists. An individual's need for identity is, therefore, directly extrapolated to the level of the collectivity such that violations or repressions of identitional expression have consequences for individual and collectivity. Burton, for example, points to such complex and protracted conflicts as the Israeli–Palestinian conflict, the Cyprus conflict and the Northern Ireland conflict, as being based on the need for identity which humans will seek to satisfy irrespective of contextual circumstances or degrees of coercion. The image which emerges is of the individual driven by the desire to satisfy his or her basic needs and of a community or collectivity which is the mere sum of its constituent parts.

The "basic human needs approach", therefore, sees the recognition of identity both as a universal need and an essential requirement for individual development.[9] Conflicts which are variously defined as "deep rooted", "protracted", or "intractable", are explained in terms of the need for free expression of identity and self-determination. The ability of leaders to mobilise support for violent conflict is explained not so much in terms of the ability of leaderships to control and manipulate the communication of issues to their masses, but in terms of the individual constituent's decision to support such action based on her or his need for identity. What emerges is a static model of already programmed individuals easily mobilised once their identity is recognised as being violated.

Individuals are, however, members of highly complex societies containing dominant norms and institutions which are deeply embedded in the histories and memory traces of collectivities. Emile Durkheim recognised the power of such cross-generational social norms in the ability of leaders to mobilise dissimilar individuals into a seemingly unified entity transformable into a fighting force against other collectivities. The "collective conscience" is manifest not merely in the leadership but in the "nature of the societies they govern". In order, therefore, to understand the ability of a leadership to mobilise entire populations, we "must observe the common beliefs, the common sentiments which, by incarnating themselves in a person or in a family, communicate each power to it".[10] Social norms are, therefore, situated within societies and adherence to them cannot simply be reduced to the individual members' innate need for identity. The basic human needs approach does not point to the construction of identity and its manifold expressions. It does not, for example, explain the predominance of one identity, usually the ethno-national, over other forms as a basis of emergent violent conflict. The ahistorical and acontextual nature of the approach suggests that it is unhelpful in understanding the relationship between the continuities of social interaction and the construction of identity, the dynamic nature of identity, and the behavioural consequences of identity formations.

The social psychological literature seeks to provide a link between the individual and group levels of analysis. Self-identity is here conceptualised as membership of a group, or as actualised through group identification. As pointed out by Abrams and Hogg, "social identity is self-conception as a group member".[11] Social identity theory assigns a central role to the "natural" human tendency to partition the world into comprehensible units. An individual's social identity is clarified through comparison with other individuals and groups, the individual's desire for positive self-evaluation providing the motive for differentiation between the in-group and the out-group. This process of differentiation is identified as the basis of inter-group discrimination and the propensity for violent inter-group interaction. Categorisation produces the search for distinguishing features through social comparison, where the need for positive identity or self-esteem is generated through selective accentuation of inter-group differences that favour the in-group. Bloom sees social identity theory as providing the explanatory link between the individual's "inherent drive" to identify and the need to "enhance and to protect the identifications he or she has made".[12]

Social identity theory has its foundations in the writings of Freud, Mead and Erikson. While the intricacies of each of their *oeuvres* will not be dealt with here, the common thread between them is the recognition that personality is a social construct which has its origins in the infant's recognition of its dependence on an "other". This differentiation has its origins in the biological drive for survival rather than being derived from "a social system's need for stability".[13] In following the psychoanalytic model propounded by Freudian psychology, Ann Norton points to this early differentiation of self and other in stating that

> Unsatisfied hunger brings with it the recognition of an other, hostile or indifferent to the self. Hunger is the passion of the infant's incompletion. Belatedly, the child recognises its separation from that collective identity that completed its being. Hunger teaches the child that it is, in want and the attendant awakening of the will, apart from the now alienated and external world of satisfaction and contentment. The infant becomes conscious of itself as difference in the denial of its

desire. The first knowledge of the self is knowledge of alienation.[14]

The differentiation of self and other has early origins in the life cycle of the individual and provides the basis of social differentiation in later social interaction.

Social identity theory has its basis, therefore, in a recognition of an early differentiation between self and other. It also recognises that individual identity is not a constant, but a shifting framework based on interactions between the individual and her or his social environment. Identity, following Erik Erikson, is the medium which bridges the self-society nexus. Erikson's contribution to the question of identity rests primarily on the relationship he discerns between identity and control or a sense of security. Identity becomes an anxiety-controlling mechanism reinforcing a sense of trust, predictability and control, disruption or threat to which, through a change in historical circumstances, results in behaviours which seek to re-establish the individual's previous identity or formulate a new one.[15]

Like the basic human needs approach, psychoanalytic models of personality development are capable of defining the temporal basis of identity formation in the individual, but remain unsatisfactory on the social construction of identity. Social identity theory of more recent social psychological work seeks to focus on group formation and group differentiation as the underlying causes of emergent conflicts. The concept of social identity is seen by conflict researchers to be the link between needs theory and inter-group relations.[16]

The aim of social identity theory as it is elaborated or utilised in social psychology is to move beyond inter-personal relations to incorporate a "non-reductionist" approach to inter-group processes. A recurrent theme in social identity theory is that social comparison processes involve individuals seeking to preserve a positive and coherent self-image where "an individual will tend to remain a member of a group or seek membership of new groups if these groups have some contribution to make to the positive aspects of his social identity, i.e. to those aspects of it from which he derives some satisfaction".[17] The need for positive self-esteem is seen to be the primary motivating force in group membership and social categorisation and consequent negative images and discrimination against outer groups.

The self-categorisation approach to social identity is considered useful in providing insights to the emergence of violent conflict. Social psychological experiments have indicated, for example, that in-group prototypes are favoured and self-group similarities accentuated. Judgement of others is mediated by the categories to which they are perceived to belong. It is important to recognise that while the aim of social identity theory, including the self-categorisation principle, is to incorporate social context in the analysis of social identity, context is only mediated through the individual's mind. According to Hogg and McGarty, "while the reality of social groups and institutions is accepted as a matter of course, it is nevertheless the case that we as social psychologists are concerned with such institutions to the extent to which they are psychologically represented".[18] Social identity and categorisation emerge from cognitive processes which seek coherence and positive self-imagery producing in their instantiation such social consequences as stereotyping, social judgement, and conformity, all of which are constitutive of the conflict process and the legitimation of violence. The problematique is whether these deeply embedded social processes may be analysed through recourse to individual cognitive imperatives.

The social psychological emphasis on human cognitive processes as the motivational underpinning of social identity and self-categorisation precludes the possibility of conceptualising the time and space implications of group identity and in-group and out-group difference. In recognising the limitations of "self-esteem" as primal mover in social identity, Hogg and Abrams argue:

> A need for self-esteem may be involved, but it may not have the status of ultimate cause . . . More often than not, it may be displaced by other, perhaps competing needs, all of which have equal causal status. Intergroup behaviour is quite likely to be multiply caused, just as self-esteem is multiply influenced . . . Interaction between different motivational pressures becomes particularly relevant when we abandon the minimal intergroup context and consider the self-esteem hypothesis in the broader context of relations between social categories which have history and content.[19]

This problem becomes highly salient when inter-group differences are "highly institutionalized and ideologically legitimated", where, importantly for the context of this book, "discriminatory practices may become ritualized and habitual: an unproblematic background to daily life which attracts little attention".[20]

In her critique of cognitive approaches to the problem of stereotyping, Susan Condor seeks to locate her analysis in the discursive and institutional construction of the social categorisation process and its social consequences. As Condor points out, the cognitive approach which underpins social identity theory analyses stereotyping as a process integral to the "natural" need for consistency and simplified information processing. In her analysis of racist and sexist stereotyping, Condor points to the need for placing stereotyping firmly within the historical and social contexts which generate and legitimate such modes of discourse. Condor situates stereotyping, which is an essential feature of conflict and the legitimation of violence, as social constructs emerging from discursive cultural continuities and contributing to their reproduction.[21] The categorisation of self and other is not, therefore, a product of cognition and information processing, but derives from discursive and institutional continuities which are reproduced through every stereotyping or categorising act.

The implications of categorisation and the communicative acts which reproduce an imagery of self and other are of central importance in understanding processes which legitimate violence in situations of conflict. As pointed out by Mitchell,[22] stereotypical images of the enemy are inextricably linked to a dehumanisation process which influences the legitimation of behaviour adopted towards the enemy. An enemy stereotypified as diabolical and inferior is, as a consequence, presented by a leadership of a conflict party as a legitimate target of direct violence or of discrimination. This process results in presenting the enemy as a monolithic whole, where populations and leaderships are perceived as one deserving target. Conflict research does not, however, move beyond the psychological processes which accompany the state of conflict and, indeed, relies on the cognitive underpinnings of such processes. It has not, therefore, recognised the discursive and institutional continuities which generate and reproduce the categorisation and differentiation processes which reproduce violence as a social continuity.

Social identity and conflict as constructed discourse

Cognitive approaches to social identity and analyses of attitudes and perceptions prevalent in time of conflict view language as an unproblematic medium of interaction. As indicated in previous chapters, the assumption taken in this book is that language has a performative function in that it is implicated in the construction of social life. Expressions of identity, formations/representations of exclusionist discourses, and processes involved in shifting identities are situated in time and space locations which link day-to-day encounters to the seemingly extraordinary time of conflict.

Conceptualising conflict as *constructed discourse* places a specific conflict within the wider discursive and institutional continuities within which the conflict is embedded. The linguistic constructs used to provide versions of a conflict by parties and observers alike are not peculiar to that conflict alone, but derive from pre-existing discursive modes which are implicated in the construction of the conflict. Furthermore, the linguistic modes surrounding a particular conflict have potent consequences more widely in the temporal and spatial domain in the reconstruction or reproduction of the discourses and institutions which render violent human conflict a social continuity in patterned social systems.

The first element of the conceptualisation of conflict as constructed discourse is that, following structurationist premises, this conceptualisation of conflict does not assume an ontological separation of agency and structure, but accepts that each is constitutive of the other in the duality of structure. It accepts the idea, developed by Giddens and articulated by Virginia Woolf's opening statement to this chapter, that individuals are knowledgeable agents who draw upon their "depths of experience" or "stocks of knowledge" in their social interactions/interpretations. Human conduct and articulations of identity are situated historically so that conditions which define the contextual frameworks of action, in the form of structures of signification and legitimation, are drawn upon reflexively and are reproduced intentionally or unintentionally through the process of interaction. Awareness of contextual and historical conditions which form the backdrop to conflict and conceptions of identity may be "practical" or "discursive", where, as indicated in chapter three, the former implies tacit knowledge while the latter indicates articulated awareness.

The challenge of the above definition of conflict as constructed discourse is to provide a conceptual link between day-to-day encounters, or the routinisation of social life, and the extraordinary time of conflict, which may also be defined as representing "critical situations".[23] The routine of the everyday provides individuals with a sense of ontological security which enables them to "go on" in their daily encounters. As pointed out by Giddens, "Routine is integral both to the continuity of the personality of the agent, as he or she moves along the paths of daily activities, and to the institutions of society, which are such only through their continued reproduction."[24] The routine encounters of daily interactions and perceptions of the self draw upon the long duree of deeply embedded social continuities through practical consciousness. Such continuities, institutionalised in social life, are reproduced through every social encounter. This reconstitutive process is illustrated in ethnomethodological research concerned with the social processes involved in the reproduction of everyday life.[25] Lawrence Wieder's study of everyday life in a half-way house for drugs offenders points to the "multiformulative" and "multiconsequential" nature of talk where routine utterances are not simply descriptions of events or rules of behaviour, but are a constitutive aspect of the rules of life within this confined setting. Talk, therefore, has a reflexive character in that it reproduces the conditions which give it meaning.[26] The routine of daily encounters implies that conduct is not always directly motivated but happens through the "reflexive monitoring of action"[27] by knowledgeable agents in situations of co-presence. In other words, the institutional and discursive continuities of social life are not only implicated in day-to-day encounters, but also reproduced by them.

The relevance of the above discussion of routine has implications for developing an understanding of conflict as constructed discourse and the role of identity therein. Social identity is not merely manifest in circumstances of adversity. Memories, myths, symbolic orders, and self-imagery form a constitutive part of the practical consciousness of situated individuals. They are not consistently referred to in social interaction but form a background which not only enables an individual to go on, but provides meaning in the daily encounters of knowledgeable human agents. The individual's articulations of a sense of self, distinguishable as a personality, provide a continual reaffirmation of the identities held by that individual and his or her relationship with the surrounding social world. Social identity is, therefore, implicated and reconstituted in daily encounters.

Individuals always stand in relation to specific histories, memories, ideologies, symbolic systems, languages and geographic locations. The identity of individuals is not always articulated through discursive consciousness, but can form the social background existing in practical consciousness. Open expressions of identity are based on a selection of attributes shared with other members of society. All individuals are "positioned" on specific locations along the structural continuities of social systems, in the form of symbolic orders, normative expectations and power relations. According to Giddens,

> Social positions are constituted structurally as specific inter-sections of signification, domination, and legitimation which relates to the typification of agents. A social position involves the specification of a definite "identity" within a network of social relations, that identity, however, being a "category" to which a particular range of normative sanctions is relevant.[28]

Identity, expressed in the form of social positioning, carries with it symbols and articulations as well as social expectations that an individual carrying a specific identity may activate at specific locations in that individual's life span. It is important to recognise, however, that identities are always located in the long duree of institutions or social continuities which provide the "frames", as containers of social rules, which render encounters or interactions both sustainable and meaningful.[29]

Articulations of identity in circumstances of conflict draw upon deeply embedded identitational continuities mobilised in the construction of bounded political groupings. The second element deriving from a conceptualisation of conflict as constructed discourse is that violent conflict is constituted around the construction of a *discourse of exclusion*. This invokes articulations of separateness, of limitations to access, of strict boundedness. It refers to dichotomous representations of the self and other, of the deserving and the guilty, and of the righteous and diabolical respectively. Such social constructs or representations as the nation-state, ethnic-nationalism, ethnic-cleansing, national sovereignty, the "bogus refugee", the "foreign worker", are expressions of a discourse of exclusion implicated in the legitimation of violence. Images/texts which represent a gendered/class/racial division of society identify an exclusionist discourse that has deep foundations which are structurated through everyday social encounters. Exclusionist discourses are not, therefore, merely manifest in specific situations of violent conflict, but are deeply embedded in discursive and institutional practices which are drawn upon and reconstituted through every articulation and practice of exclusion.

Discourses of exclusion implicated in the constitution of political violence and war as social continuity rest upon the construction of *exclusionist identities*. Identities are constructed representations of the "self" in relation to the "other". The idea of a constructed identity situates expressions of identity within the social and historical context rather than interpreting them on the basis of bio-psychological underpinnings. Expressions of identity are built out of a variety of pre-existing experiences, implicated in human conduct through practical and discursive consciousness. The construction of identity implies active selection of particular modes of representation. Active selection does not, however, imply free selection, in that social positioning is also constituted through dominant societal norms, symbolic orders, and structures of domination which are implicated in agents' choices of identiational representation. Identity is, therefore, constituted around modes of interpretation and complexes of meanings which are drawn upon in the process of self-description and articulation. Which expression of identity dominates or prevails is dependent on the degree of control different social groups exercise over discursive and institutional practices.

Structures of domination existing within administered social systems are centrally implicated in the emergence of dominant identities in society. One element of the authoritative resources implicated in the mediation of power is the organisation of human beings into mutual association. As pointed out by Giddens, "the *co-ordination* of numbers of people together in a society and their reproduction over time is an authoritative resource of a fundamental sort".[30] The ability to consolidate and reproduce authoritative power is dependent on the capacity to manipulate the memory traces of a community and control information gathering and dissemination which generate and reproduce the discursive and institutional continuities which "bind" societies. Administered systems are dependent on categorisation and surveillance in the consolidation of control.

The ability to wage war requires a high degree of control and an ability to impose and reinforce disciplinary power. Control of the body in micro-social settings is paralleled by control of the body politic in wider settings. Foucault's analysis of institutions illustrates the modes of administrative control achieved through the temporal and spatial partitioning of individuals, who may then be easily categorised according to specified principles and surveyed to ensure compliance or conformity to the rules of the institution. "Partitioning", therefore, implies a condition where "each individual has his own place; and each place its individual". Furthermore, administrative power requires uniformity and predictability so that "one must eliminate the effects of imprecise distributions, the uncontrolled disappearance of individuals, their diffuse circulation, their unusable and dangerous coagulation".[31] Foucault applies his model of the micro-social world of prisons, hospitals and armies to the constitution of the state as a system of control based on conformity and uniformity. War is the ultimate expression of control which has its parallel in the constitution of society:

> It may be that war as strategy is a continuation of politics. But it must not be forgotten that "politics" has been conceived as a continuation, if not exactly and directly of war, at least of the military model as a fundamental means of preventing civil disorder. Politics, as a technique of internal peace and order, sought to implement the mechanism of the perfect army, of the disciplined mass, of the docile, useful troop, of the regiment in camp and in the field, on manoeuvres and on exercises.[32]

Control requires that the whole is held together, that dissent is prevented or even punished, that a dominant, desirable identity is mobilised. Episodic ceremonials, symbolic representations, images of past glories and present achievements reinforce a sense of identity among the masses called upon in time of mobilisation for conflict. The control and manipulation of public discourses in time of conflict emphasise the exigencies of strategic management, regulation of behaviour, and "an ordered maximization of collective and individual forces".[33]

Exclusionist discourse, nationalism and conflict

Language is a central component in the production and reproduction of societies. Language is also a mechanism of control in
highly administered social systems. It constitutes the public domain
of political discourse and is the medium through which identity is
constructed. Moreover, it is the medium through which contestations become manifest. The implication for social identity is that,
as Nancy Fraser points out,

> people's social identities are complexes of meanings, networks
> of interpretation. To have a social identity . . . just is to live
> and to act under a set of descriptions. These descriptions, of
> course, are not simply secreted by people's bodies; still less are
> they exuded by people's psyches. Rather, they are drawn from
> the fund of interpretive possibilities available to agents in
> specific societies.[34]

The emergence of dominant constructions of identity within
specific locations in time and space suggests a point of intersection
between structures of domination, symbolic orders, and legitimation. This point of intersection defines a relation of asymmetry in
the production of dominant discourses on social identity formations. The notion of "discursive hegemony" points to the privileged
position held by dominant social groups with respect to discourse.
It also presupposes that societies are containers of a "plurality of
discourses and discursive sites".[35] Discursive hegemony does not,
therefore, produce automata, willing citizenry absorbing pro-
nouncements of identity as these are exuded from a discursively
privileged leadership. Identity is always a point of both selection
and contestation and it is through structures of domination and
control that dominant discourses on identity emerge.

Language is constitutive of all that which is public and political.
As Ann Norton points out, "The casting of thought in language
makes the private and the individual public and collective by ac-
commodating individual experience and subjectivity within the
concepts, categories, and order of a particular culture and political
system."[36] What is important here is not so much the structure of
symbolic orders which, following Saussurean linguistics, treats
language or "langue" as a code generating subjectivity, but rather,
the language of communicative practice, or "parole",[37] which

recognises the situated nature of communicative interaction. Social identity is a product of all that which is located in the realm of society, as context of communication, power relations, contestations, and dominant discursive and institutional practices.

The nation, that most commonplace of identities, is the location of discursive and institutional practices which at one and the same time generate legitimation and exclusion. It is the location of a remembered past, of repetitive symbolic reification, and of total mobilisation in time of conflict. The conflicts of our post Cold War era centre around a *discourse of origins*, where the traditions and territorial claims of forebears are relived and in whose name contemporary and future wars are legitimated. The categories of origin exemplified in constructs such as Israeli, Palestinian, Arab, Moslem, Serb, Turkish, Kurdish, Christian, Hutu, Tutsi, Catholic, Protestant, hark back to a distant past in order to mobilise a bounded, exclusionist present. This is a process of selection and definition, where a dominant identity emerges from a plethora of other possibilities. It seeks to negate and deny difference, to obliterate dissent, in the name of a mythical unified entity, an effective fighting force. A discourse of origins is at the heart of conflict as constructed discourse. Conflict is the time at which free individuality becomes submerged into a wider group affiliation defined in terms of the nation and a collective memory. Conflict is the time at which the language of politics becomes a discourse of exclusionist protection against a constructed diabolical, hated enemy who is deserving of any violence perpetrated against it. The enemy is not, however, merely an offensive leadership culpable and guilty in the generation of undesirable conditions, and therefore worthy of punishment. The enemy is another constructed entity, an entire population, whose history is reconstructed and itself represented in exclusionist terms, categorised, in turn, according to a specified attributed definition. Any conflicts and contestations within are suppressed in the name of the conflict without.

National identity, a self-perception based on history, mythology, tradition, language, culture, is an important constituent of administered social systems. It generates one identity from a plurality of other possibilities. It is based on a categorisation process which allows for ordered and rationalised rule. Extension of the administered power of the state across regions and classes is dependent upon a deeply embedded sense of identity with the state and nation.

The relationship between collective national identity and administered power establishes a "differentiation and ordering characteristic of institutional rationalization".[38] Moreover, the extension of control over networks of communication and forms of interpretation consolidate structures of domination in administered social systems, such as the state.

Individuals are born into discursive and institutional continuities which define and bind particular societies. Individuals are involved in the reproduction or transformation of social systems which are in existence through the continuity of praxis.[39] The realisation of common national identity builds up through the life cycle of the individual. He or she is integrated into society through the discursive and institutional control of his or her daily life, as a defined member of the societal whole and as conscious consumer of cultural symbols and artifacts. National identity is not necessarily an aspect of discursive consciousness, articulated in every social encounter. Rather, it forms a constituent part of a plurality of self-evident descriptions that form a background which is both pervasive and largely unacknowledged. Periods of adversity and conflict with external others or with a constructed internal enemy see dominant social groups drawing upon this generalised background identity in defining issues, interests and legitimate targets in the name of the nation.

The "nation", "national interest", "national security", "national well-being", "national sovereignty", "national self-determination" are all conceptual categories which rely on a sense of collective identity with an imagined past which binds individuals across class, gender, income levels and other forms of division amongst the citizenry. Benedict Anderson defines a nation as "an imagined political community – and imagined as both inherently limited and sovereign".[40] It is imagined in that it is constructed from a remembered past; a recollection of history as time-container of cultural, political and military achievement.[41] Such remembrances or imaginings become structurated with time into deeply founded symbolic orders and societal norms that are "carried" from generation to generation. These generally form a background of meanings which are reproduced and reconstituted through daily utterances which refer to all that which is "national". As Giddens points out, "While in the nation-state all members of the population share an array of concepts constitutive of its sovereign and polyarchic character, these may be mainly ordered in practical consciousness rather than being available to be discursively formulated as reasons for action."[42]

The concept of the nation and the national identity upon which it is based is so deeply embedded and pervasive across time and space that the division of humanity into a world of separate nation-states seems to be the natural order of things. The strength of nationalism as a doctrine, which sees the nation as the primary criterion for government, is that it has succeeded in establishing the constructed category of "nation" as a naturalised form of human development and representation. The discourse of nationalism, through its naturalisation of the nation, negates its historical and contextual underpinnings while at one and the same time relying for its legitimacy on a remembered past of a particular community.[43] Through the naturalization of what is a political construct, the "nation", as a bounded entity, is reified at the expense of other modes of representation, so that, for example, economic relations produced through the mode of production become depoliticised and almost delegitimised. The sectional interests of particular dominant groups in society are defined as being in the general "national" interest. The political construct of the "national interest" is so pervasive as to be taken as a given, natural motivation of governmental action. Government, nation and state are conceptualised as coterminous entities in interaction with other conceptually "unified" governments, nations and states in the arena of *world* politics.[44]

Elie Kedourie situates the emergence of the relationship between nationalism, sovereignty and citizenship in the French Revolution. This event established the relationship between legitimate authority and citizenship in identification with the nation.[45] Giddens sees sovereignty, citizenship, and nationalism as connected phenomena. He rejects psychological interpretations of nationalism which see its basis in the need for identity, as too limited in developing an understanding which links nationalism, as an ideological formulation, to the state and asymmetries of power. Nationalism, therefore, has a number of interrelated characteristics: a political connection with the nation-state, articulated in the construct of sovereignty; an ideological character linked to class domination; a psychological/attitudinal force linking the individual to the state; and as container of powerful symbolic forces which create an imagined community.[46] The nation is, therefore, constructed as a totality, built upon an imagined distinctive history and culture, containing a symbolic order that is utilised in times of adversity to mobilise entire collectivities against other bounded communities.

Language is not only of key importance in providing a unifying force between individual members of a community, but is the medium through which the "political as national" is constructed. For Eric Hobsbawm,

> National languages are . . . almost always semi-artificial constructs . . . They are the opposite of what nationalist mythology supposes them to be, namely the primordial foundations of national culture and the matrices of the national mind. They are usually attempts to devise a standardized idiom out of a multiplicity of actually spoken idioms, which are thereafter downgraded to dialects, the main problem in their construction being usually, which dialect to choose as the basis of the standardized and homogenized language.[47]

A standardised, constructed language comes to form a central aspect of the life of the nation-state which is replete with powerful symbols which permeate the daily lives of its citizens. National flags form not only the background image reproduced on street corners, car number plates, and roofs of restaurants, but are evident as powerful symbols of distinctiveness and segregation in sporting occasions and military ceremonies alike. National monuments are powerful reminders of past struggles and sacrifices in the name of which the continuity and survival of the nation must be assured irrespective of new sacrifices of "Unknown Soldiers". It is linguistic formulations as well as the symbolic content of cultures which perpetuate a sense of community which, in the nation-state, is a prerequisite of administrative totality.

In stressing the constructive element of discourse and in conceptualising conflict as a constructed discourse of exclusion, what is emphasised here is that accounts of events formulated by leaders and observers alike are built out of a variety of pre-existing linguistic sources and shared worlds of meaning which are drawn upon in the construction of reality. The end of the Cold War between the "superpowers" witnessed not so much the obsolescence of war, as the emergence of ethnic-nationalist conflicts, the violence of which saw massacres perpetrated against specified ethnic communities, the re-emergence of concentration camps in the European arena, and the systematic rape of women as a deliberate tactic in conflict behaviour.[48] In recording the levels of armed conflict between the years 1989–92, Peter Wallensteen and Karin Axell discovered a total of 82 armed conflicts involving at least 64 governments with a total number of fatalities estimated in six-figure proportions. The bulk of the conflicts recorded concerned "internal issues" covering demands for national autonomy and self-determination.[49] The prevalence of armed conflict based on ethno-national difference points to the dominance of exclusionist discourse in the generation of support for violent conflict.

The exclusionist discourse of violent conflict is not, however, confined to the battlefield, which is traditionally seen to involve well-defined fighting forces and their constituencies. In an essay entitled "What of Tomorrow's Nation?", Julia Kristeva speaks of a more pervasive discourse of exclusion as a "defensive hatred" where "the cult of origins easily backslides to a persecuting hatred".[50] This is where violence is turned against the "foreigner", the "incomer", the "foreign worker", or the "bogus refugee". This is a discourse of exclusion which is not confined to extreme nationalist groupings such as the British National Party in the United Kingdom, the Front National in France, or the plethora of neo-Nazi groups which have germinated in Germany and elsewhere across Europe, whose targets constitute all those defined as "other". Exclusionist categories permeate political discourse around such salient issues as immigration and the protection of boundaries against a "flood" of refugees.[51] It is a discourse which politically legitimates and reproduces a categorisation based on those who are defined as legitimately within, against all external others, who are variously targets of direct violence and/or institutionalised discrimination. The "degeneracy of the national idea",[52] which Kristeva identifies as racism, is, therefore, a pervasive form of violence that is reconstituted through every racist act and racist utterance. The link between this form of pervasive or dispersed violence and the armed conflicts identified above is that both involve discourses of exclusion which aim to typify a diversity of individuals into well-defined exclusionist categories. Both constitute structures of violence based on segmentation and opposition where the act of violence inscribes an imposed meaning upon what is essentially an unknown target.

Identity with the collective is manifest in both formalised collective modes of violence, which are characterised by structured, rule-bound institutions with a high degree of control, and informal collective violence, which incorporates unstructured entities, more or less loose political groupings. The former are associated with the state and its military establishment, while the latter are representative of non-state actors involved in conflict to achieve statehood or to remove an incumbent leadership from an existing state. Both forms of violent conflict illustrate the relationship between social identity and support for collective violence.

Formal wars associated with the state are carried out in the name of the state, which acquires its legitimacy from a collective identity with the nation. As pointed out by Ann Norton,

> The army is not only collective, it formally represents the nation, the active general will. This representative character is signified by uniforms, which disguise and formally deny individuality, and by the use of the national flag and other emblems, which announce the unity of the force and its role as representative of the nation.[53]

The violence of an army involved in war is seen as legitimate in that it is simply carrying out the "general will". The army is the outward symbol of national sovereignty. The citizenry, while uninvolved directly in the conduct of war, is incorporated into the war-fighting machine through identification, allegiance and economic production on the home front. Such identification derives from a mobilisation process which draws upon structures of signification and legitimation in the production of support for violent conflict. The process of mobilisation is not only manifest in time of specific conflicts and attributable to particular individuals or leaderships, but derives from the deeply-embedded myths that permeate the political, social and cultural aspects of society and which are reproduced through every action and utterance which glorifies the nation and/or the military.[54] Representations of the military as coterminous with the nation are carried out primarily through the mass media which comes to constitute the only source of political information and discourse.[55]

Collective identity is the medium through which the individual is related to collective violence, whether such violence is carried out by the military machinery of the state or on behalf of aspirants to statehood. War is a constitutive element of collective identity, reproduced in collective memory through national "narratives"[56] of past glories in the face of threats against national sovereignty and survival. A self-image based on notions of heroism, valour and justice draws upon such collective memories and is actively reproduced in times of conflict. The discourse of nationalism always represents wars as being fought on behalf of the "nation" and, therefore, fought for just cause. Nations are constructed around "narratives" of war, the "heroes" of which acquire symbolic significance in the reproduction of a national identity based on war. As pointed out by Hedetoft,

> A "hero" is a cluster of national meaning, in the sense that meaning is imputed to particular persons in order to serve as figures of national bravery, sacrifice and unity. But a hero is also someone who is seen to fulfil his/her innermost identity, through personal sacrifice and almost religious devotion to a worthy, noble cause . . . Heroes are socio-cultural constructs, paradoxically more useful to the cult of nationalism dead than alive.[57]

War is a product of nationalist discourse, an emblem of state sovereignty, a manifestation of individual identity with nation and state. War is also a constructed discourse, enabled through identiational discursive and institutional continuities which give it legitimacy.

In recognising the constructive element of language, discourse analysis goes some way towards contributing to an understanding of conflict as exclusionist discourse reifying a singular way of knowing. However, each observer/interpreter/party to a conflict is situated within a particular sociopolitical and historical context. As such, there can be no single interpretation or true reading of a novel, a piece of legislation, or of a historical narrative. There is, therefore, no "uniform" interpretation and no singular way of knowing.[58] Recognising the plurality of possibilities in interpretation does away with the notion of singular forms of identity, legitimate and all-encompassing. Discourses which reify ethnonationalist identity assume a uniformity in human experience which denies a pluralism of identities. It is the recognition of the plethora of legitimate readings, representations and identities that constitute individuality which must lie at the heart of transformative, critical discourses on peace. This transformative discourse forms the basis for the next chapter.

Notes

1. W. Bloom, *Personal Identity, National Identity and International Relations* (Cambridge University Press, Cambridge, 1990), p. 1.
2. J. Mayall, *Nationalism and International Society* (Cambridge University Press, Cambridge, 1990), p. 31.
3. Bloom, *op. cit.*, p. 26.
4. M.E. Clark, "Meaningful Social Bonding as a Universal Human Need", in J.W. Burton (ed.), *Conflict: Human Needs Theory* (Macmillan, London and St Martin's Press, New York, 1990), pp. 39–40.
5. J.W. Burton, *Deviance, Terrorism and War* (Martin Robertson, Oxford, 1979); E. Azar and J.W. Burton (eds), *International Conflict Resolution: Theory and Practice* (Harvester Wheatsheaf, Brighton and Lynne Reinner, Boulder, CO, 1986); D.J.D. Sandole and H. van der Merwe (eds), *Conflict Resolution Theory and Practice* (Manchester University Press, Manchester, 1993).
6. A.H. Maslow, *Motivation and Personality* (Harper and Row, New York, 1970).
7. Burton rejects the notion that needs are hierarchically organised, arguing that social needs as well as physiological needs are essential for human development. See Burton (1979), *op. cit.*
8. R.J. Fisher, "Needs Theory, Social Identity and an Eclectic Model of Conflict", in Burton (1990), *op. cit.*, p. 91.
9. K. Lederer (ed.), *Human Needs: A Contribution to the Current Debate* (Oelgeschlager, Gunn, and Hain, Cambridge, MA, 1980).
10. E. Durkheim, *The Division of Labour in Society* (Free Press, New York, 1964), p. 196.
11. D. Abrams and M.A. Hogg, "An Introduction to the Social Identity Approach", in D. Abrams and M.A. Hogg (eds), *Social Identity Theory: Constructive and Critical Advances* (Harvester Wheatsheaf, London, 1990), p. 2.
12. Bloom, *op. cit.*, p. 23.
13. Bloom, *op. cit.*, p. 33.
14. A. Norton, *Reflections on Political Identity* (Johns Hopkins University Press, London and Baltimore, 1988), p. 12.
15. E.H. Erikson, *Identity, Youth and Crisis* (Faber and Faber, London, 1968).
16. Fisher, *op. cit.*, p. 94.
17. H. Tajfel, "Social Categorisation", English manuscript of "La

categorisation sociale", in S. Moscovici (ed.), *Introduction à la Psycho-logie Sociale, Vol. I* (Larousse, Paris, 1972), quoted in Abrams and Hogg, *op. cit.*, p. 29.

18. M.A. Hogg and C. McGarty, "Self-Categorisation and Social Identity", in Abrams and Hogg, *op. cit.*, p. 24.

19. M.A. Hogg and D. Abrams, "Self-Motivation, Self-Esteem, and Social Identity", in Abrams and Hogg, *op. cit.*, p. 39.

20. *Ibid.*, p. 40.

21. Condor adopts Gergen's social constructionist approach in defining stereotypes as specifically cultural phenomena. See S. Condor, "Social Stereotypes and Social Identity", in Abrams and Hogg, *op. cit.* and K.J. Gergen and K.E. Davis (eds), *The Social Construction of the Person* (Springer Verlag, New York, 1985).

22. C.R. Mitchell, *Structure of International Conflict* (Macmillan, London, 1981), pp. 71–119.

23. A. Giddens, *The Constitution of Society* (Polity Press, Cambridge, 1984), p. 60.

24. *Ibid.*, p. 60.

25. H. Garfinkel, *Studies in Ethnomethodology* (Prentice Hall, Englewood Cliffs, NJ, 1967); J. Heritage, *Garfinkel and Ethnomethodology* (Polity Press, Cambridge, 1984).

26. L. Wieder, "Telling the Code", in R. Turner (ed.), *Ethnomethodology* (Penguin, Harmondsworth, 1974).

27. See chapter three.

28. Giddens, *op. cit.*, p. 83.

29. E. Goffman, *Frame Analysis* (Harper, New York, 1974).

30. Giddens, *op. cit.*, p. 260.

31. M. Foucault, *Discipline and Punish: The Birth of the Prison* (Penguin, London, 1991), p. 143.

32. *Ibid.*, p. 168.

33. M. Foucault, *The History of Sexuality, Vol. I*, quoted in P. Rabinow (ed.), *The Foucault Reader: An Introduction to Foucault's Thought* (Penguin, London, 1984), p. 307. Foucault applies this statement to the regulation of sex through analytical discourses. The process of identity regulation through dominant discourses is central to my understanding of violence.

34. N. Fraser, "The Uses and Abuses of French Discourse Theories for Feminist Politics", *Theory, Culture and Society*, Vol. 9 (1992), p. 52.

35. *Ibid.*, p. 54.

36. Norton, *op. cit.*, p. 46.

37. F. De Saussure, *Course in General Linguistics* (Fontana, London, 1974). For a review of the distinction between 'langue' and 'parole', see A.

Giddens, *Central Problems in Social Theory* (Macmillan, London, 1979), pp. 10–18.

38. Norton, *op. cit.*, p. 47.

39. Giddens (1984), *op. cit.*, p. 171; R. Bhaskar, *The Possibility of Naturalism* (Harvester Wheatsheaf, Hemel Hempstead, 1989), p. 42.

40. B. Anderson, *Imagined Communities* (Verso, London, 1991), p. 6.

41. Anthony Smith identifies historicity as the primary defining element of ethnic nationalism. See A.D. Smith, *The Ethnic Revival in the Modern World* (Cambridge University Press, Cambridge, 1981); *National Identity* (Penguin Books, Harmondsworth, 1991).

42. A. Giddens, *The Nation-State and Violence* (Polity Press, Cambridge, 1985), p. 211.

43. E. Kedourie, *Nationalism* (Hutchinson University Library, London, 1966), pp. 9–20.

44. Realism, as a school of thought in the discipline of international relations, takes the state as its primary, often only, unit of analysis, and has as its conceptual building blocks, the "national interest" and "sovereignty". See H.J. Morgenthau, *Politics Among Nations* (Alfred Knopf, New York, 1985); A. James, *Sovereign Statehood: The Basis of International Society* (Allen and Unwin, London and Boston, 1986).

45. Kedourie, *op. cit.*, p. 12–13.

46. Giddens (1985), *op. cit.*, pp. 215–217.

47. E. J. Hobsbawm, *Nations and Nationalism since 1780* (Cambridge University Press, Cambridge, 1990), p. 54.

48. See J.J. Mearsheimer, "Back to the Future: Instability in Europe after the Cold War", *International Security*, Vol. 15, No. 1 (1990), pp. 5–57.

49. P. Wallensteen and K. Axell, "Armed Conflict at the End of the Cold War, 1989–92", *Journal of Peace Research*, Vol. 30, No. 3 (1993), pp. 331–346.

50. J. Kristeva, *Nations without Nationalism* (Columbia University Press, New York, 1993), p. 3.

51. Richmond suggests that such terms are "actions, structures, and institutions associated with forcible isolation of people who are different". See A.H. Richmond, *Global Apartheid: Refugees, Racism, and the New World Order* (Oxford University Press, Oxford and New York, 1994), p. 206.

52. Kristeva, *op. cit.*, p. 13.

53. Norton, *op. cit.*, p. 146.

54. In seeking to establish an empirical, statistically valid relationship between support for war and the sale of war toys and war films, Patrick Regan points to the use of symbols of nationalism and patriotism in "ubiquitous forms of entertainment" in the production

of public support for the military. See P. Regan, "War Toys, War Movies, and the Militarization of the United States, 1900–85", *Journal of Peace Research*, Vol. 31, No. 1 (1994), pp. 45–58. See also P. Virilio, *War and Cinema* (Verso, London and New York, 1989).

55. S.H. Chaffee *et al.*, "Mass Communication in Political Socialization", in S.A. Renshon (ed.), *Handbook of Political Socialization: Theory and Research* (Free Press, New York, 1977), p. 227.

56. H.K. Bhabha (ed.), *Nation and Narration* (Routledge, London, 1990).

57. U. Hedetoft, "National Identity and Mentalities of War in Three EC Countries", *Journal of Peace Research*, Vol. 30, No. 3 (1993), pp. 281–300.

58. M.E. Hawkesworth, "Knowers, Knowing, Known: Feminist Theory and Claims of Truth", *Signs*, Vol. 14, No. 3 (1989), pp. 533–547.

Chapter six

A discourse on peace

> Even my
> passive eyes transmute
> everything I look at to the pocked
> black and white of a war photo,
> how
> can I stop myself
>
> It is dangerous to read newspapers
>
> Each time I hit a key
> on my electric typewriter,
> speaking of peaceful trees
>
> another village explodes

Margaret Atwood,
The Oxford Book of War Poetry (1988)

The aim of this chapter is to investigate ideas on the condition of peace. No critical discourse on political violence can be complete in the absence of consideration of the means by which humanity could transcend the condition of war. Peace, however, remains as enigmatic a concept as it is in achievement. Any discourse on war as a social phenomenon must incorporate practices and thoughts which may contribute to the transformation of the discursive and institutional continuities which legitimate it. Such would be the emancipatory component of this study. In seeking to situate this discourse within the overall framework of the book, there is a recognition of the transformative capacity of agents – the ability to make a difference – but always within a complex combination of structural enablement and constraint. Inclusion of this chapter also points to the view held by this author that social inquiry and the textual articulations it produces have some role, albeit beyond specifiable measures, in the reproduction and/or transformation of the social world which forms its subject matter. This investigation has sought to move the study of violent human conflict towards understanding it as a social continuity sustained by deeply embedded discursive and institutional structures existent in patterned social systems. A discourse on peace assumes a basis for the transformation of symbolic and institutional orders which underpin violent human conflict. A discourse on peace is necessarily a counter-discourse which seeks to understand the structurated legitimation of violence and challenge the militarist order and exclusionist identities which encompass it.

The chapter starts with a review of ideas on peace which have prevailed as foundations of international thought and considers the problematic nature of the concept of peace. It then considers peacemaking and mediation as practices which generate a move away from violent confrontation between specified entities towards outcomes based on resolution. The argument presented is that while the study of conflict resolution provides valuable insights into the transformation of specific conflicts, it has not challenged the discursive and institutional continuities implicated in the legitimation of violent human interaction. The chapter, therefore, seeks to locate the construct of peace within a wider conception of communicative action and utilises as baseline a Habermasian conception of dialogic relations emerging through discourse. What is required first is a brief consideration of the substantive suggestions which have been formulated as "answers" to the question of "what is to be done about war?"

Some preliminaries on the question of war and peace

War has variously been considered as a "natural" aspect of human existence, a "necessary evil", the highest expression of individuality, or an abomination. War has also generated discourses concerned with its total elimination or, less ambitiously, at least its rational management, only to be adopted in conditions of adversity where no other option could suffice. Under the Christian edicts of St Augustine and later St Thomas Aquinas, war and the death and destruction it caused had to be fought for "just" cause and through "just" means.[1] Later, in the writings of Vattel, Pufendorf and Grotius, war had to be regulated through a set of international laws, to which states were subject.[2] An international "society", analogous to the domestic society, could thus be superimposed upon the anarchical inter-state system where states would recognise their loose contractual obligations to a set of rules and norms which would constrain their behaviour. International institutions would uphold the rule of international law where any transgression on the part of "deviant" states would invite a collective response in the name of collective security. A primary role was to be given to powerful states whose remit was to ensure balance, which was seen as a necessary component of regulated international relations. Order was to be the priority and war a necessity where such order was violated. Within an anarchical international system of states founded upon the construct of sovereignty, order was a possible, achievable outcome where peace was not.

The later discipline of international relations, itself established following the devastation of the First World War to analyse the question of war and define the conditions of peace, was to concentrate on these founding principles. The "idealism" or "utopianism"[3] which established both the discipline and the League of Nations placed emphasis upon the management and regulation of war rather than its total elimination. Though the discipline was later to emphasise power as the determinant of order within the system, it nevertheless remains the case that the structuring ideas of the discipline were/are centred around the dual notions of power and regulated order. The central premise which linked the former idealism and later realism was the view that, as Howard states, "for better or worse war was an institution which could not be eliminated from the international system. All that could be done about it was, so far as possible, to codify its rationale and to civilise its means."[4]

The development of what came to be known as the idealist tradition in international relations may be located in the sixteenth and seventeenth centuries with the emergence of ideas on the "law of nations". International law came to represent efforts to regulate relations between states for the establishment and continuation of order. Hedley Bull suggests international law gave precedence to order over justice;[5] what is more relevant is that it gave precedence to order over peace.

The idea of an "international society" emergent from a set of regulated relations between states as the unit members of this society was rejected by Immanuel Kant, who argued instead that the notion of "society" could only incorporate individuals connected across state boundaries. For Kant, there is no state of nature defining external relations between states, for just as states are a product of human creation, so too are relations between them in the global arena. Nature gave the individual reason and reason was the connecting force in the community of humankind, the first step towards which was the creation of a "just civil constitution".[6] However, "The problem of establishing a perfect civil constitution is subordinate to the problem of a law governed external relationship with other states, and cannot be solved unless the latter is also solved."[7] The first requirement for the establishment of "perpetual peace" is, in turn, the creation of a "republican" civil constitution founded upon three principles: the principle of freedom, a single common legislation, and legal equality.[8] Public opinion becomes a primary consideration from which emanate constraints on declarations of war. Just as reason creates the civil constitution, so too reason, "as the highest legislative moral power, absolutely condemns war as a test of rights and sets up peace as an immediate duty".[9] A "federation" of states could only guarantee perpetual peace if its constituent parts were based on individual freedom within the bounds of legislative justice.

Kant established the will for peace in reason and individual freedom within representative states. Public opinion and free unhindered commerce as a basis for world peace later became the primary ideas in the peace movements which emerged after the Napoleonic wars.[10] As Howard points out,

> In the education of public opinion, then, in the spread of commerce, and in the advent to power of those classes which derived their wealth from commerce, these liberal thinkers of the early nineteenth century saw the answer to the problem of war. It was in order to work on public opinion that the first peace movements were founded; but the initiative came from men whose objection to war was not so much utilitarian as moral.[11]

In unifying the ideas of the peace movements and those of the free trade movement, these early views on the destructiveness of war have their remnants in later international relations thought relating increasing interdependence to the prevention of war.[12]

The concept of peace

Just as peace as a condition has eluded humanity, its meaning as a linguistic construct has been a subject of contestation within the research field of confict and peace studies. Like the discipline of international relations, this research field was established with the view that understanding war laid the first foundation stone for defining the conditions of peace. The behaviouralist methodology which characterised the research programme of this endeavour soon came to focus on the quantitative study of various aspects of conflict at the expense of developing a philosophical conception of peace. Recognition of this negation reached its height in the 1960s when neo-Marxist West European peace researchers called for an explicit statement on "peace" as a clearly-defined value-orientation for the field.[13] The drive for replicating the methodology of the natural sciences had obscured the value-orientation of the field, which was centred around the concept of peace. The most influential statement on peace, made by Johan Galtung, also proved to be the most controversial. In an article entitled "Violence, Peace, and Peace Research", Galtung produced a definitional distinction between direct and structural violence suggesting that a "positive" conception of peace pointed to the elimination of structures of exploitation and dependency which, he argued, were as destructive of human life and well-being as the direct violence experienced in times of war.[14] According to critics of Galtung's approach, the concept of "positive peace" was so wide in scope as to have diverted conflict and peace studies from the problems and challenges associated with direct violence.[15]

Others within conflict and peace studies, led primarily by John Burton, concentrated their efforts on addressing the dynamics of specific conflicts and processes which lead to conflict resolution. This area of research has produced ideas on the suitability of different modes of conflict resolution, from negotiation to mediation to "problem-solving" in specific types of conflict situation.[16] While this approach will be returned to later, it is important to state that its aim is not so much to define a general condition of peace, but to address the conditions which could transform a specific conflict towards de-escalation and ultimately resolution.

It is evident that "peace" as a linguistic construct has not been an uncontested concept, even within a research field that concentrates its attentions towards it. The everyday use of this concept places it in juxtaposition to war such that peace is the absence of war. Responses to violent conflicts, such as (peace)keeping and (peace)making, assume peace as that end state of conflict where violent interaction has been terminated. Peace is thus defined as the opposite of war, or as describing the absence of the use of force or violence. This "peace = non-war" formula fails to incorporate the fact that during phases of non-war, humanity, organised into sovereign states and politically aspirant communities, continues to uphold institutions and identities which allow for the re-emergence of violent conflict. Militarism, both as a value system and as institutionalised in the world military order is a constant presence which renders war not only a desirable and feasible option in times of conflict, but also a deeply-embedded continuity reinforced through dominant discursive and institutional frameworks. Peace, if defined as that interim period, that transition phase, only makes further wars possible.

Jean Elshtain suggests that "peace is an ontologically suspicious concept, as troubling in its own way as war".[17] Similarly, Senghaas suggests that "peace . . . is to be understood as a civilizational achievement which is extremely difficult to attain".[18] A rejection of the above formula, peace = non-war, would seem to suggest, in place of transition, permanence. Such was Kant's presupposition, when he wrote of a "perpetual" peace. Rejected for its seeming idealism, nevertheless this was an effort to construct upon the notion of peace as non-violence a number of specific conditions which would allow its potential realisation. The construct of peace, therefore, must aim to incorporate both a rejection of violence and its institutional underpinnings in combination with a defined process which would enable its realisation.

(Peace)making as conflict resolution

Conflict resolution currently forms a major research programme in the field of conflict and peace studies and a recent review of the literature is testimony to the wide cross-disciplinary interest in the area.[19] Two important conclusions may be drawn from this review. Firstly, that mediation as a process of conflict resolution is a pervasive form of behaviour across levels of social interaction, from the inter-personal to the international, and secondly, that mediation, far from constituting a uniform activity, is carried out by a variety of actors who have in common only that they are accepted in such a role by the protagonists in conflict. From non-official Quaker intermediaries to representatives of powerful states and international organisations, mediation as a process of peace-making traverses social domains and forms a central component of human conduct.

Does conflict resolution provide an adequate conception of peace? Does conflict resolution as practice and theory generate a critical discourse on peace? The vast majority of the mediation literature covers case study material which attempts to generate hypotheses relating to negotiation and mediation processes, the nature of third parties intervening in specific conflict situations, and the suitability of different types of third parties and processes in the resolution of conflicts varying in causes, parties and other contextual features.

Traditional forms of conflict resolution are based on negotiation and bargaining between the parties in conflict. These are adversarial interactions where the parties articulate mutually exclusive positions using the arena of negotiation as well as the surrounding social environment to induce a change in the position of the adversary which is perceived as the source of grievance and obstacle to achieving desired outcomes. The primary aim of negotiation and the bargaining context is to win through the manipulation of information surrounding the conflict and the use of coercive resources to induce concessions. The process of communicative interaction between the parties is determined by a motivation to gain favourable outcomes to the negotiator's own side in the dispute. The issues under discussion are defined in zero-sum terms, where a gain for one is a direct loss for the other. The surrounding social environment of the conflict is utilised to acquire support from external observers and affected third parties in combination with attempts to suppress the claims of the adversary or question their legitimacy. In international conflict situations, such negotiations are often accompanied by continued violent interaction in order to "strengthen the hand of the negotiator". Violence is, therefore, used as a bargaining counter aimed at inducing concessions from the opponent.

The process of bargaining and negotiation between opponents is often accompanied by the presence of a third party functioning in the role of mediator. Most of the literature on mediation concerns itself with the effectiveness of specific mediation techniques, mediator qualities defined in terms of interests and influence potential, and mediator decision-making processes. Third parties intervening as mediators aim to achieve a settlement between the conflicting parties through the facilitation of communication, through the formulation of proposals on substantive outcomes, and through the use of influence tactics and inducements to facilitate concession-making. While traditionally the role of mediator has been conceived as an impartial outsider, the literature illustrates that, in certain conflicts, bias and influence may be effective in moving the parties towards compromise as opposed to continued conflict behaviour. It is also important to recognise that third parties may be interested in the substantive issues in the conflict where, as well as carrying out intermediary functions focusing on facilitating the process of communication, the third party may also transform the dyadic bargaining situation into a triadic relationship where the mediator becomes directly involved in bargaining with the parties. Mediation is thus a facilitated bargaining process which does not challenge the exclusionist discourse of the conflict. Moreover, mediation may reinforce such discourse by replicating an agenda of violence based on territorial separation, ethnicity and so on. Mediation may thus be process-oriented, where the aim is to facilitate communication through the transfer of positional statements between the parties and the clarification of issues, as well as being outcome-oriented, where the emphasis is on the substantive content of the conflict and the pursuit of the third party's own interests.[20] The move from a process-oriented to an outcome-oriented approach is dependent on the influence potential of the third party. Mediation may thus be conceived as a spectrum of activity ranging from facilitation to bargaining depending on the third party's access to resources which may be utilised in the inducement of concessions.

The mediation of conflict may thus centre around facilitative tactics, where the emphasis is on removing the obstacles to effective communication between the parties, or on more directive procedures, where the third party effectively becomes another bargainer seeking to induce concessions in pursuit of a settlement suited to the protagonists or even the third party's own sectional interests. The mode adopted seems to depend upon a number of interrelated factors situated in the dynamics of the conflict or in the third party's own evaluative and situational context.

Research on mediation has become a central focus of inquiry in the field of conflict and peace research. The specifically practical orientation of this research seeks to suggest prescriptions as to the most effective means by which conflicts may be resolved. Those who view the international system as a Hobbesian sphere of conflicts of interest emphasise the vital role played by coercive mediation.[21] Advocates of more innovative approaches which focus on non-official interactive facilitation suggest that outcomes based on coercion preclude the possibility of achieving a resolution of the underlying causes of conflict which could only be a possibility through a facilitated communicative process that aims at understanding and mutual recognition as a basis for more lasting, mutually-reinforcing outcomes.[22] The thrust of the latter argument is that while traditional, coercive mediation may achieve a settlement of issues, it cannot produce resolution of the fundamental causes of protracted conflicts centred around identity and security concerns.

That the two positions are not mutually exclusive is suggested by the fact that facilitative and coercive procedures may be suitably applicable at different stages of a conflict[23] and that individual third parties (official and non-official) may shift along the spectrum of third party activity depending on the circumstances of the conflict.[24] Moreover, wholesale condemnation of traditional negotiation and mediation processes seems to negate the possibility that protracted positional adversarial negotiations may result in a gradual transformation of relations between adversaries such that non-violent interaction becomes a preferred option.[25] As pointed out by Rothman, "the fact of putting forward these types of positions and counter-positions illustrates that the conflict and discussion about its management has perhaps unalterably moved beyond the battlefields, where there is no room even for positions, as there is no recognition of a legitimate opponent".[26]

Peacemaking as conflict resolution varies, therefore, along dimensions of context and third party characteristics. A conflict resolution process which emphasises "problem-solving" seeks mutual understanding between the protagonists. A process based on adversarial bargaining has its focus primarily on substantive outcomes, but may through the process of communication also incorporate an element of improved understanding where possibilities other than violence become apparent. In summarising the aims of problem-solving processes, Rothman suggests the following components:

1 There is a mutual recognition of each party's existence and legitimate participation in a process of communication.

2 Participants gain insights into the position of the adversary, their central concerns and fears, and the attitudinal and structural constraints which limit their flexibility.

3 A gradual recognition develops of any changes in the attitudes and positions of the adversary along with an ability to recognise any peace signals which the adversary projects. Rothman describes this as "a kind of learning that is especially important because the dynamics of conflict create a strong tendency to dismiss the occurrence and the possibility of change on the part of the adversary".[27]

4 Within the workshop setting, participants become aware of the actions they can adopt that would be meaningful to the other side which would entail little cost to themselves.

The interactive problem-solving process incorporates an aim of mutual understanding of the positions of self and adversary as well as the structural contextual constraints which limit their room for manoeuvrability. The focus is primarily on process rather than outcome and precludes manipulation and coercion.

With the above brief review of the conflict resolution process, we may now assess its importance in developing a conception of peace that challenges war as a social continuity. As is evident from the above, conflict resolution processes and the developing vast literature on mediation concentrate on the effectiveness of different types of intervention within the contexts of specific conflict situations. The practical aim is to generate an understanding of the processes which transform conflict from violent interaction towards mutual recognition by adversaries of other possibilities leading gradually towards resolution. While traditional modes of negotiation and mediation may adopt processes and seek outcomes that either fail to challenge or reinforce the exclusionist discourse of the adversaries, the very fact of their occurrence provides scope for transformation. Facilitative processes place an emphasis on communicative interaction between the parties aiming towards mutual understanding of the causes of conflict and the uncovering of the cognitive and structural obstacles to resolution. The process of conflict resolution, therefore, seeks the transformation of conflictual relationships away from violent interaction.[28] While coercive mediation may be criticised for failing to change its power political base in its dependence on the use of threat and reward tactics for gaining concessions, the latter facilitative approach may also be criticised for negating power asymmetry in its discourse, thereby creating a myth of equals involved in unobstructed dialogue. Such is the critique articulated by Edward Said in relation to facilitative processes applied to the Israeli-Palestinian conflict:

> One of the most striking features of . . . attempts at representing the conflict as if from the outside has been the notion that Palestinians and Israelis are equal, symmetrically balanced, polarized at dead centre . . . It will hardly come as a revelation, however, when I say . . . that no such symmetry has ever existed, no matter how tempted we might be by the nicely balanced rhetorical form of the polarity. If there is one thing that deconstructive philosophy has effected it is to have shown definitively that bipolar oppositions always, regularly, constitutively mystify the domination of one of the terms by the other . . . to place the Palestinian and the Israeli sides within the opposition on what appears to be an equal, opposite and symmetrical footing is also to reduce the claims of the one by elevating the claims of the other.[29]

The above statement effectively summarises the impact of uncritical approaches to conflict resolution. The facilitation process is represented as being conducted by outsiders, uninvolved observers whose interpretations of the conflict are excluded from the communicative process. Interpretation is, however, centrally involved in the process of facilitation, in its assumption of what constitutes the core set of grievances, the identity of the "parties" in conflict, and the premise that facilitation as a process may be extracted from the wider structural asymmetries of the conflict.

In seeking to define a critical approach to conflict resolution, Rothman defines a model which situates peace within conflict resolution as a process. Rothman's is an activist "conflict management training methodology", which, he states, is designed to encourage a critical approach, in theory and practice, to conflict and its management. As with education for critical thinking, conflict management training is designed to help parties clarify their own epistemologies and question their own assumptions about conflict in ways that lead to enhanced creativity and imagination in planning for its management.[30]

The model for training parties involved in conflict utilises an "adversarial", "reflexive" and "integrative" framework (ARI) where the adversarial component guides parties to make explicit their adversarial frames about their conflict while the reflexive component is defined as a "transitional vehicle for moving parties from adversarial into integrative frames".[31] The reflexive process involves parties in a public introspection of their hopes, fears, aspirations and behaviours generating a shift from a framework of blame towards recognising the conflict as a shared problem within a process aimed at mutual understanding. Rothman suggests that this method of approaching conflict resolution is "critical" in orientation in that it incorporates a normative component in seeking the transformation of adversarial relations into integrative, mutually reinforcing processes.

Rothman's is a training programme aimed specifically at the resolution of conflict involving situated actors. While it does not make an explicit theoretical statement regarding the construct of peace, it nevertheless provides a basis from which we may locate peace in the conflict resolution process. In its emphasis on conflict resolution training in particular conflicts, it does not challenge the institutional and discursive underpinnings of war as a social continuity. It does not, furthermore, challenge the basis of the militarist and exclusionist identities which enable war as a form of human conduct.

What the next concluding section seeks to achieve is precisely to define a theoretical/philosophical basis for situating peace within discourse. The section does not address the possibilities of transforming particular conflicts, but rather suggests a moral discourse which both challenges war as a social continuity and provides a conception of peace that is located in communicative/dialogic relations.

Situating peace in discourse

War as an institution is reproduced through discourses which confer legitimacy on it. It is upheld by militarist institutions which have used war as a vehicle through which specific ends against adversaries could be achieved, and as an arena for testing innovations in weaponry, the research and development policies for which feed back into the civilian sphere, thus militarising the world of work and daily encounters. The legitimation of war is situated in discursive practices based on exclusionist identities. Is it therefore possible to conceive of peace as situated in a critical discursive process which, rather than reifying exclusion, incorporates difference? Is this a basis which provides a challenge to the seemingly overwhelming forces which have enabled war in human history?

What the previous chapters have argued is that every single instance of war, every decision by leaders to utilise force in time of conflict, every individual's practical support for violence as a mode of conflict behaviour adopted by their community, draws upon continuities located in discourse and in deeply held social norms institutionalised across time and space and reinforced through structures of domination. Each such action reconstitutes or reproduces war as a social continuity, itself institutionalised across time and space. As was argued in earlier chapters, the language of every war is based on strategic imperatives and moral justifications. Every war is a "war that will end war"[32] just as every war is seen as the inevitable consequence of an international system built upon the construct of sovereignty. Those who lack sovereignty seek it, often through resort to violence. The violent conflicts we witness today and the massacres which seem to form such an integral part of these conflicts predominantly involve ethnic-national categories. The construct of sovereignty lies at the core of a dominant discourse based on reification and exclusion. The state is "naturalised" under ethnic-nationalism as a dominant form of ideological representation dependent on a mythical construction of an exclusionist identity. The emergence of such a dominant mode of representation precludes other possibilities in discourse and negates the pluralities of identity which have their expressions in every individual.

Domination and control always have a dialectic character,[33] in that, through the transformative capacity of individuals and groups as agents, they remain at varying degrees, always ultimately contested and contestable. The efforts of the early peace movements and women's movements were aimed precisely to form counter-discourses to the prevailing ideologies of their day, the nationalism and jingoism which fed the war fever at the outset of the First World War.[34] The counter-discourse of the peace and women's movements defined them as "outsiders", challenging ideological hegemony while seeking free and open discourse based on reason. The inspiration for the peace movement derived from a Kantian belief in the possibility of peace based on freedom, reason and the ability of an active public sphere to make a difference. War was a game favoured by rulers for sectional interests. An informed public had the potential to prevent war since, ultimately, the costs of war in terms of sacrifice were not borne by leaders but by their publics.

The problem with the above separation of leaders and led in relation to war is that our observations indicate that publics can be active supporters of war and can, as in the cases of the former Yugoslavia and in Rwanda, be active and willing participants in violence. The overwhelming support for war in the Gulf expressed by the majority in the UK and elsewhere in the West indicates that support for war may be mobilised irrespective of the structure of governance or internal political dispensation.[35] What these observations indicate is that war incorporates not just the state and its military machinery, but the wider publics which may become directly involved in combat or indirectly through support.

As has been stated in earlier chapters, the relationship between the individual and the state/community is situated in identity constructed along exclusionist lines and perpetuated through discursive and institutional structures which legitimate violent human conflict. The symbolic orders and interpretative schemes upon which identity is based constitute "public" or political space. The transformative capacity of counter-discourses must also be located in the public space. It is the domination of this space which generates hegemonic discourses based on exclusionist ideologies which are used to legitimate the onset of war and the manipulation of information in time of war. Structures of domination point to the existence of asymmetrical access to public space such that the counter-discourses generated by social movements opposed to war are marginalised or rendered invisible. Public space is, therefore, a place of contestation and conflict – it is a space which must be understood if we are to uncover the processes which lead to its

control and manipulation as well as those involved in the emergence of dissident voices and counter-discourses.[36]

One of the challenges of the late modern era is that the public
space is not confined within the territorial domain of the sovereign
state but expands beyond into what has been termed a "global
society". According to Martin Shaw, global society is "the largest
existing, and also the largest possible, framework or context of
social relations, but not necessarily the immediately defining context of all social relations".[37] The process of globalisation, through
the world economic system, the world military order, the mass
media and advanced telecommunications, has generated a changing, multi-layered contextualisation of social relations wherein the
global comes into direct confrontation with the local and the particular. This global public space is the arena of contestation between a universalist economistic discourse and local assertions of
ethnic and/or religious identity. The global public space is also,
however, the location of migration, exile and individual movements
traversing bounded territories and identities. Any conception of a
counter-discourse situates it within a politics of emancipation. The
challenge of the late modern period is to define emancipation within
this complex array of social relations. A further challenge to an
emancipatory discourse on peace is to situate it within this global
public space which by definition contains both uniformity and
difference and where identity-based conflicts reify the local while
making use of the global military order.

The constitutive element of an emancipatory discourse on peace
is the recognition of the individual's capacity not only to make a
difference, but to assert difference in a distinct individuality located
in wider social relations. For Giddens, "emancipatory politics" is a
"generic outlook concerned above all with liberating individuals
and groups from constraints which adversely affect their life
chances".[38] Where emancipatory politics is concerned with issues
of justice and equality, its primary focus is on the question of
participation in political discourse as a process of enablement aimed
at the transformation of structural and relational constraints. Emphasis on participation implies a recognition of collective normative
life encompassing individual autonomy. A conception of peace
located in emancipatory politics would, therefore, stress the interrelated elements of public space, participation and individuality.

For Habermas, public space or the "public sphere" is a "realm of social life in which something approaching public opinion can be formed" where citizens "behave as a public body when they confer in an unrestricted fashion."[39] Habermas's emphasis is on *process* rather than content where "the procedures and presuppositions of free argument are the basis for the justification of opinions".[40] An unrestricted public sphere provides a basis for a social order based on individual autonomy situated within a distinctly public consciousness. However, there is always a discrepancy between free speech within the public sphere and the constraints and manipulations of economic and political structures. Agency, in other words, comes up against structures of domination. The public sphere becomes an arena within which the manipulation of information and the enhancement of sectional interests result in distorted communication. Using the premises of structuration theory, we may state that the intersection of structures of signification, legitimation and domination is that point where a hegemonic discourse emerges and dominates the public sphere. It is also, however, the point at which contestation is directed, where nonconformity is at its most blatant, and dissent the ultimate expression of agency.

The discourse of war seeks to conceal dissent, individuality and nonconformity. It is couched in terms of instrumental reason, strategic calculation and technological innovation in combination with statements of justification of cause and method. The benefits of war are presented in terms of general interests and conceal the idiosyncratic calculations of leaders. The generation of a technocratic consciousness in time of war places emphasis on innovations in weaponry which allow, as occurred in the Gulf war, the use of linguistic constructs such as "precision accuracy", "surgical strikes", and mere "classification error" when no such precision is achieved. The implication, as Virilio points out, is a distancing of war achieved through new forms of weaponry but also in the images brought back to publics from the "war front".[41] The imagery of war itself is taken up by the military where computer-generated images of bombed targets are used by the mass media in their reporting of war. Such images have a distancing effect which does not allow reflection upon the effects of war. War is thus reduced to a video-game, a subjectless, automated fight which precludes ethical reflection. Such is the convergence of war with the technocratic consciousness that reduces agency to instrumental reason.

The reduction of agency to instrumental reason negates the constructive role of language and shared worlds of meaning which constitute social life. The socio-cultural aspect of life emerges through linguistic communication and every such interaction draws upon and reproduces a rich mosaic of symbolic and interpretative meanings as well as the normative expectations which become structurated through time and space. Communicative action, through the duality of structure, draws upon symbolic orders, interpretative schemes, norms and resources, in the reproduction of structures of signification, legitimation and domination. Social institutions are, therefore, implicated both in the enablement of communication and in its constraint or distortion.[42] The ability to "make a difference" or to overcome institutional constraint in order to generate unhindered, open communication, constitutes what Habermas calls "emancipatory interest".[43]

In seeking to situate peace in discourse the suggestion being put forward is that the condition of peace incorporates a process of unhindered communicative action which involves *participation* and *difference*. Situating peace in the unhindered process of intersubjective communication recognises two indisputable assumptions: (a) that only humans enact war and (b) that only humans enact what we call linguistic communication.[44] This process is, by definition, between "self" and "other", a structure which is both the basis of conflict and of dialogue. Communication implies a process of common discovery, the emergence of a "we", through a process of unrestricted questioning and dialogue. This may be distinguished from what Chanteur calls "pseudodialogues", which incorporate dogma, rhetoric and ideology.[45] The pseudodialogue is not so much a "common search" but a wish to impose an unshiftable opinion. For Chanteur, Plato's *Dialogues* provide the ideal form of human communication or "true discourse". The process of dialogue provides for Chanteur a basis for conceptualising peace:

> Such is the voice of peace – harmonized speech that, in moving from the particular "I" to the impersonal "I", forms the strands binding humans in authentic relations of *philia*, because affection is the feeling that expresses the completeness of their reconciled being.[46]

While Chanteur recognises that peace may be located in dialogue, she nevertheless fails to elaborate or develop the theme.

The conception of peace elaborated in the present study is that it is situated within the process of discourse. Peace is a normative construct which incorporates an understanding of the processes which have institutionalised war as a social continuity as well as an emancipatory component aimed at transforming the present condition. Peace is here conceptualised as a process located in discursive social relations. Locating peace in discourse suggests Habermas's "discursive ethics" as a framework where there is an emphasis on process rather than substantive content. While it is not within the scope of this book fully to evaluate Habermas's "Theory of Communicative Action" and its philosophical grounding, the aim is to argue that such a framework is helpful in developing an understanding of peace based in discourse.

In arguing against positivism's supposition of language as an unproblematic vehicle for the description of an "objective" world, Habermas places language and inter-subjective communication at the centre of his critical theory, the core component of which is emancipation. Understanding emerges through a process of communicative action which is not reducible to instrumental action. Communicative interaction in time of conflict involves subjects situated in specific life-contexts which could potentially hinder mutual knowledge or mutual understanding. The process of communication that constitutes "true discourse" requires that the subjects shed any ideological distortions prior to an engagement aimed at understanding. How do we, therefore, incorporate difference in our conceptualisation of peace as situated in the discursive, dialogic process? Can there be a "mediation of traditions" where understanding is a possibility despite the "framework of concepts, beliefs and standards"[47] which participants carry into the process?

It could be argued that an unquestioning inclusion or acceptance of tradition as a component of the process of communicative interaction and understanding means that every individual, text and artifact is interpreted in terms of the "tradition" from which it emerged. Tradition is taken as unquestionably constitutive of the subjectivity expressed in actions, utterances and texts of the "other". Such interpretations seem to preclude the possibility of "free-standing" individuality or of tradition as the location of coercion and prejudice. Tradition is taken as unproblematic and absolute rather than being situated in relation to other social processes and structures of domination.[48] The communicative process is enabled and constrained by power relations structurated in asymmetrical social systems. For Habermas, emancipation is achieved through uncovering the forces which generate distorted communication and through a discursive process which incorporates critical self-reflection and understanding. Language is, therefore, a medium of understanding as well as domination:

> It makes good sense to conceive of language as a kind of meta-institution on which all social institutions are dependent; for social action is constituted only in ordinary language communication. But this meta-institution of language as tradition is evidently dependent in turn on social processes that are not reducible to normative relationships. Language is also a medium of domination and social power; it serves to legitimate relations of organized force. Insofar as the legitimations do not articulate the power relations whose institutionalization they make possible, insofar as these relations merely manifest themselves in the legitimations, language is also ideological.[49]

Given this dual role of language, its use in social encounters cannot be taken for granted since doing so would imply, as Bernstein points out, "providing the existing self-interpretation of groups with a kind of normative inviolability, an ontological defence mechanism, against the interrogation of the truth of fundamental beliefs and the justice of operative social norms and values".[50] An emancipatory critical theory allows self-reflection and understanding through uncovering the causes of distorted communication and defining a process of free, unhindered communication, the counterfactual "test" for which is the "ideal speech situation". The emancipatory component emerges since, as Giddens points out, "The more social circumstances approximate to an ideal speech situation, the more a social order based on the autonomous action of free and equal individuals will emerge."[51]

A discourse free of distorted communication has its point of validity with respect to the ideal speech situation which is an aspect of the structure of discourse. As suggested by Habermas,

> The ideal speech situation is neither an empirical phenomenon nor simply a construct, but a reciprocal supposition unavoidable in discourse. This supposition can, but need not be, counterfactual; but even when counterfactual it is a fiction which is operatively effective in communication. I

would therefore prefer to speak of an anticipation of an ideal speech situation . . . This alone is the warrant which permits us to join to an actually attained consensus the claim of a rational consensus. At the same time it is a critical standard against which every actually realized consensus can be called into question and tested.[52]

The ideal speech situation assumes equal participation and the right to question the validity claims of normative and factual statements in a dialogic process which aims at reaching free rational consensus about such claims. Furthermore, participants must be symmetrically situated with respect to social norms and material conditions if unhindered communication is to take place. Discourse is the process through which normative statements are treated as hypotheses in need of justification and defence. Consensus is possible, but it is not imposed.

Can we, therefore, develop a concept of peace situated in Habermasian "discourse ethics"? The basic assumption of discourse ethics is that a process of dialogue, or a dialogic relationship, may produce validity claims on questions of morality. Such a process allows conditions for making "impartial judgements" of moral-practical questions based on reason. Since normative statements are open to criticism, justification and refutation, such claims incorporate speech acts which assume the presence of another in a process of communicative action. An ethics of discourse is situated in communicative action in that it assumes participation by agents in a process of dialogue which is acceptable to both, where agreement emerges or is evaluated in terms of the "intersubjective recognition of validity claims."[53] Such validity claims must rest upon propositions being linguistically comprehensible; that it is "right" with reference to a shared external world; and that it is "truthful" with respect to the speaker's own subjective world. Furthermore, given that "communication oriented to reaching understanding has a validity basis, a speaker can persuade a hearer to accept a speech-act offer by guaranteeing that he will redeem a criticizable validity claim. In doing so, he creates a binding/bonding effect between speaker and hearer that makes the continuation of their interaction possible."[54] The discursive, dialogic process, therefore, incorporates both rights and obligations; the right to unhindered and unconstrained questioning normative propositions and the obligation to persuade through force of argument and discursive guarantees.

The central premises of discourse ethics are outlined by Habermas in the following statement:

> Discourse ethics . . . stands or falls with two assumptions: (a) that normative claims to validity have cognitive meaning and can be treated *like* claims to truth and (b) that the justification of norms and commands requires that a real discourse be carried out and thus cannot occur in a strictly monological form, i.e., in the form of a hypothetical process of argumentation occuring in the individual mind.[55]

In this, Habermas suggests that the structure of discourse is a basis for establishing the validity claims of normative statements. Discourse contains within it reciprocal behavioural expectations that are themselves "raised to normative status".[56] Universalisation results from a common interest in discursive practice and access to participation in the process. The emergent "rational consensus" results from unhindered dialogue and argumentation where every statement is interrogated in terms of its validity claims. The ideal speech situation serves as standard for the critique of systematically distorted communication.

Individuals and groups involved in social relations do not always reach rational consensus. Where disagreement occurs, a variety of options are available. Groups and individuals may adopt strategic behaviour where actors may seek to influence communicative interaction through, for example, the direct manipulation of information on their intentions or the shared external world. Groups may also break off communication and resort to violence where, as Bernstein points out, "the rules of communication are supplanted by the 'rules' of war".[57] A process situated in discursive ethics, however, rejects these options and enters a dialogic relationship of free objection and justification.

Discourse ethics claims to overcome objections to the abstract, formal moral individualism of Kantian philosophy through locating morality in the inter-subjective understanding of participants engaged in a dialogic relationship. The starting-point is not so much individual moral autonomy and consciousness but free expression actualised in the inter-subjective process. As Habermas suggests, "In Kant, autonomy was conceived as freedom under self-given laws, which involves an element of coercive subordination of subjective nature. In discourse ethics the idea of autonomy is intersubjective."[58] *Participation, understanding* and a commitment to a *process* are at the core of discourse ethics and define its relevance to the conception of peace that is being suggested here.

The Habermasian model of discursive ethics has been subject to criticism on the basis that its universality is dependent upon its abstraction from concrete situations. It does not address concrete dilemmas over ethical issues of concern to politically and historically situated actors. The force of the model in conceptualising peace is, however, in its capacity to locate a process which allows for the emergence of dialogic relationships. Such relationships can only exist in an environment that is free of coercion and manipulation where dissent against the validity claims of those in authority is legitimately open for argumentation. As pointed out by O'Neill, "Discourse ethics relates specifically to the moralization of the social world that occurs when the normativity of existing institutions is brought into question. These can no longer enjoy a naive social acceptance but are potential subjects of a practical discourse."[59] The model, therefore, does not provide a substantive definition of the contents of peace, but provides for a process of which peace is by necessity constitutive. It also provides a framework through which war as an institution may be put to question.

The study of conflict presents a number of challenges to the normative conception of peace provided in this chapter. More specifically, the challenge relates to the constitutive assumptions of peace based upon discourse. As highlighted above, discourse ethics contains universalist assumptions underlying advocacy of a process of communicative action. The process defines or makes possible an inter-subjective moral understanding based on participation, empathy and recognition. The accent is upon a procedural framework which enables an interactive questioning of dominant norms and institutions. Once participants enter discourse they also enter, according to the contentions made in this chapter, a zone of peace based upon dialogic principles.

The challenge of empirical observations of conflict situations involving violence, specifically those centred around issues of belief, relates to differing conceptions of the moral worth of discourse itself. Discourse ethics as process is a locale of emancipation from the constraints of tradition, prejudice, and myth. However, some of the most pervasive conflicts of late modernity concern issues of religious belief which preclude a questioning of norms, where the text and image considered sacred are not allowed into an inter-subjective space of equal interpretation and contestation. This defines a situation where it is not merely inter-subjective consent as an outcome of discourse that is the problem. This is, in fact, a condition which does not allow the occurrence of discourse and precludes any possibility of an emergent dialogic relationship.

Even where consent as the test of Habermas's principle of "universalisation" is rejected, discourse ethics assumes agreement on the worth of the communicative process. In *Situating the Self*, Seyla Benhabib rejects the principle of consent as the test of validity for normative claims, suggesting instead that communicative discourse, by definition, incorporates both process and moral substance. She thus expands Habermas's framework by suggesting that discourse ethics applies to considerations of both abstract conceptions of justice and evaluative questions relating to lived experience:

> Since practical discourses do not theoretically predefine the domain of moral debate and since individuals do not have to abstract from their everyday attachments and beliefs when they begin argumentation, we cannot preclude that it will be not only matters of justice but those of the good life as well that will become thematised in practical discourses or that the presuppositions of discourse themselves will be challenged.[60]

To incorporate concrete issues of lived experience into the frame-work of communicative ethics renders it more responsive to the challenges of contextualised social relations. While the process contains universal constitutive rules framing communicative action, it concedes that it must take place within conditions of value differentiation and heterogeneity. A peace located in discourse ethics must therefore recognise difference as a formative compo-nent of subjectivity. As will be argued in the concluding chapter, one of the central questions emerging from this study of violent conflict relates to subjectivity and the construction of identity in situated social relations.

Notes

1. See chapter four for the continuation of the just war doctrine in present day discourses on war.
2. E. de Vattel, *The Law of Nations* (AMS Press, New York, 1987); S. von Pufendorf, *The Law of Nature and Nations* (Clarendon Press, Oxford, 1934); H. Grotius, *The Law of War and Peace* (Bobbs-Merrill, New York, 1925).
3. E.H. Carr, *The Twenty Years Crisis, 1919–1939* (Harper and Row, New York, 1964 and Macmillan, London, 1981).
4. M. Howard, *War and the Liberal Conscience* (Temple Smith, London, 1978), p. 18.
5. H.N. Bull, *The Anarchical Society: A Study of World Order* (Macmillan, London and Columbia University Press, New York, 1977).
6. I. Kant, "Idea for a Universal History with a Cosmopolitan Purpose", in I. Kant, *Political Writings*, ed. H. Reiss (Cambridge University Press, Cambridge, 1991), p. 46.
7. *Ibid.*, p. 47.
8. I. Kant, "Perpetual Peace", in Kant, *op. cit.*, p. 100.
9. *Ibid.*, p. 104.
10. Howard, *op. cit.*, pp. 36–47.
11. *Ibid.*, p. 39.
12. The most explicit statement on the relationship between the disutility of war and interdependence is Norman Angell's *The Great Illusion* published before the First World War. See J.B.D. Miller, *Norman Angell and the Futility of War* (Macmillan, London, 1986); C. Navari, "*The Great Illusion* Revisited: The International Theory of Norman Angell", *Review of International Studies*, Vol. 15, No. 4 (1989), pp. 341–358.
13. See H. Schmid, "Peace Research and Politics", *Journal of Peace Research*, Vol. 5 (1968), pp. 217–232; A. Eide, "Dialogue and Confrontation in Europe", *Journal of Conflict Resolution*, Vol. 16 (1972), pp. 511–522.
14. J. Galtung, "Violence, Peace and Peace Research", *Journal of Peace Research*, Vol. 6, No. 3 (1969), pp. 167–191.
15. K. Boulding, "Future Directions in Conflict and Peace Studies", *Journal of Conflict Resolution*, Vol. 22, No. 2 (1978), p. 344.
16. See V. Jabri, *Mediating Conflict* (Manchester University Press, Manchester, 1990); K. Kressel and D. Pruitt (eds), *Mediation Research* (Jossey-Bass, San Francisco, 1989); C.R. Mitchell and K. Webb (eds), *New Approaches to International Mediation* (Greenwood Press, Westport, CT, 1989).

17. J.B. Elshtain, *Women and War* (The Harvester Press, Brighton, 1987), p. 253.
18. D. Senghaas, "Transcending Collective Violence: The Civilizing Process and the Peace Problem", in R. Vayrynen (ed.), *The Quest for Peace: Transcending Collective Violence and War among Societies, Cultures and States* (Sage, London, 1987).
19. J.A. Wall and A. Lynn, "Mediation: A Current Review", *Journal of Conflict Resolution*, Vol. 37, No. 1 (1993), pp. 160–194.
20. See Jabri, *op. cit.* and M. Hoffman, "Third Party Mediation and Conflict Resolution in the Post-Cold War World", in J. Baylis and N.J. Rengger (eds), *Dilemmas of World Politics* (Clarendon, Oxford and New York, 1992).
21. J. Bercovitch, J.T. Anagnoson, and D.L. Wille, "Some Conceptual Issues and Empirical Trends in the Study of Successful Mediation in International Relations", *Journal of Peace Research*, Vol. 28, No. 1 (1991), pp. 7–17; S. Touval, "Biased Intermediaries: Theoretical and Historical Considerations", *Jerusalem Journal of International Relations*, Vol. 1, No. 1 (1975), pp. 51–69.
22. E. Azar, *The Management of Protracted Social Conflict* (Dartmouth, Aldershot, 1990); J.W. Burton, *Resolving Deep-Rooted Conflict: A Handbook* (University Press of America, Lanham, MD, 1987); J.W. Burton, *Conflict: Resolution and Provention* (Macmillan, London, 1990).
23. R.J. Fisher and L. Keashley, "The Potential Complementarity of Mediation and Consultation Within a Contingency Model of Third Party Intervention", *Journal of Peace Research*, Vol. 28, No. 1 (1991), pp. 29–42.
24. Jabri, *op. cit.*, pp. 15–37.
25. In an investigation of the relationship between "conflict management" and "conflict resolution" in the Arab-Israeli conflict, Yaacov Bar-Siman-Tov argues that "a protracted conflict lingering over time with violent hostilities, cannot be resolved without a prerequisite prolonged and successful conflict management" which is defined as a "learning process". Y. Bar-Siman-Tov, "The Arab-Israeli Conflict: Learning Conflict Resolution", *Journal of Peace Research*, Vol. 31, No. 1 (1994), p. 75.
26. J. Rothman, *From Confrontation to Cooperation: Resolving Ethnic and Regional Conflict* (Sage, London, 1992), p. 26.
27. *Ibid.*, p. 30.
28. According to Wallensteen, "a successful case of conflict transformation is one where the parties, the issues and the expectations are changed so that there is no longer a fear of war arising from the relationship". P. Wallensteen, "The Resolution and Transformation

of International Conflict: A Structural Perspective", in R. Vayrynen (ed.), *New Directions in Conflict Theory: Conflict Resolution and Conflict Transformation* (Sage, London, 1991), p. 130.

29. E. Said, "The Burdens of Interpretation and the Question of Palestine", paper presented to the conference of the International Society of Political Psychology, Amsterdam, July 1986.

30. Rothman, *op. cit.*, p. 75.

31. *Ibid.*, p. 58.

32. H.G. Wells was the author of a pamphlet entitled "The War That Will End War", written as a propaganda piece during the First World War. See P. Buitenhuis, *The Great War of Words: Literature as Propaganda 1914–1918* (Batsford, London, 1987).

33. Giddens defines the "dialectic of control" as "The two-way character of the distributive aspect of power (power as control); how the less powerful manage resources in such a way as to exert control over the more powerful in established power relations." A. Giddens, *The Constitution of Society* (Polity Press, Cambridge, 1984), p. 374.

34. On the role of the women's movement at the outset of the First World War, see S. Ouditt, *Fighting Forces, Writing Women: Identity and Ideology in the First World War* (Routledge, London and New York, 1994).

35. See special issue of the *Journal of Peace Research* devoted to the empirical investigation of the relationship between war and democracy. *Journal of Peace Research*, Vol 29, No. 4 (1992), pp. 369–434.

36. Gramsci is one of the foremost post-Marxist theorists of ideology as hegemonic discourse. See A. Gramsci, *Selections from the Prison Notebooks of Antonio Gramsci*, trans. Q. Hoare and G.N. Smith (Lawrence and Wishart, London, 1971). For the application of Gramscian premises in the field of international relations, see S. Gill (ed.), *Gramsci, Historical Materialism, and International Relations* (Cambridge University Press, Cambridge, 1993).

37. M. Shaw, *Global Society and International Relations* (Polity Press, Cambridge, 1994), p. 17.

38. A. Giddens, *Modernity and Self-Identity: Self and Society in the Late Modern Age* (Polity Press, Cambridge, 1991), p. 211.

39. J. Habermas, "The Public Sphere", *New German Critique*, Vol. 3 (1974), p. 42. Quoted in J.M. Bernstein, *Recovering Ethical Life: Jurgen Habermas and the Future of Critical Theory* (Routledge, London and New York, 1995), p. 38.

40. D. Held, *Introduction to Critical Theory: Horkheimer to Habermas* (Polity Press, Cambridge, 1980), p. 260.

41. P. Virilio and S. Lotringer, *Pure War*, trans. Mark Polizotti (Semiotext, New York, 1983), p. 31.

42. See chapter three for a review of structuration theory.

43. J. Habermas, *Knowledge and Human Interests*, trans. J.J. Shapiro (Heinemann, London, 1972).

44. According to Gadamer, language is the medium through which we "know" the world and is a precondition to understanding and dialogue, both constitutive of humanity. See H.-G. Gadamer, *Truth and Method*, trans. G. Barden and J. Cumming (Sheed and Ward, London, 1975), p. 431.

45. J. Chanteur, *From War to Peace*, trans. S.A. Weisz (Westview Press, Boulder, CO, 1992), p. 232.

46. *Ibid.*, p. 232.

47. Gadamer, *op. cit.*, and Held, *op. cit.*, p. 312.

48. J. Habermas, "A Review of Gadamer's *Truth and Method*", in F. Dallmayr and T. McCarthy (eds), *Understanding Social Inquiry* (Notre Dame Press, Notre Dame, IN, 1977), quoted in Held, *op. cit.*, p. 316.

49. *Ibid.*, p. 360. Quoted in Bernstein, *op. cit.*, p. 45.

50. *Ibid.*, p. 46.

51. Giddens, *op. cit.*, p. 213.

52. Quoted in Held, *op. cit.*, p. 344.

53. J. Habermas, *Moral Consciousness and Communicative Action*, trans. C. Lenhardt and S.W. Nicholson (Polity Press, Cambridge, 1992), p. 58.

54. *Ibid.*, p. 59.

55. *Ibid.*, p. 68.

56. J. Habermas, *Legitimation Crisis*, trans. T. McCarthy (Heinemann, London, 1975), p. 108.

57. Bernstein, *op. cit.*, p. 49.

58. Habermas (1992), *op. cit.*, p. 207.

59. S. O'Neill, "Morality, Ethical Life and the Persistence of Universalism", *Theory, Culture and Society*, Vol. 11, No. 2 (1994), p. 133.

60. S. Benhabib, *Situating the Self: Gender, Community, and Postmodernism in Contemporary Ethics* (Polity Press, Cambridge, 1992), p. 74.

Chapter seven

Back to the future: some critical reflections

*In the Symposium . . . Diotima's teaching will be very dialectical –
but different from what we usually call dialectical. Unlike Hegel's,
her dialectic does not work by opposition to transform the first term
into the second, in order to arrive at a synthesis of the two. At the
very outset, she establishes the intermediary and she never abandons
it as a mere way or means.*
> Luce Irigaray, *Sorcerer Love*, trans. E.H. Kuykendall (1984)

This study has argued that understanding violent conflict as a
form of human interaction requires a conception of action that
incorporates both agency and structure. Violent conflict emerges
as a result of concrete decisions made by actors situated in specific
social relations. It involves defined incompatibilities which underpin the issues in conflict, and evaluations of the effectiveness of
means utilised to achieve desired outcomes. Conflict is not, however, confined to the decision-making elite but involves the mobilisation of both material and human resources towards generating
support for violent action. The study argued that decisions for war
and support for war cannot be simply understood in terms of
instrumentality but must locate conduct within the wider
contextualities of social life. Using structurationist premises, the
underlying assumption of the study is that human conduct,
including war as a specifically human phenomenon, is situated
historically so that the conditions which define the contextual
framework of action are drawn upon reflexively and are reproduced
intentionally or unintentionally through the process of interaction.
Every action, every decision, image, text, declaration of support, is
also an act of reproduction of the social structures which render

these actions possible. Violent conflict is seen as an aspect of social systems reproduced through the dialectical interplay between agency and the structural continuities of social life. The continuity of war is, therefore, a product of the recursive character of social relations, constituted through deeply embedded discursive and institutional practices and constitutive of these continuities in patterned social systems.

The framework developed in chapter three suggests that the structural continuities of social systems are drawn upon and reproduced by actors in strategic interaction. The relevance of the theory of structuration for the study of conflict lies in its concern with the reproduction of institutional practices ordered across time and space. In developing a structurationist theory of conflict, chapter three sought to situate violent conflict within a wider theory of social reproduction and transformation.

Implicated in the reproduction of war as a social continuity are structures of signification, legitimation, and domination drawn upon and reproduced by actors in situated interactive social relations. Structures of signification and legitimation are reproduced through shared interpretative schemes, symbolic orders and normative expectations defining a language of war, which, as argued in chapter four, contains constructs of rationalisation and justification which are drawn upon in the mobilisation of support for violent conflict. The state, as a highly administered social system, was seen to be centrally implicated in the reproduction of war both as a focus of legitimating dominant discourses on war and as the manifest institutionalisation of the war process.

The structurationist theory of conflict developed in this study also focused on the construction of identity and its relationship to violent human conflict. The main argument developed in chapter five is that expressions of identity and representations of exclusionist discourses involve actors situated in time and space locations which link day-to-day encounters with the extraordinary time of conflict. Articulations of identity draw upon deeply embedded identiational continuities mobilised in the construction of bounded political groupings. As was argued in chapter five, conflict constitutes a discourse of exclusion based upon a linguistically and institutionally constructed identity involving separation, classification and strict boundedness. While expressions of identity are built out of a variety of individual experiences, the emergence of dominant constructions of identity within specific locations in time and space points to structures of domination as implicated in the generation of hegemonic identity defining discourses. As was pointed out in chapter five, identity is always a domain of selection and contestation and it is through structures of domination and control that dominant identiational discourses emerge and become highly defined in time of conflict with a constructed enemy.

The structurationist theory of violent conflict developed in this study is of central relevance to developing a specifically critical, post-positivist approach to the study of international relations in general and the study of violent conflict in particular. Recent debates in international relations suggest that the so-called "agency-structure problem" is of central concern in epistemological debates within the discipline. Alexander Wendt has suggested that the theory of structuration overcomes problems of reductionism associated with the neo-realist school and structural reification associated with world system analysis.[1] Hollis and Smith, on the other hand, have argued that the agency-structure problem is not merely one of ontology; because of an assumed causal relationship between agency and structure, questions of epistemology are as important.[2] These debates are conducted within the boundaries of international relations as a discipline and rarely engage directly with discourses occurring in other social science disciplines.

Any international relations discourse must be situated within wider social theoretical concerns which bridge the gap between the various social science disciplines. Understanding conflict in world society cannot confine analysis to inter-state relations conducted between governmental decision-makers. Conflict is a social phenomenon involving governments, communities and individuals, and instrumental reason as the basis of conflict decisions does not provide any indication of the discursive and institutional continuities situated within societies and across state boundaries which are drawn upon and reproduced by actors in interaction. A critical, post-positivist international relations requires a shift away from an assumed universalist epistemology towards understanding the ontological underpinnings of international political life. Similarly, understanding violent conflict requires an ontological discourse on the construction of self and society and the place of war therein. The importation of social theory, specifically Giddens's theory of structuration which has centralised ontology, is, therefore, of central importance in developing a critical post-positivist approach to international relations concerned with understanding the reproduction of social formations and institutional practices across time and space. International relations is premised upon exclusionist discourses which conceive the state and sovereignty as given ahistorical entities forming the defining point of world politics. A critical discourse on violence as centrally located in international relations uncovers the contextualities of social formations and discourses implicated in the reproduction of violence as an aspect of social systems, domestic and international. An ontological discourse problematises agency and structure, subjectivity and collective experience.

Of primary importance in understanding war as a social phenomenon is the structurationist premise that the starting-points for social theoretical discourse are conceptions of being, of subjectivity and its relation to social formations and social transformation. The generalising and homogenising discourse contained in universalised epistemologies is rejected through recognition that actors are situated in time and space and their acts cannot be understood as an "aggregate or series of separate intentions, reasons and motives",[3] but as reflexively and recursively implicated in the production and reproduction of the historical continuities of situated social life. By emphasising the ontological basis of self and society, structuration theory provides an "ontology of potentials"[4] recognising that agents are knowledgeable entities whose social interactions, worlds of meaning, discursive and institutional practices are always instantiated in specific time and space locations. The ontological basis of the theory of structuration moves the agenda of international relations and the study of conflict away from a descriptive, uncritical account of events presented in universalist terms. In utilising structuration theory, this particular study has sought to consider the production and reproduction of practices, forms of meanings, discourses and institutional frameworks which are implicated in the reproduction of war as a social continuity manifest across levels of social interaction.

Critical reflections on the theory of structuration and understanding violence in world society

This study suggests that all aspects of conflict involve both structure and agency. The decision to utilise violence, the specificity of desires sought, the mobilisation of support for violent interaction, the construction of dominant modes of discourse on identity, and representations of the enemy, are based on the activities of situated agents acting within and reproducing the structural continuities of specific social formations. In moving beyond the polarity expressed in the structuralist-individualist divide, the aim of the theory of structuration is to "analyse social structure so that we can clearly discern how it *requires* agency and analyse human agency in such a manner that we grasp how all social action *involves* social structure".[5] Given the ontological underpinnings of the theory of structuration, one of the primary questions relates to its relevance in social research.

Giddens rejects the view that empirical research is conducted to validate or refute theoretical statements, arguing instead that social theory may be utilised as a sensitising device in the formulation of research problems and the interpretation of research results.[6] However, one reaction to the level of abstraction manifest in structuration theory is that it remains unhelpful in concrete empirical research. Nicki Gregson, for example, suggests that

> Structuration theory is concerned essentially with developing an ontology of human society. What this means in terms of the concepts which Giddens provides in structuration theory is that, for the most part, these will be specific to the ontological level; they will relate more to the nature of being, of existence, in human society generally than to the contingencies of how this might work out in particular periods or places.[7]

This study has shown that ontological concerns are of central importance in developing understandings of social phenomena, including violence as a mode of human interaction. Empirical research is not devoid of ontologies but is founded upon an implicit set of ontological assumptions which largely remain unstated and beyond reflective consideration.

A related issue is the question of whether the theory of structuration constitutes a specifically "critical" social theory. Giddens follows Charles Taylor's premise that in the social sciences, unlike the natural sciences, "the practice is the object of the theory. Theory in this domain transforms its own object".[8] This defines what Giddens refers to as the "double hermeneutic" which he defines as

> The intersection of two frames of meaning as a logically necessary part of social science, the meaningful social world as constituted by lay actors and the metalanguages invented by social scientists; there is a constant "slippage" from one to the other involved in the practice of the social sciences.[9]

The double hermeneutic points to the role of the social sciences in the constitution of social life. Social theory thereby becomes inherently critical in that it is implicated in the constitution and transformation of the social life which forms its subject matter. This, according to some critics, is too minimal a conception of what constitutes a critical orientation in social theory. According to Bernstein, "Sometimes Giddens confuses the issue of the *practical* consequences of social science on the social world with its *critical* impact."[10] Giddens calls for an awareness of the practical impact of social research and theory on wider social relations and more specifically a reflective understanding of its constitutive role in sociopolitical practices. This reflective component is central to developing a critical understanding of the social domain and the place of inquiry therein. As will be argued below, conflict research has not reflected on the constitutive impact of its discourses on the conflicts it studies from an assumption of exteriority.

Does a specifically critical social theory contain an emancipatory element? We may acknowledge the constitutive role played by social research, but a critical social theory must point to some criteria as to how we may discriminate between the practical connotations of different social theories. While social theory may have technical consequences, the uses to which social research is put by authorities and others becomes of crucial importance in developing an emancipatory transformative social theory. It seems, therefore, that a more precise conception of critical theory is required if we are to move beyond technical knowledge about violence in world society. This study has argued that the application of structurationist premises to understanding violence provides a critical conception of this human phenomenon in that it is centrally concerned with uncovering the discursive and institutional continuities which generate and legitimate violence in world society. However, in seeking an emancipatory discourse, that is one which was distinctly concerned with the transformation of such continuities, the discourse on peace articulated in chapter six relied specifically on Habermas's conception of emancipation and situated peace within the moral domain of discourse ethics.

A central component of the theory of structuration is that structure is both constraining and enabling. Giddens's stratification model of action defined in chapter three of this book suggests that agents' actions are bounded by unintended consequences which later become the unacknowledged conditions of further actions. This is the way in which action is related to structure, for actors unintentionally reproduce the structural continuities of social life just as they draw upon these in their strategic interaction. It is in this way that structure, for Giddens, is both enabling and constraining. Rules as an aspect of structure enable actors to "go on" in daily life while at the same time constraining particular modes of behaviour. Giddens distinguishes between "material constraints", deriving from the character of the material world, "negative sanctions", which define constraints deriving from punitive measures enacted by some agents against others, and "structural constraints", which derive from the "contextuality of action" or the structural properties of social systems *vis-à-vis* situated actors.[11] It is important to recognise that the structural properties of social systems, even where these are deeply embedded in institutions, are both enabling and constraining. Shared worlds of meaning contained in structures of signification, for example, allow communication between situated social actors but also limit the possibilities of expressive statements available to actors. The context of action and interaction, therefore, becomes of primary importance in whether the structural properties of social formations are constraining or enabling.

A central concern in understanding violent human conflict relates to the choices available to actors in situated conflictual social relations. It could be stated that this study has primarily concentrated on the enabling aspect of structure; that is, those discursive and institutional continuities which enable and legitimate the occurrence of war as a form of conflict behaviour. It could be argued that the above conceptualisation of structural enablement and constraint does not inform the conflict researcher on the circumstances which render structures either enabling or constraining. The question of why some forms of conflict become manifest while others remain largely hidden social contradictions is of central importance when considering questions of differential enablement and constraint. According to Thompson,

> One of the key tasks of social analysis is to explore this space of possibilities, both in terms of the differential distribution of options according to class, age, sex, and so on, but also of the kinds of wants and desires, the interests and needs, which are themselves differentially possessed . . . To explore the space between the differential distribution of options, on the one hand, and the wants and needs of different kinds and of different categories of individuals, on the other, is to examine the degrees of freedom and constraint which are entailed by social structure.[12]

If structural constraint and enablement are conceived as situated in persistently reproduced social interaction, and if these are differentially applicable within and across collectivities, it becomes necessary to align the nature of individual wants and needs with the structural properties which inhibit (or enable) their manifestation. As will be seen below, the construction of individual identity is always enabled through discursive practices and modes of legitimation reproduced in the structural properties of social systems, but it is also constrained in the possibilities and options available to situated actors. Structure, therefore, allows some modes of representation while censoring others. This is of central concern to conflict processes and will be returned to below.

One of the central components of Giddens's theory of structuration is its emphasis on the knowledgeability of social agents. Actors are knowledgeable in that they reflexively monitor the conditions of action in "practical consciousness" which is invoked in the routine processes of daily life but remains unarticulated. Discursive consciousness, on the other hand, is "what actors are able to say, or to give verbal expression to, about social conditions, including especially the conditions of their own action". It is awareness which has a discursive form.[13] The attraction of this conception of individual knowledgeability as being situated in both practical and discursive consciousness is that it points to the nature of day-to-day encounters and the routines which confer "onto-logical security" on social agents. The challenge to the social theorist is to provide a conceptual link between practical and discursive consciousness. The challenge for understanding violence and its legitimation is to uncover the daily modes of representation and imagery which are implicated and drawn upon in times of conflict to generate exclusionist modes of discourse. The relevant question for conflict research is how the tacit knowledge contained in practical consciousness becomes articulated in discourse in conditions of adversity. Chapter five argued that identity formations and their role in conflict represent the interplay between the practical tacit knowledge of the everyday and the critical encounters constituting the extraordinary time of conflict.

The application of structurationist premises to the question of identity raises a number of questions of relevance to a critical discourse in international relations generally and the study of conflict in particular. The construction of identity involves an interplay of the knowledgeability of situated social agents and the structural properties of specific social formations. Identity is a product of social relations and forms a constitutive element of day-to-day social encounters. Agents draw upon specific constructions of identity in times of adversity and perceived threat. Some modes of identity, the ethno-national, for example, constitute a dominant mode of representation which is assumed by agents in conflict and observers alike. Chapter five of this study argued that the construction of identity and the emergence of dominant modes of exclusionist discourse point to the positionality of actors at the intersection of structures of signification, legitimation and domination. Violent conflict generates a hegemonic discourse which seeks to subsume subjectivity and its multiple forms of representation into a singular entity involved in a confrontational interaction with another assumed/constructed monolithic entity. Such hegemonic discourses are not simply a product of dominant agents drawing upon deeply embedded symbolic orders, but are reproduced through the representations of observers, conflict researchers and third parties attempting mediation. The assumption of the latter group is that their definitions of the conflict reflect the definitions of the protagonists. This premise of exteriority derives from a behaviouralist imperative which states that analysis is based upon objective observation. Interpretations of a conflict based on the definitions and identifications of protagonist leaders, however, reconstitute that conflict and reproduce the exclusionist, violent discourses and practices which perpetuate it.

Questions that are of relevance in understanding the relationship between identity and conflict relate to unravelling its construction, the basis upon which some modes of representation come to dominate others, and the emergence of exclusionist identities implicated in violent human conflict. A survey of post Cold War conflicts points to the central role played by ethno-nationalist identity in the emergence of intense and protracted social conflicts. In a survey of armed conflicts occurring within the period 1989–93, Wallensteen and Axell point to the predominance of territorial incompatibilities involving governments and non-state actors. Even where conflicts concerned governmental structures, the parties involved seemed, in the majority of cases, to have a self-definition based on ethnicity or religious identity. What is also of significance in this survey is that of the ninety armed conflicts recorded for this short period, involving one-third of the UN membership and a plethora of non-state actors, only four were of the conventional inter-state variety.[14] Given the sheer number of armed conflicts occurring in world society, some of these involving the massacre of civilian populations,[15] the level of violence, even within this four-year duration, has not been of negligible proportions. Given that ethnicity and religious modes of identity are at the core of contemporary violent conflicts, we cannot confine interest to inter-state conflicts but must recognise that violence involves communities and states alike. The central component of any analysis of violence in contemporary world society must be a recognition that war continues to be a constitutive aspect of state formation and its scope and intensity are reinforced through a global military order.

The boundary-defining texts within the discipline of international relations have concentrated on the state as an ahistorical and unproblematised unit of analysis and on inter-state relations as the discipline's legitimate concern. In neo-realist discourses on international relations, war was seen as a product of the anarchical structure of the inter-state system. It came to constitute one of the regulative mechanisms of geopolitical imperatives. The state is considered a pre-given entity, precluding both ontological and normative discourses which could situate the state in specific historic locations, and as implicated in the relationship between self and society. That the state, as a highly administered social system of control, is implicated in the institutionalisation of violence, in legitimating discourses on the rationalisation and justification of war, and in dominant identity-forming discourses, suggests that any understanding of war – including inter-state war – requires a conception of self and society, of worlds of meaning, and the recursive relationship between individuality and collective social life. The state is not an ontologically pre-given entity nor is it simply a product of modes of production and exchange relations. The state is a product of historical social formations emerging largely through a combination of external conflict and internal pacification. The state is an administered social system built upon institutional frameworks containing structures of signification, legitimation and domination.

An ontological discourse on violence in world society focuses on the nature of self, collective social life, institutional and discursive practices and transformations. An ontological discourse does not assume a pre-given distinction between inter-state or intercommunal violence. While these may be distinguished along degrees of formalisation, both require an ontological discourse which problematises individuality, collectivity and structural continuity.

The ontological discourse which constitutes the theory of structuration utilised in this study situates violent conflict, both interstate and inter-communal, within the ontological relationship between self and society, agency and structure. The state is not, as in Wendt's application of structuration to international relations, considered as agent interacting with the structure of the inter-state system or the world capitalist system.[16] The state, as indicated above, is a social system, a power-container, historically reproduced through the activities of social agents situated in relation to institutional formations of administration and control. Agency relates to the transformative capacity of situated agents, positioned at specific intersections of structures of signification, legitimation and domination. Actors may be positioned within political or economic institutions of the state, they may be positioned in relation to bounded social groupings within the wider society, but their activities, in daily encounters and in the most critical situations, are always reflexively and recursively implicated in the reproduction of the structural properties of social systems. The state, as a mode of human organisation, contains situated agents and deeply embedded structural properties. The state is a symbolic and institutional container of power – a system of control developed historically through processes of segregation and administered classification as modes of control.

A central component of an ontological discourse on violence is centrally concerned with the nature of self, self-identity, subjectivity and representation. The tendency in conflict research is to define specific conflict situations in terms of bounded communities or entities. Reference is made, for example, to the "Bosnian-Serb" conflict, the "Hutu-Tutsi" conflict, the "Israeli-Palestinian" conflict. Such representations confer on the parties a singular identity, reproducing the exclusionist discourses of protagonist leaders. Singular subjectivities and monolithic identities are, however, always constructed through hegemonic discourses which contribute to a dominant form of identity. To take identity formations as pre-given definitions of social entities would, therefore, render unproblematic the nature of self-identity, of subjectivity, difference and conformity. These are, however, constructs emerging from discursive and institutional practices which must be questioned if we are to develop an understanding of the constitutive relationship between self and society and the place of war therein.

The construction of identity is, therefore, of central concern in a discourse on violence. Identity always implies positionality and difference. It incorporates inter-subjectivity and dialogue. It also involves transience and provisionality and as such is always a place of selection and contestation. Lived experience in daily encounters always involves self-knowledgeability and others' interpretations mediated through embodied co-presence. Identity is constructed through a social process involving subjective representation and inter-subjective recognition. It is always multiple and varied based on a plethora of experiences and positionalities of individuals existing as women, men, Jews, Arabs, Christians, Black, White, and so on. There is no singular experience of being any of these identities. These are always social positions emerging through a multiplicity of locations and reflecting different modes of representation.

As indicated previously in this study, a central component of violent conflict is the emergence of dominant discourses which seek to subsume multiple subjectivities into singular modes of identity requiring conformity and allegiance. Control, however, generates counter-discourses, resistance and non-conformity. The question of resistance to hegemonic discourses on identity is of central value not only in understanding the relationship between identity, mobilisation and violence, but for developing emancipatory, critical approaches to conflict resolution which recognise difference and diversity. As pointed out by Henrietta Moore,

> As types of agency, resistance and complicity are notoriously difficult to analyse. What makes individuals resist or comply? It has become increasingly clear that one cannot answer such a question in purely social terms. Issues of desire, identification, fantasy and fear all have to be addressed. Each individual has a personal history and it is in the intersection of this history with collective situations, discourses and identities that the problematic relationship between structure and praxis, and between the social and the individual resides.[17]

For Moore, complicity and resistance are types of agency as well as being aspects of subjectivity "marked through with structures of difference based on gender, race, ethnicity, and so on".[18] Identity and expressions of difference are always situated in contextualised social relations and cannot be assumed in advance as is the tendency in ahistorical discourses in conflict research and international relations.

Feminist discourses on gender identity contribute to understanding the dialectical interplay between agency and structure in the construction of identity and the multiple ways in which modes of identiational representation are implicated in violence. Feminist discourses recognise that gender identity has both individual and collective dimensions. Both social representation and subjective constructions of identity are interrelated within complex intersubjective locations situated within discursive and institutional frameworks.

Conflict research and international relations assume that collectivities are composed of unitary rational individuals. It is the collective, and more importantly its leadership, that is of analytic and conflict resolutionary concern. However, problematising both individuality and collectivity points to the post-structuralist premise that the individual is a site of multiple subjectivities. Conflict research equates individuality and subjectivity where there is no valid basis for such an equation. As indicated by post-structuralist feminist discourses on gender identity, individuals are not simply carriers of a single imposed identity but have multiple subjectivities lived and expressed differently within different contextualities. According to Moore's analysis of gender identity,

> Individuals are multiply constituted subjects, and they can, and do, take up multiple subject positions within a range of discourses and social practices. Some of these subject positions will be contradictory and will conflict with each other.[19]

Identity is located in social discourse, networks of interpretation, and relations of power. Identity is also an expression of the multiplicity of subjectivities that individuals express within different circumstances in social relations. Recognising the multiple subjectivities of individuals in relation to emergent conflict is specifically relevant to conflict resolution processes which, rather than reconstituting monolithic views of identity, recognise diversity, the articulation of multiple subjectivities and the potentiality of crosscutting modes of discourse which transcend ethno-national conflict divides. Conflicts are constructed along one major axis of difference. Conflicting societies are, however, composed of individuals who in themselves have multiple, shifting subjectivities situating along a number of intersecting axes of difference both within each group and across the conflict divide. Hegemonic discourses seek the production of a singular, unified mode of representation and in times of conflict with a perceived enemy are intolerant towards resistance and assertions of difference. A transformative discourse seeking peace situated in dialogic relations must seek to uncover processes which generate dominant identity formations and the possibilities existing in the multiple subjectivities of the self which transcend the conflict divide of an inter-societal conflict.

This book has sought to develop a critical discourse on violence and peace. It is normative in orientation, seeking understanding of a human phenomenon, of the continuities which have established violence itself as a continuity. The study is also normative in that it seeks the transformation of the human condition, its exclusionist discourses and institutions, and situates such transformation in a discursive ethics which not only incorporates difference but celebrates such agency. Normativity does not indicate idealism or a belief in utopian futures free of violence against a targeted "other". Normativity asserts a recognition of the complex combination of differentially located enablements and constraints, of the multiplicity of subject positions "carried" by situated agents, and of the plethora of social formations, cultures and traditions which constitute the diversity that is the human condition. The contextuality of the human condition, however, also contains the seeds of its transformation. The transformation this book seeks is located in the discourses and institutions we alone construct.

Notes

1. For a debate on the agency-structure problem within international relations, see A.E. Wendt, "Bridging the Theory/Meta-Theory Gap in International Relations", and M. Hollis and S. Smith, "Beware of Gurus: Structure and Action in International Relations", both in *Review of International Studies*, Vol. 17, No. 4 (October 1991).

2. See M. Hollis and S. Smith, "Two Stories about Structure and Agency", *Review of International Studies*, Vol. 20, No. 3 (1994), pp. 241–251. For a reply asserting the importance of ontology in a post-positivist international relations, see V. Jabri and S. Chan, "The Ontologist Always Rings Twice: Two More Stories about Structure and Agency in Reply to Hollis and Smith", forthcoming in *Review of International Studies*.

3. A. Giddens, *The Constitution of Society* (Polity Press, Cambridge, 1984), p. 3.

4. I.J. Cohen, *Structuration Theory: Anthony Giddens and the Constitution of Social Life* (Macmillan, London, 1989), p. 29.

5. R. Bernstein, "Social Theory as Critique", in D. Held and J.B. Thompson (eds), *Social Theory of Modern Societies: Anthony Giddens and His Critics* (Cambridge University Press, Cambridge, 1989), p. 25.

6. Giddens, *op. cit.*, p. 326.

7. N. Gregson, "On the (Ir)relevance of Structuration Theory To Empirical Research", in Held and Thompson, *op. cit.*, p. 244.

8. C. Taylor, "Political Theory and Practice", in C. Lloyd (ed.), *Social Theory and Political Practice* (Clarendon Press, Oxford, 1983), p. 74. Quoted in Giddens, *op. cit.*, p. 348.

9. *Ibid.*, p. 374.

10. Bernstein, *op. cit.*, p. 30.

11. Giddens, *op. cit.*, p. 176.

12. J.B. Thompson, "The Theory of Structuration", in Held and Thompson, *op. cit.*, p. 74.

13. Giddens, *op. cit.*, p. 374.

14. P. Wallensteen and K. Axell, "Conflict Resolution and the End of the

Cold War, 1989–1993", *Journal of Peace Research*, Vol. 31, No. 3 (1994), pp. 333–350.

15. Rudolph Rummel estimates this century's battle deaths at 38,500,000 and numbers of civilians massacred ("killing in cold blood, aside from warfare") at 151,000,000 in international and civil wars up to 1987. See R.J. Rummel, "Power, Genocide and Mass Murder", *Journal of Peace Research*, Vol. 31, No. 1 (1994), pp. 2–3.

16. A.E. Wendt, "The Agent-Structure Problem in International Relations Theory", *International Organisation*, Vol. 41, No. 3 (1987).

17. H.L. Moore, *A Passion for Difference* (Polity Press, Cambridge, 1994), pp. 49–50.

18. *Ibid.*, p. 50.

19. *Ibid.*, p. 55.

Bibliography

Abrams, D. and M.A. Hogg, "An Introduction to the Social Identity Approach", in D. Abrams and M.A. Hogg (eds), *Social Identity Theory: Constructive and Critical Advances* (Harvester Wheatsheaf, London, 1990).

Anderson, B., *Imagined Communities* (Verso, London, 1991).

Appignanesi, L. and S. Maitland (eds), *The Rushdie File* (Fourth Estate, London, 1989).

Archer, M.S., *Culture and Agency: The Place of Culture in Social Theory* (Cambridge University Press, Cambridge, 1988).

Aubert, V., "Competition and Dissensus: Two Types of Conflict and Conflict Resolution", *Journal of Conflict Resolution*, Vol. 7 (1963), pp. 26–42.

Austin, J.L., *How To Do Things With Words* (Harvard University Press, Cambridge, MA, 1962).

Azar, E., *The Management of Protracted Social Conflict* (Dartmouth, Aldershot, 1990).

Azar, E. and J.W. Burton (eds), *International Conflict Resolution: Theory and Practice* (Harvester Wheatsheaf, Brighton and Lynne Reinner, Boulder, CO, 1986).

Bar-Siman-Tov, Y., "The Arab-Israeli Conflict: Learning Conflict Resolution", *Journal of Peace Research*, Vol. 31, No. 1 (1994), pp. 75–92.

Barrow, R.H. (trans.), *Introduction to St Augustine: City of God* (Faber and Faber, London, 1950).

Bazin, N.T. and J.H. Lauter, "Virginia Woolf's Keen Sensitivity to War: Its Roots and its Impact on Her Novels", in M. Hussey (ed.), *Virginia Woolf and War: Fiction, Reality and Myth* (Syracuse University Press, Syracuse, NY, 1992).

Benhabib, S., *Situating the Self: Gender, Community, and Postmodernism in Contemporary Ethics* (Polity Press, Cambridge, 1992).

Bercovitch, J., J.T. Anagnoson and D.L. Wille, "Some Conceptual Issues and Empirical Trends in the Study of Successful Mediation in International Relations", *Journal of Peace Research*, Vol. 28, No. 1 (1991), pp. 7–17.

Berghahn, V.R., *Militarism: The History of an International Debate 1861–1979* (Berg Publishers, Leamington Spa, 1981).

Bernstein, J.M., *Recovering Ethical Life: Jurgen Habermas and the Future of Critical Theory* (Routledge, London and New York, 1995).

Bernstein, R., "Social Theory as Critique", in D. Held and J.B. Thompson (eds),

Social Theory of Modern Societies: Anthony Giddens and His Critics (Cambridge University Press, Cambridge, 1989).

Best, G., *Humanity in Warfare: The Modern History of the International Law of Armed Conflicts* (Weidenfeld and Nicolson, London, 1980).

Best, S. and D. Kellner, *Postmodern Theory: Critical Interrogations* (Macmillan, London, 1991).

Bhabha, H.K. (ed.), *Nation and Narration* (Routledge, London, 1990).

Bhaskar, R., *The Possibility of Naturalism* (Harvester Wheatsheaf, Hemel Hempstead, 1989).

Biddle, B.J., "Recent Developments in Role Theory", *Annual Review of Sociology*, Vol. 12 (1987), pp. 67–92.

Bilmes, J., *Discourses and Behaviour* (Plenum Press, New York, 1986).

Blalock, H., *Power and Conflict: Toward a General Theory* (Sage, London, 1989).

Bloom, W., *Personal Identity, National Identity and International Relations* (Cambridge University Press, Cambridge, 1990).

Boulding, K., "Future Directions in Conflict and Peace Studies", *Journal of Conflict Resolution*, Vol. 22, No. 2 (1978).

Brock, P., *Pacifism in Europe to 1914* (Princeton University Press, Princeton, NJ, 1972).

Brown, C., *International Relations Theory: New Normative Approaches* (Harvester Wheatsheaf, Hemel Hempstead, 1993).

Bueno de Mesquita, B., *The War Trap* (Yale University Press, New Haven, CT, 1981).

Buitenhuis, P., *The Great War of Words: Literature as Propaganda 1914–1918* (Batsford, London, 1987).

Bull, H.N., *The Anarchical Society: A Study of World Order* (Macmillan, London and Columbia University Press, New York, 1977).

Burman, E. and I. Parker, *Discourse Analytic Research: Repertoires and Readings of Texts in Action* (Routledge, London, 1993).

Burton, J.W., *Deviance, Terrorism and War* (Martin Robertson, Oxford, 1979).

Burton, J.W., *Resolving Deep-Rooted Conflict: A Handbook* (University Press of America, Lanham, MD, 1987).

Burton, J.W., "Introduction", in J.W. Burton and F. Dukes (eds), *Conflict: Readings in Management and Resolution* (Macmillan, London, 1990).

Burton, J.W., *Conflict: Resolution and Provention* (Macmillan, London, 1990).

Cady, D.L., *From Warism to Pacifism: A Moral Continuum* (Temple University Press, Philadelphia, 1989).

Callinicos, A., "Anthony Giddens: A Contemporary Critique", *Theory and Society*, Vol. 14 (1985), pp. 133–166.

Campbell, D. and M. Dillon, "The End of Philosophy and the End of International Relations", in D. Campbell and M. Dillon (eds), *The Political Subject of Violence* (Manchester University Press, Manchester, 1993).

Canovan, M., *Hannah Arendt: A Reinterpretation of Her Political Thought* (Cambridge University Press, Cambridge, 1992).

Carlsnaes, W., "The Agency-Structure Problem in Foreign Policy Analysis", *International Studies Quarterly*, Vol. 36, No. 3 (1992), pp. 245–270.

Carr, E.H., *The Twenty Years Crisis, 1919–1939* (Harper and Row, New York, 1964, and Macmillan, London, 1981).

Caygill, H., "Violence, Civility and the Predicaments of Philosophy", in D. Campbell and M. Dillon (eds), *The Political Subject of Violence* (Manchester University Press, Manchester, 1993).

Ceadel, M., *Thinking about Peace and War* (Oxford University Press, Oxford, 1989).

Chaffee, S.H. *et al.*, "Mass Communication in Political Socialization", in S.A. Renshon (ed.), *Handbook of Political Socialization: Theory and Research* (Free Press, New York, 1977).

Chanteur, J., *From War to Peace*, trans. S.A. Weisz (Westview Press, Boulder, CO, 1992).

Clark, M.E., "Meaningful Social Bonding as a Universal Human Need", in J. Burton (ed.), *Conflict: Human Needs Theory* (Macmillan, London and St Martin's Press, New York, 1990).

Clausewitz, C. von, *On War*, trans. J.J. Graham (Routledge and Kegan Paul, London, 1966).

Clausewitz, Carl von, *On War*, ed. and trans. M. Howard and P. Paret (Princeton University Press, Princeton, NJ, 1976).

Cohen, I.J., *Structuration Theory: Anthony Giddens and the Constitution of Social Life* (Macmillan, London, 1989).

Collier, A., *Critical Realism: An Introduction to Roy Bhaskar's Philosophy* (Verso, London, 1994).

Condor, S., "Social Stereotypes and Social Identity", in D. Abrams and M.A. Hogg (eds), *Social Identity Theory: Constructive and Critical Advances* (Harvester Wheatsheaf, London, 1990).

D'Entreves, A.P. (ed.), *Aquinas: Selected Political Writings* (Blackwell, Oxford, 1965).

De Saussure, F., *Course in General Linguistics* (Fontana, London, 1974).

Der Derian, J., "The Value of Security: Hobbes, Marx, Nietzsche and Baudrillard", in D. Campbell and M. Dillon, *The Political Subject of Violence* (Manchester University Press, Manchester, 1993).

Deutsch, M., "Subjective Features of Conflict Resolution", in R. Vayrynen (ed.), *New Directions in Conflict Theory* (Sage, London, 1991).

Diehl, R.F., "What are they Fighting For? The Importance of Issues in International Conflict Research", *Journal of Peace Research*, Vol. 29, No. 3 (1992), p. 335.

Draculic, S., *Balkan Express* (Hutchinson, London, 1993).

Druckman, D., "An Analytical Research Agenda for Conflict and Conflict Resolution", in D.J.D. Sandole and H. van der Merwe (eds), *Conflict Resolution Theory and Practice* (Manchester University Press, Manchester, 1993).

Durkheim, E., *The Division of Labour in Society* (Free Press, New York, 1964).

Eide, A., "Dialogue and Confrontation in Europe", *Journal of Conflict Resolution*, Vol. 16 (1972), pp. 511–522.

Elshtain, J.B., *Women and War* (The Harvester Press, Brighton, 1987).

Elshtain, J.B. (ed.), *Just War Theory* (Blackwell, Oxford, 1992).

Elster, J., *Sour Grapes: Studies in the Subversion of Rationality* (Cambridge University Press, Cambridge, 1983).

Elster, J., *Nuts and Bolts for the Social Sciences* (Cambridge University Press, Cambridge, 1989).

Erikson, E.H., *Identity, Youth and Crisis* (Faber and Faber, London, 1968).

Ferguson, R.B. (ed.), *Warfare, Culture and Environment* (Academic Press, Orlando, FL, 1984).

Fisher, R.J., "Needs Theory, Social Identity and an Eclectic Model of Conflict", in J.W. Burton (ed.), *Conflict: Human Needs Theory* (Macmillan, London and St Martin's Press, New York, 1990).

Fisher, R.J. and L. Keashley, "The Potential Complementarity of Mediation and Consultation Within a Contingency Model of Third Party Intervention", *Journal of Peace Research*, Vol. 28, No. 1 (1991), pp. 29–42.

Foucault, M., *Discipline and Punish: The Birth of the Prison* (Penguin, London, 1991).

Fraser, N., "The Uses and Abuses of French Discourse Theories for Feminist Politics", *Theory, Culture, and Society*, Vol. 9 (1992), pp. 51–71.

Freedman, L. (ed.), *War* (Oxford University Press, Oxford, 1994).

Gadamer, H.-G., *Truth and Method*, trans. G. Barden and J. Cumming (Sheed and Ward, London, 1975).

Gallie, W.B., *Philosophers of Peace and War* (Cambridge University Press, Cambridge, 1989).

Galtung, J., "Violence, Peace and Peace Research", *Journal of Peace Research*, Vol. 6, No. 3 (1969), pp. 167–191.

Garfinkel, H., *Studies in Ethnomethodology* (Prentice Hall, Englewood Cliffs, NJ, 1967).

Gergen, K.J. and K.E. Davis (eds), *The Social Construction of the Person* (Springer Verlag, New York, 1985).

Giddens, A., *New Rules of Sociological Method: A Positive Critique of Interpretative Sociologies* (Hutchinson, London, 1976).

Giddens, A., *Central Problems in Social Theory: Action, Structure and Contradiction in Social Analysis* (Macmillan, London, 1979).

Giddens, A., *The Constitution of Society* (Polity Press, Cambridge, 1984).

Giddens, A., *The Nation-State and Violence* (Polity Press, Cambridge, 1985).

Giddens, A., *Modernity and Self-Identity: Self and Society in the Late Modern Age* (Polity Press, Cambridge, 1991).

Gill, S. (ed.), *Gramsci, Historical Materialism, and International Relations* (Cambridge University Press, Cambridge, 1993).

Gilpin, R., *War and Change in World Politics* (Cambridge University Press, Cambridge, 1981).

Goffman, E., *Relations in Public: Microstudies of the Public Order* (Harper and Colophon, New York, 1972).

Goffman, E., *Frame Analysis* (Harper, New York, 1974).

Gramsci, A., *Selections from the Prison Notebooks of Antonio Gramsci*, trans. Q. Hoare and G.N. Smith (Lawrence and Wishart, London, 1971).

Gregson, N., "On the (Ir)relevance of Structuration Theory to Empirical Research", in D. Held and J.B. Thompson (eds), *Social Theory of Modern Societies: Anthony Giddens and His Critics* (Cambridge University Press, Cambridge, 1989).

Groom, A.J.R., "Paradigms in Conflict: The Strategist, the Conflict Researcher and the Peace Researcher", in J.W. Burton and F. Dukes (eds), *Conflict: Readings in Management and Resolution* (Macmillan, London, 1990).

Grotius, H., *The Law of War and Peace* (Bobbs-Merrill, New York, 1925).

Habermas, J., *Knowledge and Human Interests*, trans. J.J. Shapiro (Heinemann, London, 1972).

Habermas, J., "The Public Sphere", *New German Critique*, Vol. 3 (1974), p. 42.

Habermas, J., *Legitimation Crisis*, trans. T. McCarthy (Heinemann, London, 1975).

Habermas, J., "A Review of Gadamer's *Truth and Method*", in F. Dallmayr and T. McCarthy (eds), *Understanding Social Inquiry* (Notre Dame Press, Notre Dame, IN, 1977).

Habermas, J., *Moral Consciousness and Communicative Action*, trans. C. Lenhardt and S.W. Nicholson (Polity Press, Cambridge, 1992).

Haney, P.J., *et al.*, "Unitary Actors, Advisory Models, and Experimental Tests", *Journal of Conflict Resolution*, Vol. 36, No. 4 (1992), pp. 603–633.

Hardimon, M.O., *Hegel's Social Philosophy: The Project of Reconciliation* (Cambridge University Press, Cambridge, 1994).

Hawkesworth, M.E., "Knowers, Knowing, Known: Feminist Theory and Claims of Truth", *Signs*, Vol. 14, No. 3 (1989), pp. 533–547.

Hebdige, D., "Bombing Logic", *Marxism Today* (March 1991).

Hechter, M., *Internal Colonialism: The Celtic Fringe in British National Development 1536–1966* (University of California Press, Berkeley, 1975).

Hechter, M., "Rational Choice Theory and the Study of Race", in J. Rex and D. Mason (eds), *Theories of Race and Ethnic Relations* (Cambridge University Press, Cambridge, 1986).

Heckman, S.J., *Gender and Knowledge: Elements of a Postmodern Feminism* (Polity Press, Cambridge, 1990).

Hedetoft, U., "National Identity and Mentalities of War in Three EC Countries", *Journal of Peace Research*, Vol. 30, No. 3 (1993), pp. 281–300.

Hegel, G.W.F., *The Philosophy of Right*, trans. T.M. Knox (Oxford University Press, Oxford, 1942).

Held, D., *Introduction to Critical Theory: Horkheimer to Habermas* (Polity Press, Cambridge, 1980).

Held, D. and J.B. Thompson (eds), *Social Theory of Modern Societies: Anthony Giddens and His Critics* (Cambridge University Press, Cambridge, 1989).

Heritage, J., *Garfinkel and Ethnomethodology* (Polity Press, Cambridge, 1984).

Higonnet, M.R. and P.L.R. Higonnet, "The Double Helix", in M.R. Higonnet, J. Jenson, S. Michel, and M.C. Weitz (eds), *Behind the Lines: Gender and the Two World Wars* (Yale University Press, New Haven, CT, 1987).

Himes, J.S., *Conflict and Conflict Management* (Georgia University Press, Athens, GA, 1980).

Hobbes, T., *Leviathan* (Penguin Classics, Harmondsworth, 1985).

Hobsbawm, E.J., *Nations and Nationalism since 1780* (Cambridge University Press, Cambridge, 1990).

Hoffman, M., "Critical Theory and the Inter-Paradigm Debate", *Millennium*, Vol. 16, No. 2 (1987), pp. 231–250.

Hoffman, M., "Third Party Mediation and Conflict Resolution in the Post-Cold War World", in J. Baylis and N.J. Rengger (eds), *Dilemmas of World Politics* (Clarendon, Oxford and New York, 1992).

Hogg, M.A. and D. Abrams, "Self-Motivation, Self-Esteem, and Social Identity", in D. Abrams and M.A. Hogg (eds), *Social Identity Theory: Constructive and Critical Advances* (Harvester Wheatsheaf, London, 1990).

Hogg, M.A. and C. McGarty, "Self-Categorisation and Social Identity", in D. Abrams and M.A. Hogg (eds), *Social Identity Theory: Constructive and Critical Advances* (Harvester Wheatsheaf, London, 1990).

Hollis, M., *The Cunning of Reason* (Cambridge University Press, Cambridge, 1987).

Hollis, M. and S. Smith, *Explaining and Understanding International Relations* (Clarendon, Oxford, 1991).

Hollis, M. and S. Smith, "Beware of Gurus: Structure and Action in International Relations", *Review of International Studies*, Vol. 17, No. 4 (1991), pp. 393–410.

Hollis, M. and S. Smith, "Two Stories about Structure and Agency", *Review of International Studies*, Vol. 20, No. 3 (1994), pp. 241–251.

Holsti, O., "Crisis Management", in B. Glad (ed.), *Psychological Dimensions of Conflict* (Sage, London, 1990).

Holsti, K.J., *Peace and War: Armed Conflicts and International Order 1648–1989* (Cambridge University Press, Cambridge, 1991).

Howard, M., *War and the Liberal Conscience* (Temple Smith, London, 1978).

Howard, M., "Temperamenta Belli: Can War be Controlled?", in J.B. Elshtain (ed.), *Just War Theory* (Blackwell, Oxford, 1992).

Howell, S. and R. Willis (eds), *Societies at Peace: Anthropological Perspectives* (Routledge, London and New York, 1989).

Hussey, M. (ed.), *Virginia Woolf and War: Fiction, Reality and Myth* (Syracuse University Press, Syracuse, NY, 1992).

Jabri, V., *Mediating Conflict: Decision-making and Western Intervention in Namibia* (Manchester University Press, Manchester, 1990).

Jabri, V. and S. Chan, "The Ontologist Always Rings Twice: Two More Stories about Structure and Agency in Reply to Hollis and Smith", *Review of International Studies*, forthcoming.

James, A., *Sovereign Statehood: The Basis of International Society* (Allen and Unwin, London and Boston, 1986).

Janis, I.L., *Groupthink* (Houghton Mifflin, Boston, 1982).

Jervis, R., *Perception and Misperception in International Politics* (Princeton University Press, Princeton, NJ, 1976).

Jowett, G.S. and V. O'Donnel, *Propaganda and Persuasion* (Sage, London, 1992).

Kant, I., *The Moral Law*, trans. H.J. Paton (London, 1961).

Kant, I., "Idea for a Universal History with a Cosmopolitan Purpose", in *Political Writings*, ed. H. Reiss.

Kant, I., "Perpetual Peace", in *Political Writings*, ed. H. Reiss.

Kant, I., *Political Writings*, ed. H. Reiss (Cambridge University Press, Cambridge, 1991).

Kedourie, E., *Nationalism* (Hutchinson University Library, London, 1966).

Kratochwil, F.V., *Rules, Norms, and Decisions: On the Conditions of Practical and Legal Reasoning in International Relations and Democratic Affairs* (Cambridge University Press, Cambridge, 1989).

Kressel, K. and D. Pruitt (eds), *Mediation Research* (Jossey-Bass, San Francisco, 1989).

Kriesberg, L., *Social Conflicts* (Prentice Hall, Englewood Cliffs, NJ, 1982)

Kriesberg, L., "Conflict Resolution Applications to Peace Studies", *Peace and Change*, Vol. 16, No. 4 (1991), pp. 400–417.

Krippendorff, E., "Peace Research and the Industrial Revolution", *Journal of Peace Research*, Vol. 10 (1973).

Kristeva, J., *Nations without Nationalism* (Columbia University Press, New York, 1993).

Lakatos, I., "Falsification and the Methodology of Scientific Research Programmes", in I. Lakatos and A. Musgrove (eds), *Criticism and the Growth of Knowledge* (Cambridge University Press, Cambridge, 1970).

Lasswell, H.D., "The Garrison State and the Specialists on Violence", *American Journal of Sociology* (January 1941), pp. 455–468.

Lederer, K. (ed.), *Human Needs: A Contribution to the Current Debate* (Oelge-schlager, Gunn, and Hain, Cambridge, MA, 1980).

Linklater, A., *Men and Citizens in the Theory of International Relations* (Macmillan, London, 1990).

Linklater, A., "The Question of the Next Stage in International Relations Theory: A Critical-Theoretical Point of View", *Millennium: Journal of International Studies*, Vol. 21, No. 1 (1992), pp. 77–98.

Lukes, S., *Power: A Radical View* (Macmillan, London, 1974).

Machiavelli, N., *The Prince and the Discourses* (Modern Library, New York, 1950).

Machiavelli, N., *The Prince* (Penguin Classics, London, 1981).

Mann, M., "Capitalism and Militarism", in M. Shaw (ed.), *War, State, and Society* (Macmillan, London, 1984).

Mann, M., "The Roots and Contradictions of Modern Militarism", *New Left Review*, No. 162 (1987), pp. 35–50.

Mann, M., *The Sources of Social Power, Vol. II* (Cambridge University Press, Cambridge, 1993).

March, J.G. and J.P. Olsen, *Rediscovering Institutions: The Organizational Basis of Politics* (Free Press, New York, 1989).

Marsh, P. and A. Campbell (eds), *Aggression and Violence* (Blackwell, Oxford, 1982).

Maslow, A.H., *Motivation and Personality* (Harper and Row, New York, 1970).

Mayall, J., *Nationalism and International Society* (Cambridge University Press, Cambridge, 1990).

Mearsheimer, J.J., "Back to the Future: Instability in Europe after the Cold War", *International Security*, Vol. 15, No. 1 (1990), pp. 5–57.

Miller, J.B.D., *Norman Angell and the Futility of War* (Macmillan, London, 1986).

Mills, C. Wright, *The Power Elite* (Oxford University Press, Oxford and New York, 1956).

Mills, C. Wright, *The Causes of World War Three* (Secker and Warburg, London, 1959).

Mitchell, C.R., *Structure of International Conflict* (Macmillan, London, 1981).

Mitchell, C.R., "Conflict Research", in M. Light and A.J.R. Groom (eds), *Contemporary International Relations: A Guide to Theory* (Pinter, London and New York, 1994).

Mitchell, C.R. and K. Webb (eds), *New Approaches to International Mediation* (Greenwood Press, Westport, CT, 1989).

Moore, H.L., *A Passion for Difference* (Polity Press, Cambridge, 1994).

Morgenthau, H.J., *Politics Among Nations* (Alfred Knopf, New York, 1985).

Mulhall, S. and A. Swift, *Liberals and Communitarians* (Blackwell Publishers, Oxford, 1992).

Muller, E.N. and K.-D. Opp, "Rational Choice and Rebellious Collective Action", *American Political Science Review*, Vol. 80, No. 2 (1986), pp. 472–487.

Nardin, T., "Theory and Practice in Conflict Research", in T.R. Gurr (ed.), *Handbook of Political Conflict* (Free Press, New York, 1980).

Navari, C., "*The Great Illusion* Revisited: The International Theory of Norman Angell", *Review of International Studies*, Vol. 15, No. 4 (1989), pp. 341–358.

Nicholson, M., *Rationality and the Analysis of International Conflict* (Cambridge University Press, Cambridge, 1992).

Nisbett, R. and L. Ross, *Human Inference: Strategies and Shortcomings of Social Judgement* (Prentice Hall, Englewood Cliffs, NJ, 1980).

Norris, C., *Uncritical Theory: Postmodernism, Intellectuals, and the Gulf War* (Lawrence and Wishart, London, 1992).

Norton, A., *Reflections on Political Identity* (Johns Hopkins University Press, London and Baltimore, 1988).

O'Neill, S., "Morality, Ethical Life and the Persistence of Universalism", *Theory, Culture and Society*, Vol. 11, No. 2 (1994), pp. 129–149.

Ostrom, E., "Rational Choice Theory and Institutional Analysis: Toward Complementarity", *American Political Science Review*, Vol. 85, No. 1 (1991), pp. 237–243.

Ouditt, S., *Fighting Forces, Writing Women: Identity and Ideology in the First World War* (Routledge, London and New York, 1994).

Paret, P., B.I. Lewis and P. Paret, *Persuasive Images: Posters of War and Revolution* (Princeton University Press, Princeton, NJ, 1992).

Pick, D., *War Machine: The Rationalisation of Slaughter in the Modern Age* (Yale University Press, New Haven, CT and London, 1993).

Popkin, S., *The Rational Peasant: The Political Economy of Rural Society in Vietnam* (University of California Press, Berkeley, 1979).

Potter, J., "What is Reflexive about Discourse Analysis?", in S. Woolgar (ed.), *Knowledge and Reflexivity* (Sage, London, 1988).

Potter, J. and M. Whetherell, *Discourse and Social Psychology: Beyond Attitudes and Behaviour* (Sage, London, 1987).

Pufendorf, S. von, *The Law of Nature and Nations*, trans. W. Simons (Clarendon Press, Oxford, 1934).

Rabinow, P. (ed.), *The Foucault Reader: An Introduction to Foucault's Thought* (Penguin, London, 1984).

Rawls, J., "Kantian Constructivism in Moral Theory", *Journal of Philosophy*, Vol. 27 (1980), pp. 409–425.

Regan, P., "War Toys, War Movies, and the Militarization of the United States, 1900–85", *Journal of Peace Research*, Vol. 31, No. 1 (1994), pp. 45–58.

Reid, H.G. and E.J. Yanarella, "Toward a Critical Theory of Peace Research in the United States: The Search for an 'Intelligible Core'", *Journal of Peace Research*, Vol. 13 (1976).

Richardson, L.F., "War Moods", *Psychometrica*, Vol. 13, Part 1 (1948), pp. 147–174.

Riches, D., *The Anthropology of Violence* (Blackwell, Oxford, 1986).

Richmond, A.H., *Global Apartheid: Refugees, Racism, and the New World Order* (Oxford University Press, Oxford and New York, 1994).

Roosevelt, G.G., *Reading Rousseau in the Nuclear Age* (Temple University Press, Philadelphia, 1990).

Rosenberg, J., "A Non-Realist Theory of Sovereignty: Giddens' *The Nation-State and Violence*", *Millennium*, Vol. 19 (1990), pp. 249–270.

Ross, M.H., *The Culture of Conflict: Interpretations and Interests in Comparative Perspective* (Yale University Press, New Haven, CT and London, 1993).

Rothman, J., *From Confrontation to Cooperation: Resolving Ethnic and Regional Conflict* (Sage, London, 1992).

Rousseau, J.-J., *On the Social Contract*, trans. D. Cress (Hackett Publishing, Indiana, 1983).

Rummel, R.J., "Power, Genocide and Mass Murder", *Journal of Peace Research*, Vol. 31, No. 1 (1994), pp. 1–10.

Ruthven, M., *A Satanic Affair: Salman Rushdie and the Wrath of Islam* (The Hogarth Press, London, 1991).

Said, E., "The Burdens of Interpretation and the Question of Palestine", paper presented to the conference of the International Society of Political Psychology, Amsterdam, July 1986.

Said, E., *Orientalism: Western Conceptions of the Orient* (Penguin Books, London, 1991).

Sandole, D.J.D. and H. van der Merwe (eds), *Conflict Resolution Theory and Practice* (Manchester University Press, Manchester, 1993).

Schlesinger, P., *Media, State and Nation: Political Violence and Collective Identities* (Sage, London, 1991).

Schmid, H., "Peace Research and Politics", *Journal of Peace Research*, Vol. 5 (1968), pp. 217–232.

Searing, D.D., "Roles, Rules, and Rationality in the New Institutionalism", *American Political Science Review*, Vol. 85, No. 4 (1991), pp. 1239–1260.

Senghaas, D., "Transcending Collective Violence: The Civilizing Process and the Peace Problem", in R. Vayrynen (ed.), *The Quest for Peace: Transcending Collective Violence and War Among Societies, Cultures and States* (Sage, London, 1987).

Shapiro, M.J., "That Obscure Object of Violence: Logistics and Desire in the Gulf War", in D. Campbell and M. Dillon, *The Political Subject of Violence* (Manchester University Press, Manchester, 1993).

Shaw, M. (ed.), *War, State, and Society* (Macmillan, London, 1984).

Shaw, M., *Dialectics of War* (Pluto Press, London, 1988).

Shaw, M., "War and the Nation-State in Social Theory", in D. Held and J.B. Thompson (eds), *Social Theory of Modern Societies: Anthony Giddens and His Critics* (Cambridge University Press, Cambridge, 1989).

Shaw, M., *Global Society and International Relations* (Polity Press, Cambridge, 1994).

Siann, G., *Accounting for Aggression: Perspectives on Aggression and Violence* (Allen and Unwin, Boston, 1985).

Skocpol, T., *States and Social Revolutions: A Comparative Analysis of France, Russia, and China* (Cambridge University Press, Cambridge, 1979).

Smith, A.D., *The Ethnic Revival in the Modern World* (Cambridge University Press, Cambridge, 1981).

Smith, A.D., *National Identity* (Penguin Books, Harmondsworth, 1991).

Taylor, C., "Political Theory and Practice", in C. Lloyd (ed.), *Social Theory and Political Practice* (Clarendon Press, Oxford, 1983).

198   *Discourses on violence*

Taylor, M., "Structure, Culture and Action in the Explanation of Social Change", *Politics and Society*, Vol. 17, No. 2 (1989), pp. 115–162.
Thompson, J.B., *Studies in the Theory of Ideology* (University of California Press, Berkeley, 1984).
Thompson, J.B., "The Theory of Structuration", in D. Held and J.B. Thompson (eds), *Social Theory of Modern Societies: Anthony Giddens and His Critics* (Cambridge University Press, Cambridge, 1989).
Tilly, C., "Do Communities Act?", *Sociological Inquiry*, Vol. 43 (1974), pp. 209–240.
Tilly, C., *From Mobilization to Revolution* (Addison-Wesley, Reading, MA, 1978).
Tilly, C., "War Making and State Making as Organized Crime", in P.B. Evans, D. Rueschemeyer and T. Skocpol (eds), *Bringing the State Back In* (Cambridge University Press, Cambridge, 1985).
Touval, S., "Biased Intermediaries: Theoretical and Historical Considerations", *Jerusalem Journal of International Relations*, Vol. 1, No. 1 (1975), pp. 51–69.
Touval, S. and I.W. Zartman (eds), *International Mediation in Theory and Practice* (Westview Press, Boulder, CO, 1985).
Tversky, A. and D. Kahneman, *Judgement Under Uncertainty: Heuristics and Biases* (Cambridge University Press, Cambridge, 1982).
Vagts, A., *A History of Militarism* (Meridian Books, New York, 1959).
Van Dijk, T.A. (ed.), *Handbook of Discourse Analysis, Vols 1–4* (Academic Press, London, 1985).
Vasquez, J.A., *The War Puzzle* (Cambridge University Press, Cambridge, 1993).
Vattel, E. de, *The Law of Nations* (AMS Press, New York, 1987).
Verene, D.P., "Hegel's Account of War", in Z.A. Pelczynski (ed.), *Hegel's Political Philosophy: A Collection of New Essays* (Cambridge University Press, Cambridge, 1971).
Virilio, P., *War and Cinema* (Verso, London and New York, 1989).
Virilio, P. and S. Lotringer, *Pure War*, trans. Mark Polizotti (Semiotext, New York, 1983).
Von Wright, G.H., *Explanation and Understanding* (Cornell University Press, Ithaca, NY, 1971).
Wall, J.A. and A. Lynn, "Mediation: A Current Review", *Journal of Conflict Resolution*, Vol. 37, No. 1 (1993), pp. 160–194.
Wallensteen, P., "The Resolution and Transformation of International Conflict: A Structural Perspective", in R. Vayrynen (ed.), *New Directions in Conflict Theory: Conflict Resolution and Conflict Transformation* (Sage, London, 1991).
Wallensteen, P. and K. Axell, "Armed Conflict at the End of the Cold War, 1989–92", *Journal of Peace Research*, Vol. 30, No. 3 (1993), pp. 331–346.
Wallensteen, P. and K. Axell, "Conflict Resolution and the End of the Cold

War, 1989–1993", *Journal of Peace Research*, Vol. 31, No. 3 (1994), pp. 333–350.

Wallerstein, I., *The Capitalist World Economy* (Cambridge University Press, Cambridge, 1979).

Wallerstein, I., "The Future of the World Economy", in T.K. Hopkins and I. Wallerstein (eds), *Processes of the World System* (Sage, London, 1980).

Waltz, K., *Man, the State and War: A Theoretical Analysis* (Columbia University Press, New York, 1954).

Waltz, K.N., *Theory of International Politics* (Addison-Wesley, Reading, MA, and London, 1979).

Walzer, M., *Just and Unjust Wars: A Moral Argument with Historical Illustrations* (Basic Books, New York, 1977).

Weber, M., *Economy and Society* (University of California Press, Berkeley, 1978).

Wendt, A.E., "The Agent-Structure Problem in International Relations Theory", *International Organisation*, Vol. 41, No. 3 (1987), pp. 335–370.

Wendt, A.E., "Bridging the Theory/Meta-Theory Gap in International Relations", *Review of International Studies*, Vol. 17, No. 4 (1991), pp. 383–392.

White, R.K., *Nobody Wanted War: Misperception in Vietnam and Other Wars* (Doubleday/Anchor, New York, 1970).

White, R.K., *Fearful Warriors: A Psychological Profile of US–Soviet Relations* (Free Press, New York, 1984).

Wieder, L., "Telling the Code", in R. Turner (ed.), *Ethnomethodology* (Penguin, Harmondsworth, 1974).

Woolf, V., *Three Guineas* (The Hogarth Press, London, 1938; Penguin, Harmondsworth, 1977).

Wright, Q., *A Study of War* (University of Chicago Press, Chicago and London, 1966).

Wuthnow, R., *Communities of Discourse* (Harvard University Press, Cambridge, MA, 1989).

Index

Durkheim, E., 123

ecological variables, 3
Elshtain, J., 47, 104, 150
emancipatory politics, 159
Enlightenment epistemology, 47,
175
Erikson, E., 124–5
ethnic nationalism, 18, 120, 133–
41
exclusionist identities, 131

Falklands/Malvinas conflict, 64
feminist theory
gender identity, 184
individuality, 185
post-structuralist, 184
public-private dichotomy, 45
war, 47
First World War, 98, 147, 157
Foucault, M., 113, 132
Freud, S., 124

Galtung, 11, 149
gendered self, 45–50
Giddens, A., 3, 4, 77–86, 99, 102,
112, 113, 128, 135, 159, 176
Gilpin, R., 10
global society, 159
Groom, A.J.R., 11
group loyalty, 58
groupthink, 57
Gulf war, 108–9, 158, 160

Habermas, J., 159–67
Hegel
critique of Kant, 44
discourse of war, 105
individuality, 46
project of reconciliation, 43
public-private dualism, 105
state, 42–4
heroism, 140
Hobbes, T., 6, 33–5, 110, 122

Hollis, M., 66–8
Holsti, K.J., 3, 9
Holsti, O., 57
Howard, M., 105, 107, 147–8
human needs theory, 121–4

idealism, 110
ideal speech situation, 163
identity
as discursive consciousness, 128,
179
as human need, 122
as practical consciousness, 128,
179
conflict resolution, 119
daily routines and, 129
differentiation of self and other,
124–5
exclusionist discourses, 120, 131
language of war, 108, 140
self as positioned entity, 120,
130
source of deep-rooted conflict,
123

imagined nation, 120
inclusion-exclusion dichotomy, 7,
24, 104
individualism, 76
individuality, 31, 36, 160, 184
institutional continuities, 31, 90
instrumental reason, 4, 13, 160
inter-communal violence, 16
inter-group processes, 125
international relations, 147, 174
international society, 147
international system, 3, 4, 10,
110, 147
interpretative schemes, 96, 158
Irigaray, L., 172
Israeli-Palestinian conflict, 18, 20,
123, 155

Journal of Conflict Resolution, 11